D0279493

The Railways of
Southern England:
Independent and
Light Railways

To a railway enthusiast of the future:
Magnus Edwin George Course, born 1974

The Railways of Southern England: Independent and Light Railways

Edwin Course

B. T. Batsford Ltd
London

© Edwin Course 1976
First published 1976

All rights reserved. No part
of this publication may be reproduced
in any form, or by any means,
without permission from the publisher.

ISBN 0 7134 3196 2

Filmset by Servis Filmsetting Ltd, Manchester

Printed in Great Britain by Biddles Ltd, Guildford, Surrey
for the publisher
B.T. Batsford Ltd, 4 Fitzhardinge Street,
London W1H 0AH

Contents

List of Illustrations   vii
List of Diagrams and Maps   ix
Preface   I
Sources and Acknowledgments   3
Abbreviations   6

1   Independent and Light Railways in Southern England   7
2   Light Railways in Hampshire   15
3   Light Railways in Kent and Sussex   32
4   East Kent Light Railways   72
5   Independent Railways open to the Public   107
6   Private Railways   125

Appendix 1   The Colonel Stephens Railways   157
2   Opening and Closure of Light or Independent
    Railways   159
3   Opening and Closure of Passenger Stations on
    Light or Independent Railways   165
4   Steep Grade Railways and Pleasure Lines   171
5   Lines Constructed for Public Services,
    Utilities and the Government   173
6   Lines Constructed for Industry and
    Commerce   176
Notes   180
Index   186

The Illustrations

		Between Pages
1	Lee-on-the-Solent station on 14 April, 1928	38–39
2	The last train from Lee-on-the-Solent on 2 October, 1935	38–39
3	Herriard station on 13 June, 1931	38–39
4	Bordon station in use on 7 September, 1957	38–39
5	Bordon station abandoned in July 1971	38–39
6	Typical passenger train of the late 1920s on a Col. Stephens railway	38–39
7	Hunston station on 15 February, 1975	38–39
8	St Michael's tunnel near Tenterden in late 1953	38–39
9	Rolvenden station on 2 January, 1954, the last day of passenger traffic on the KESR	38–39
10	Rolvenden station on 19 October, 1958	38–39
11	The 10.55 a.m. to Leysdown at Queenborough on 3 December, 1950	38–39
12	The 10.55 a.m. from Queenborough at Brambledown halt on 3 December, 1950	38–39
13	Hythe, the eastern terminal of the RHDR on 19 August, 1973	38–39
14	The 2.10 p.m. to New Romney at Hythe on 19 August, 1973	38–39
15	Shepherd's Well viewed from the embankment to the north of the station on 22 August, 1946	38–39
16	The southern portal of the EKLR's Golgotha tunnel on 20 May, 1967	38–39
17	Mixed train approaching Eythorne from Shepherd's Well in September, 1921	86–87
18	Eythorne junction in October 1954	86–87
19	Knowlton, a wayside station on the EKLR on 15 August, 1956	86–87
20	Site of Knowlton station viewed from the south, 28 January, 1969	86–87

vii

Between Pages

21 Bridges carrying the EKLR over the Minster to Deal
    railway and the River Stour, 14 April, 1947   86–87
22 The unopened station at Richborough in 1937   86–87
23 Aquarium station, Brighton, on 25 July, 1955   86–87
24 The car, 'Pioneer', seen from the Banjo Groyne,
    Brighton, on 28 November, 1896   86–87
25 A view of the BRSER car approaching the Brighton
    terminal   86–87
26 The 1.45 p.m. from Golf Links at Rye, 18 July, 1914 86–87
27 Golf Links station on the RCT, 20 June, 1950   86–87
28 Pier Head terminal of the Herne Bay Pier Railway
    before 1914   86–87
29 Sandgate Hill terminal of the Sandgate steep-grade
    railway before 1914   86–87
30 Devil's Dyke steep-grade railway c. 1900   86–87
31 Site of Devil's Dyke steep-grade railway in May 1975 86–87
32 An 0-6-0 locomotive of 1934 on Hastings Miniature
    Railway, 7 April, 1974   86–87
33 A special passenger train on the Hellingly Mental
    Hospital Railway, 4 April, 1959   134–135
34 North station on the Brookwood Cemetery line   134–135
35 North station platform at Brookwood Cemetery on
    23 November, 1974   134–135
36 Train ferry, 'TF4', at her berth in Southampton in
    1918   134–135
37 A special train at Bisley on 23 November, 1952   134–135
38 Bisley station on 16 May, 1964   134–135
39 Riflemen joining the 'train' at Bisley c. 1913   134–135
40 Deepcut Camp station at its opening in 1917   134–135
41 Booking-hall at Deepcut Camp station   134–135
42 A special train on the Longmoor Military Railway,
    4 October, 1958   134–135
43 The motive power depot at Longmoor on 4 October,
    1958   134–135
44 A geared well tank of 1926 at A.P.C.M. Ltd's
    Holborough Work, 26 June, 1946   134–135
45 A special train at Burley crossing, on the
    Sittingbourne & Kemsley Railway, 30 March, 1974   134–135
46 The locomotive 'Corrall Queen' at Dible's Wharf,
    Southampton, 16 December, 1972   134–135

Diagrams and Maps

		Page
I	Lines and stations, east of the Brighton main line	8
2	Lines and stations, west of the Brighton main line	9
3	Key to diagrams: Fort Brockhurst to Lee-on-the-Solent; Basingstoke to Alton; Bentley to Bordon	16
4	Chichester to Selsey Beach; Robertsbridge to Headcorn	33
5	Queenborough to Leysdown; Hythe to Dungeness; Rye to Camber Sands; Ramsgate Harbour to Ramsgate, Hereson Road	54
6	Shepherd's Well to Wingham, Canterbury Road; Eastry to Richborough Port; Guilford Colliery Branch; Herne Bay Pier Railway; Aquarium, Brighton to Black Rock; Paston Place, Brighton to Rottingdean	75
7	East Kent coal-field	76

Acknowledgments

The author and publishers would like to thank the following for permission to reproduce the illustrations:
H C Casserley for nos 1 and 3; A A Jackson for 9, 10, 16, 23, 27, 33, 35, 42 and 43; Ken Nunn Collection of Locomotive Club of Great Britain for 26; H J Patterson Rutherford for 17 and 18; Collection of Miss Lay for 36; A G Wells for 15, 19, 21, 22 and 44. Nos 2, 6, 24, 25, 28, 29, 30, 34, 39, 40 and 41 are from the collections of A A Jackson and the author; and 4, 5, 7, 8, 11, 12, 13, 14, 20, 31, 32, 37, 38, 45 and 46 were photographed by the author.

Preface

This volume, the last of three describing the railways of southern England, differs slightly in character from the other two. The geographical limits are identical – the coastline, the southern boundary of the London Transport area, and the London to Southampton main line railway. However, while Volume One covered every mile of main lines, and Volume Two treated all the secondary and branch lines in a similar comprehensive way, Volume Three is, in some respects, more selective. It completes the picture by describing all the lines not included in the other volumes. The few omissions are confined to lines of less than ten-and-a-quarter-inch gauge, temporary railways, and some minor private lines. Independently owned public passenger-carrying railways are treated in the same way as the routes of the main line companies, with detailed diagrams and full historical, archaeological and geographical descriptions. However, the 'itinerary' approach is not practical for the numerous private railways. They are listed, but the treatment is varied according to the character of the line.

The variety of the lines described is far greater than in the previous volumes. Even within such coherent groups as the light railways, there was a great deal of difference between say, the Sheppey Light Railway, with its strong resemblance to a normal branch line, and the self-contained Romney, Hythe & Dymchurch Railway. Other groups such as the steep-grade railways, showed an even greater range: in this case from the early industrial line at Offham to the passenger-carrying cliff lifts associated with sea-side resorts and the Edwardian period. Narrow-gauge lines of the same gauge vary from the passenger-carrying line in the grounds of Drusilla's Tea Rooms at Berwick to the internal lines of many of the cement works.

While the character of the lines described requires some variation of approach, this volume, like its companions, is intended for the general reader who is interested in looking at railways and for the type of railway enthusiast who reads the itineraries so carefully prepared for the rail tours of the established societies. Again, the text is not overloaded with references or footnotes, but an indication of the 'credentials' for the text is given in Sources and Acknowledgments. Readers concerned with the evidence for particular statements made in previous volumes have requested these from the author, who will be pleased to provide this information in the same way for the present volume. The text is concentrated on the railways themselves, although it would be foolish to suggest that they operate in a social and economic vacuum. In the case of the industrial lines, the close linkage with specific industries is obvious, but an enterprise like the Dreamland Miniature Railway is very dependent on the tourist industry. The railways form an important part of the social and economic history of the south of England and the present volume concentrates on enumerating and describing them.

It is intended primarily as a travellers' companion for those who enjoy looking at railways and the sites of railways. Like its predecessors, this book can be read at home, but the ideal reader will wish to see what is left of the lines described, even though he may no longer be able to reach them by train.

Sources and Acknowledgments

Although this book has one author, it has many contributors. It relies partly on people and institutions whose help is acknowledged below, and partly on numerous people who, in times past, produced the documents which have provided the source material.

Documentary source material falls into two main categories – the primary material, arising from the operation of the railways, and the secondary material consisting of things that have been written about them. Each of the main categories may be sub-divided. For instance, primary material was produced by the railways themselves, by government departments with a responsibility for the railways, and by publishers, such as Bradshaw, who produced railway time-tables and shareholders' guides. In addition to material which concentrates on railways, local papers, Ordnance Survey maps, local guide books, personal diaries and other writings all provide information. In fact, the problem for the writer may well be not to discover primary sources but rather to decide when he has enough, and may stop searching. The same problem applies to some extent with secondary sources, but in this case it is usually possible to read everything relevant which has been published. In this connection, George Ottley's monumental *Bibliography of British Railway History* is invaluable.

It is not intended to give an exhaustive list of everything consulted, but readers who are interested in the evidence for a particular statement are invited to write to the author for details of his source of information. However, the acknowledgments that follow will give a sufficient indication of the 'pedigree' of the book, and also provide an indication of where information is to be found. First, the most valuable thing an author can have is well-informed criticism, and two people in particular have contributed greatly in this way. Professor M.J. Wise supervised the writing of the thesis on which this book is based, and Alan A. Jackson has read and criticised both the thesis and the book. Other people have read all, or parts of either the thesis or the book: in particular, Mr L.C. Johnson, former Archivist, British Transport Commission, and Mr Charles E. Lee. With apologies for names omitted, I retain correspondence with the following:

G. Barlow (RHDR); H.V. Borley (dates); Rixon Bucknall (Channel ports); C.R. Clinker (dates and Acts of Parliament); W. Dray (traffic statistics); Professor H.J. Dyos (railways and housing); S.R. Garrett (light railways); C. Hadfield (canals); H.W. Hart (Southern Railway); the late P. Hollands (worked on railway construction); R. Job (Kent coalfield); the late R. Kirkland (commuter traffic); C. Maguire (Southern electrification); G.T. Moody (Southern Railway); B.N. Nunns (dating of pictures); F.O. Randall (Hundred of Hoo); R.C. Riley (LBSCR); H.J.P. Rutherford (pictorial records); Dr K.R. Sealy (railways and airports); J.G. Spence (Southern Railway); R.H.G. Thomas (local lines); R. Townsend (railway plans); J. Howard Turner (Southern Railway); A.G. Wells (East Kent) and the late C. Wright (ganger, SECR, SR and BR).

Companies who have provided information include: United Glass Bottles, Pilkingtons, Cellactite and British Uralite, A.P.C.M. and N.C.B. The following public libraries were visited: Brighton, Dover, Gravesend, Hastings, Maidstone, Portsmouth, Tonbridge and Southampton. Record offices providing information were as follows: East Sussex (Lewes), Hampshire (Winchester), Kent (Maidstone), London, Portsmouth, Southampton, Surrey (Kingston) and West Sussex (Chichester). Considerable material was made available in the House of Lords Record Office, and in the libraries of the Institution of Civil Engineers and the Chartered Institute of Transport. Finally, this book could not have been written in its present form without the co-operation of the British Transport Record Office with its three successive Archivists, Messrs Johnson, Atkinson and Foulkes. Acknowledgment is made to the staff at all these places who have helped me at some point during the last 15 years. With regard to secondary sources, the relevant publications are listed in George Ottley's *Bibliography*. However, publications which have been especially useful or have appeared since the *Bibliography*, are mentioned in the Notes. Numerous railway periodicals have been consulted, but probably the *Railway Magazine* more than any other.

While those mentioned above had provided information, others have helped in different ways. Typing, including the interpretation of unusually obscure handwriting, has been undertaken by Mrs Irene Candy, Mrs Susan Willgoss and my wife. Most of the diagrams were drawn by Miss Jane Holdsworth. Two people who have provided not only material help, but also encouragement are Mr Peter Kemmis Betty of B.T. Batsford and my wife. In conclusion, acknowledgment is due to the staff of the Southern Region. The author would hesitate to assess the number of hours spent in conversation with them during the last fifteen years and earlier, in the course of which all kinds of information has come to light. As will be appreciated from the text, in addition to verbal and documentary evidence, this book relies heavily on what might be called archaeological evidence. For instance, the remains of an abandoned station may be more informative than pages of a vaguely written book. But the men who built the railways and worked on them provide the essential element in the railway system which this book describes.

Abbreviations

BR	British Rail
BRSER	Brighton & Rottingdean Seashore Electric Railway
EKLR	East Kent Light Railways (absorbed by BR)
GNR	Great Northern Railway (absorbed by LNER)
GWR	Great Western Railway (absorbed by BR)
HBP	Herne Bay Pier Company (absorbed by Herne Bay Urban District Council)
KESR	Kent & East Sussex Railway, initially Rother Valley Railway (absorbed by BR)
LBSCR	London, Brighton & South Coast Railway (absorbed by SR)
LCDR	London, Chatham & Dover Railway (absorbed by SECR)
LMSR	London, Midland & Scottish Railway (absorbed by BR)
LMR	Longmoor Military Railway
LNER	London & North Eastern Railway (absorbed by BR)
LSR	Lee-on-the-Solent Railway (absorbed by SR)
LSWR	London & South Western Railway (absorbed by SR)
RCT	Rye & Camber Tramway
RHDR	Romney, Hythe & Dymchurch Railway
SER	South Eastern Railway (absorbed by SECR)
SECR	South Eastern & Chatham Railway (absorbed by SR)
SR	Southern Railway (absorbed by BR)
TA	Thanet Amusements Ltd
VER	Volk's Electric Railway (absorbed by Brighton Corporation)
WSR	West Sussex Railway, initially Selsey & Hundred of Manhood Railway

1

Independent and Light Railways in Southern England

Volumes One and Two of *The Railways of Southern England* described lines owned and operated by the main line companies. Volume One covers 462 miles of main line with 209 passenger stations, the corresponding figures for Volume Two being 450 miles of secondary and branch lines and 198 stations. On the same basis of lines open to passengers, Volume Three covers 91 miles of independent or light railways with 80 passenger stations. However, in addition it includes descriptions of a number of railways not open to the general public, such as the Chattenden & Upror line and the line to Hellingly Mental Hospital.

All the lines described were either owned and operated by concerns other than the main line railway companies or else were constructed as light railways. The latter varied in character. The Bordon branch, although constructed under light railway legislation, apart from an ungated crossing, was indistinguishable from other branches of the LSWR company. On the other hand, the line from Shepherd's Well to Wingham, with its antique rolling stock and minimal stations, was unlikely to be taken for part of a main line undertaking. However, in every case their operation was covered by light railway legislation. By the 1860s legal requirements for the promotion, construction and operation of railways had reached a stage when rural areas were unlikely to be able to support them. This was appreciated, and the Railways Construction Facilities Act of 1864 provided for authorization by Board of Trade Certificate instead of Act of Parliament. Little use was made of it, as it could only be invoked in the absence of competition. However, both the Lee-on-the-Solent Railway and the West Sussex Railway operated with Certificates granted under this Act, in the latter case some years after the opening of the line. The Regulation of Railways Act of 1868

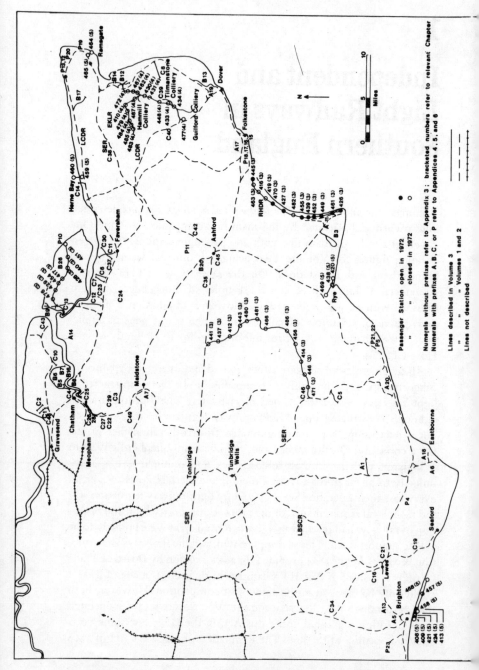

1 Lines and stations, east of the Brighton main line

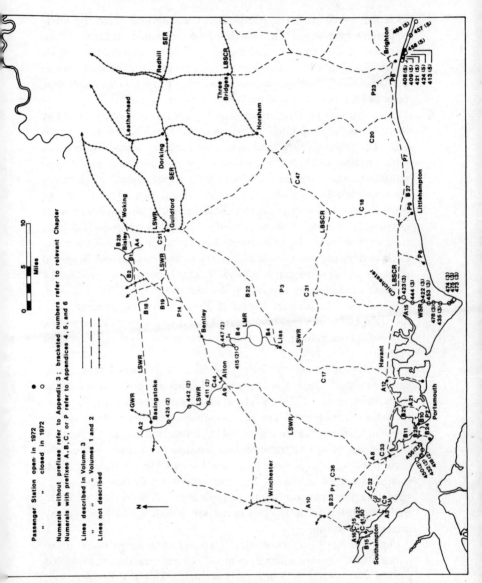

2 Lines and stations, west of the Brighton main line

included provision for applications for exemptions from the safety requirements specified. The main line companies made little use of these Acts and by the 1890s the need for light railways was more fully appreciated. The Light Railways Act of 1896 provided for the avoidance of parliamentary expenses, the reduction of construction and operating costs and the availability of financial assistance.

Applications to form companies and construct lines were received by three Light Railway Commissioners in May and November of each year. They subsequently conducted a local inquiry whose function was rather similar to that of a parliamentary committee. If this proved satisfactory they submitted a draft Order to the Board of Trade for confirmation. Local authorities could construct their own lines, or provide financial assistance. In fact, local authorities showed little interest in railways, although in some parts of the country they promoted street tramways under the Light Railways Act. The raising of capital was also facilitated by the power of the Treasury to make loans, and, in special cases, to provide free grants. Operating expenses could be reduced by clauses forbidding any increase in the rateable value of the land used, and also by relaxation of Board of Trade safety requirements. The speed limit of 25 miles per hour was reduced near ungated level crossings, on gradients exceeding 1 in 50, and on curves sharper than nine-chains radius.

Twice a year the Light Railway Commissioners reported to the Board of Trade (after 1919, to the Ministry of Transport), giving details of the applications received, the capital and mileage involved and the decisions taken for lines in Britain. The peak was reached as early as 1898, with 39 applications for 557 miles of light railway, estimated to cost £3,300,939. But the age of motor transport was imminent, so that by 1914, the corresponding figures were three applications for 13½ miles with an estimated cost of £192,316. In 1926 there was only one application; 1932 was the first year with no applications. The revival of Light Railway Orders in the 1960s catered for branch lines taken over by preservation groups.

On a mileage basis, the south of England attracted its fair share of light railway schemes with rather more materializing than the national pattern would suggest. Some, such as the Cuckmere Valley Railway, projected in 1897 from Berwick on the LBSCR through the South Downs to the Birling Gap, were rejected by the commissioners. Lines authorized but not built included that from Cranbrook to Tenterden in 1898, Hollingbourne, on the LCDR, to Faversham in 1899, and a number of

lines based on the Kent and East Sussex Railway. If the two lines certi-
ficated under the 1864 Act are included, 87 miles of light railway were
opened in the south between 1894 and 1929. By 1972, 13¾ miles remained
open to passengers only, two miles to freight only, and the re-opening
of one-and-a-half miles to passengers was imminent.

Although the intention of the 1896 Act was to encourage the provision
of railway facilties for the benefit of areas with little traffic potential, the
motives behind the promotion of light railways in the south were mixed.
They all served rural areas, but of the two promoted by the LSWR, the
Basingstoke & Alton was a blocking line, built to secure a route from
possible GWR penetration, and the Bordon line served a military camp.
The LBSCR did not promote any light railways and the SECR confined
themselves to one. This was on the commissioners' list for November
1899 for a line from Hythe to New Romney, but was withdrawn before
the inquiry was held. In addition to the lines which they promoted
themselves, the LSWR began to operate the Lee-on-the-Solent Railway
some years after its opening, but the SECR provided the services on the
Sheppey Light Railway from the start. Both these lines were speculative,
built in the hope that Lee-on-the-Solent and Leysdown would become
second Bournemouths. A similar hope was entertained by the promoters
of the Hundred of Manhood & Selsey Tramway, which, although
opened in 1897, only achieved formal light railway status in 1924. The
Kent & East Sussex was mainly designed to carry the traffic of its district,
although it did hope to supplement this with summer visitors to Bodiam
Castle. The East Kent Light Railway was in a class of its own, being
designed to serve the Kent coal-field which, in the event, got no nearer
to Yorkshire standards than Leysdown did to Bournemouth. In 1925,
the Kingsnorth Light Railway was authorized to take over the Chattenden Naval Tramway, but never carried passengers. The eighth and last
of the fully fledged light railways was the Romney, Hythe & Dymchurch,
authorized from Hythe to New Romney in 1925, and on to Dungeness
in 1928.

All the other lines were of standard gauge, and carried freight wagons
from the main lines, but the RHDR was constructed to a gauge of 15
inches. The main saving achieved by narrow gauge was that it made
possible curves of about two-chains radius as compared to about ten-
chains with standard gauge, and in hilly country, this could save considerable amounts on engineering and earthworks.[1] They did, of course,
reduce speed but on light railways, low speeds were obligatory. However, far from penetrating hilly country, the RHDR ran across Romney

Marsh, and although there would have been some saving over the amount of land purchased, earthworks were virtually non-existent. The scaling down of the locomotives did produce some saving on bridges, but the main argument for the narrow-gauge and miniature locomotives was the novel one that they would attract more passengers. The correctness of this assumption is borne out by the fact that the RHDR is the only one of the light railways which has survived with all its mileage intact.

They were essentially cut-price railways, built and operated as cheaply as possible where revenue was very limited. Their sharp curves and steep gradients, and moderately powered, venerable locomotives ensured that the legal 25 miles-per-hour speed limit was rarely achieved. Because of the light track (usually with rails of 70 lbs per yard or less) and the limited strength of the underbridges, it was unusual to employ locomotives with axle loads exceeding 16 tons. Their limited power blended happily enough with the low speeds of the short, mixed trains of coaches and wagons which conveyed the sparse traffic.

The stations were as modest as everything else, and passenger accommodation frequently consisted of no more than a platform. Sometimes a shelter of wood or corrugated iron was provided, and occasionally a name-board to assist the passenger new to the district. Although an ability to handle the horse and carriage traffic of the local gentry was usually claimed, it would have required an unusually intrepid horse with an even more remarkable carriage to join say, an East Kent train from the platform at Knowlton station. The facilities for handling freight were also decidedly modest, cranes or goods sheds being virtually unknown. Money was saved in other ways which had no direct effect on the appearance of the line, such as an easing of the regulations concerning hours of duty of the staff.

With their low speeds and simple if not primitive facilities, the light railways were extremely vulnerable to road competition and, despite a reprieve during the Second World War, with the rather special exception of the RHDR, the last opportunity for passenger riding was in 1957. Now gorse and bramble or the farmer's plough have obliterated much of the short-lived permanent way. The station buildings, where they existed, were not of a type destined for longevity, and by now it needs a very discerning eye to appreciate that, for instance, a railway ever ran from Chichester to Selsey.

Whereas the lines operating with light railway orders are fairly easily identified, the listing of all other railways is a formidable task.[2] Strictly speaking, a Hornby O Gauge track forming a circle on the dining room table at Christmas is a temporary railway, in a similar way to 'Jubilee' track in a sand pit. Motive power may be clockwork, manual, animal, hydraulic, electric, steam or sail. Definition is inevitably hazardous, but reasonably firm guide-lines have been used in deciding which independent lines shall be included in this text. First, lines with a gauge of less than ten-and-a-quarter inches are usually ignored. Second, those that provided service for less than a year are excluded. Third, those less than a mile in length are also generally disregarded. The last characteristic presents the most difficulty. For instance, not all railways merely connect one point to another. A system such as that in Chatham dockyard connects many points, and its track mileage is not easily distinguished from its route mileage. So this guide is applied rather loosely, and lines such as the Herne Bay Pier Railway or the Ramsgate Tunnel Railway, both with mileages of less than a mile, are included. At the margin come the passenger-carrying inclines or cliff railways, the shortest, that at Margate, consisting of 69 feet of five-feet-gauge track.

The independent railways are divided into those that carried public traffic, including passengers, and the private lines which only carried goods and in some cases passengers nominated by their owners. Bowaters Railway or the Netley Hospital Railway are examples of the latter type. As a number of the lines had no direct connection with the main-line system, gauges varied widely. The RHDR was built to a gauge of 15 inches; the Brighton & Rottingdean Seashore Electric Railway, with its unusual rolling stock, had a gauge of 18 feet. Steam was the commonest form of motive power, but one of the passenger-carrying lines, Volk's Electric Railway, was opened with electric power in 1883. Hydraulic power was confined to the cliff railways, and sail power was used on Herne Bay Pier and informally on a disused industrial line at Cliffe. Manual and animal power were more common, one of the more extensive systems relying on human motive power being that at Gosport.[3]

Nearly all the lines described were built to convey passengers or freight from one place to another, even if it was only the length of a pier. But a small number of passenger-carrying lines were constructed purely for pleasure riding, frequently returning passengers to the point at which they had boarded the train. With this characteristic, in extreme cases, such as the railway at Drusilla's Tea Rooms at Berwick, the track was laid to form a circuit rather than a line. The most meaningful definition of a pleasure line is one on which most of the passengers make a round trip without leaving the train. On this basis, such undertakings as the RHDR, may be classified as deriving much of their revenue from pleasure traffic. This must be distinguished from the use of say, the West Sussex Railway to Golf Course halt, where the motive for travel was the pleasure of playing golf, and not of travelling on the West Sussex Railway.

If track mileage is the criterion, the largest group of independent railways were the industrial lines. The scarcity of heavy industry makes them a trifle rarer in the south of England than in the north, but such systems as the cement railways of north Kent were once common. Conversely, lines associated with defence are more easily found in the south, perhaps the most interesting example being the Longmoor Military Railway, whose main function was the training of soldiers in railway operating. No examples survive of branch lines to aerodromes, of which that to Manston, near Margate, was the longest. Another type of line, now extinct, was that to a particular hospital. Such lines as these to Netley, Park Prewett and Hellingly were of special interest.

Whereas the total mileage in any given year of public railways can be readily ascertained, comparable figures for private railways are harder to determine. Large-scale maps are probably the best guide, but they only provide information for given areas at given points in time. In general, there is little doubt that the rise and decline of independent railways are comparable to those of branch lines, for many of them were vulnerable to alternative forms of transport. For such functions as the conveyance of chalk to pit to works, the railway has often given place to the pipeline, but more commonly motor vehicles, sometimes with wide tyres for crossing soft ground, have displaced rail transport. As with the light railways, the student of private lines must for the most part concentrate on history and archaeology rather than working railways. But as this volume shows, there is still much to be seen.

2

Light Railways in Hampshire

Hampshire passengers has their first opportunity to ride on a light railway in 1894, and their last in 1957.

The Lee-on-the-Solent Railway

The Lee-on-the-Solent Railway was opened in 1894. As it was too early to take advantage of powers under the 1896 Light Railways Act, the promoters used the Railways Construction Facilities Act of 1864. Motivated by high hopes of a second Bournemouth, they looked forward to the rapid development of the new resort.

The land was owned by Sir J. Robinson of Newton Manor near Swanage, and, until development began in 1885, was occupied by a few farmhouses and the hamlet of Lee Britten. The manor house was converted into the Victoria Hotel.

The Railway World of July 1894 referred to the way the 'estate has been carefully laid out with several miles of good wide roads in lieu of the narrow thoroughfares disfiguring many old towns which have come into being without any plan'. The contemporary edition of *Mate's Illustrated Guide* proclaimed that 'a glance at the map of the estate will show how numerous are the plots of building land which have been sold to the public at the auctions which are held periodically by Mr F. G. Wheatley, and handsome villas are rapidly increasing in number. One essential for a resort was a promenade, and Mr C. Newton-Robinson, Sir J. Robinson's son 'who was the first to discover the advantages of the site for a future town', provided 'a Marine Parade more than a mile in length and 50 feet in width, between which and the sea runs a belt of grass 150 feet wide, which has been reserved as a park'. This belt of grass

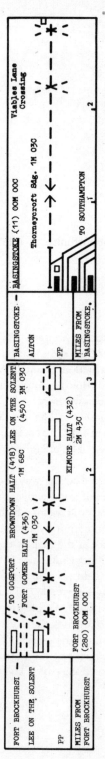
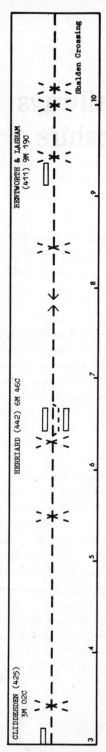
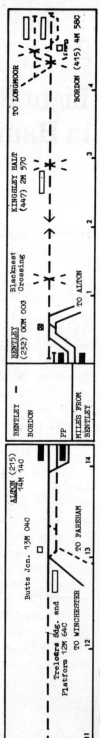

3 Key to diagrams: Fort Brockhurst to Lee-on-the-Solent; Basingstoke to Alton; Bentley to Bordon

provided a convenient way for the railway to reach the 'centre' of the nascent resort.

The new town having been laid out and provided with a name, its other two requirements were a pier and a railway. A pier was constructed under powers obtained in 1885 by Sir J. Robinson, sold to the Lee-on-the-Solent Pier Company, and formally opened on 3 April, 1888 by Lady Robinson. The *Princess Beatrice* was the first steamer to land passengers at the new, 750-foot long pier which could be reached at all states of the tide, and shortly afterwards the steam launch *Venus* was making six trips a day to Lee-on-the-Solent from the Clarence Pier at Southsea.

Apart from its steamer traffic, the pier was intended to act as a promenade and pleasure centre being 'provided with seats and glazed shelters with a pavilion for the band in the centre'. During 1893, the *Venus* carried 4,500 passengers, but she only operated from May until September, and, especially for residents, a link with the railway system was essential.

A company was formed and a Board of Trade Certificate was obtained in 1890 for three miles of railway between Lee-on-the-Solent and Fort Brockhurst on the LSWR Gosport line. Work started in 1891, but the first contractor defaulted, and the company had to be rescued with financial assistance from Sir J. Robinson. In 1893, a new contract was made with Pauling & Elliott of Westminster, who completed the line ready for its opening on 12 May, 1894.

Among its more substantial features were the platforms at its terminals and two intermediate stations. In fact, the concrete platform faces at Privett (later Fort Gomer) and Browndown survived until demolished for road improvements in 1961, and that at Fort Brockhurst is still in position.

Although the platform at Fort Brockhurst was constructed at the back of the LSWR station, there was no direct connection with the LSWR Fareham to Gosport line, and wagons were transferred by means of a double shunt. In this way, the cost of points leading direct from the main line to the branch was avoided, but the arrangement would have been highly disadvantageous if through passenger trains had ever been operated.

From the terminal platform, the track curved round to run alongside Military Road as far as its junction with Bury Road. Here it crossed the road by a level crossing. Privett Station, which consisted of a single platform, was situated on the far side of the road. In the early days of the line, its staff consisted of a boy who displayed a red flag by day or a red lamp after dark if the train was required to stop for a passenger.

Its traffic increased after 1906 when the Gosport electric trams reached Bury Cross only three-quarters-of-a-mile short of the platform. On summer days before the coming of the motor bus, the delights of electric tram, walking, and the tram-like train could be experienced in that order by the people of Gosport. However, by 1913 there was no service on Sundays, and even on weekdays there was no train until 10.18 a.m.

Having left its roadside location, the line struck across heath country to rejoin the road at Browndown, where there was a military camp and a shooting range. This section included a simple bridge over a stream, the bridge consisting of four steel girders laid on wooden stringers resting on piles. Like Privett, Browndown was on the far side of a level crossing. The track was laid on the south side of the road to the point at which it reached the coast, near Elmore Farm, where a curve of ten-chains radius brought it out on the top of the cliff.

The last half mile to the terminus, situated just short of the pier, traversed the 'Park' which had been left between Marine Parade and the top of the cliff. Unfortunately this quite narrow strip was not flat, and, although a modest cutting was provided, beyond Elmore trains had to climb at 1 in 66.

The terminal at Lee-on-the-Solent consisted of a concrete-faced platform with a shelter, but in contrast with other stations, here there were other buildings. A red-brick edifice consisted of a single storey block with two wings, and contained a booking office, waiting rooms and conveniences.

Because it was authorized as a light railway, various restrictions applied. There was an overall speed limit of 25 miles per hour and a maximum load of eight tons on each pair of wheels, but the whole line was fenced. Signalling was not required as the single track was operated under the Board of Trade 'one engine' rules, which were based on the fact that with only one locomotive on the line, collisions were impossible. Despite the weight restriction, flat-bottomed rails weighing 60 lbs to the yard and spiked to the sleepers were provided. Sufficient land was purchased to allow for double track if traffic required it.

Perhaps wisely, the LSWR showed no inclination to work the new line, so the light railway company had to make do with one tank locomotive[1] and some tramcar-like coaches which could carry ten first-class and 24 second-class passengers. However, in 1909 the LSWR made financial arrangements to operate the line but were careful not to buy it.

Before the First World War the service was usually maintained by one rail motor-car.[2] As the LSWR already had a Privett station on their Meon Valley line, in October 1909 they re-named the Lee-on-the-Solent's Privett as Fort Gomer. In 1910 a new halt was opened at Elmore. LSWR timetables also described the stopping places at Fort Gomer and Browndown as halts.[3] The Lee-on-the-Solent company was regularly unable to pay its debenture holders and by 1922 had an accumulated debt of £14,000. The newly formed Southern Railway was reluctant to take over either the line or the debt associated with it. Lee had developed as a dormitory for Gosport, to which it was linked by direct motor bus services with which the railway could not possibly compete.[4] However, it was ruled that under the Railways Act of 1921 the Southern was bound to take on the Lee-on-the-Solent, and so in 1923, the latter became part of the Southern system.

Rail motor-cars were not perpetuated, the Southern preferring motor trains, with separate locomotives and coaches. As a result of the grouping, they had plenty of the eminently suitable LBSCR 'Terrier' class tank locomotives available, and a photograph taken in 1928 shows No. B661 of this class hauling a single LSWR coach. Another view of the same period shows a mixed train of two LSWR coaches and two freight wagons alongside the platform at Lee-on-the-Solent. This was hauled by an LBSCR tank locomotive of the D1 class. On the opposite side to the platform was the road leading to the goods siding, and beyond that, the bathing huts at the top of the beach.

By 1930 it was clear that there was no future for railway passenger services to Lee-on-the-Solent and they were withdrawn at the end of that year. Freight continued until 1935. A photograph of 2 October, 1935 shows an LBSCR D1 class tank locomotive No. 2239 removing empty coal wagons from Lee.[5] At this date both the terminals and the intermediate stations had been neglected, but were not much damaged.

This was still the case when I paid my first visit to the line in 1937. The track was still in position, but especially between Fort Gomer and Elmore, gorse was rapidly obscuring it. It was removed in 1942 but on a return visit, after the war, the platforms at Fort Brockhurst, Fort Gomer, Browndown and Elmore were all intact, although obscured by varying amounts of vegetation. At Lee-on-the-Solent the bathing huts had been moved across the station yard on to the site of the platform. While this had gone, the station buildings had found a new use. The two wings had been removed but the main block had become an amusement parlour. In this role, its takings were probably substantially greater than as a booking office for the railway.

Subsequent demolition has removed almost every trace of the line, except the station building at Lee and the platform at Fort Brockhurst. Coastal erosion and infilling have combined to obliterate the cliff-top section. The platforms and the alignment between Privett and Brown-down, including the girders of the bridge over the stream, were replaced by a new road in 1961. An LSWR metal warning plate which somewhat illogically survived after the removal of the track at the level-crossing over Cambridge Road was removed at about the same time. Now the line to Gosport has been closed to freight, and if the LSWR Fort Brock-hurst station is demolished the Lee-on-the-Solent platform will go as well. The only involuntary preservationists will be the providers of amusement machines on what was once Lee-on-the-Solent station.

The Basingstoke & Alton Railway

The next light railway to be opened in Hampshire was the Basingstoke & Alton line opened on 1 June, 1901. In 1895 plans had been deposited for a new railway from the Great Western at Basingstoke to Alton and Portsmouth. Although it was not overtly a Great Western promotion the LSWR had little doubt that its principal rival would be interested in obtaining a share of the Portsmouth traffic, if it were given an opportunity. Sir Charles Scotter, the general manager of the LSWR, decided that the best method of protection was to occupy the route from Basingstoke to Alton and on to Fareham. Once LSWR track was laid, Parliament would never agree to a rival route through the same country. Powers were obtained under the Light Railways Act of 1896, the Basingstoke & Alton being the first line to take advantage of it.

Mr E.C. Griffith records that for what was hardly a major project the LSWR organised quite an impressive show for the beginning of the works.[6] A party of directors came down from London by special train, and the first sod was cut with the traditional silver spade by the Rt Hon. C.T. Ritchie, President of the Board of Trade. As he could hardly have been concerned with celebrating the fact that the LSWR had secured the route against any possible Great Western threat, he presumably agreed to perform the ceremony because the Basingstoke & Alton was the first line authorized under the Light Railways Act. The proceedings received a musical accompaniment by the band of the Basingstoke

Mechanics Institute, and after all the principal guests had wielded the spade, it was presented to Mr Ritchie, and the party adjourned for luncheon.

The estimated cost of construction, £67,000 for 13 miles, was low (only a trifle dearer than the Rother Valley which followed a valley with very little in the way of earthworks). It would appear that land-owners were unusually helpful in the prices they accepted, presumably looking forward to an appreciation in the value of their property after the opening of the line.

In fact, the only considerable altercation during the construction period seems to have been with Cliddesden Parish Council. The railway was to cross over the main road at the end of the village and the council had understood that this was where the station would be. There was clearly a breakdown in communications as this would have placed the platforms on a 1 in 60 gradient. The company wanted to open the station by a level-crossing about three-quarters-of-a-mile from the village, where the track was level, but in the end it was built by a crossing half-a-mile from the village on a 1 in 330 gradient.

The contractor for the line was Mr J.T. Firbank, who, having under-taken major contracts on the London extension of the Great Central, should not have been unduly taxed by the Basingstoke & Alton, and in fact he could have finished the line by the end of 1900. However, having joined the LSWR main line half-amile west of Basingstoke, the Basingstoke & Alton was to have an independent track through the goods yard to a bay platform on the down side. The down goods yard was being rebuilt on chalk taken from suitable points on the new line, and the LSWR intimated that the contractor should arrange for the completion of the line to synchronize with that of the yard, which was to be in early June the following year. Whereas such modest under-takings as the Selsey Tramway had opened with a flourish of mayors and councillors, the Basingstoke & Alton came into being almost surrepti-tiously. Perhaps the LSWR, having effectively blocked the Great Western, wished to forget about its new line. Certainly the service of three trains per day was unlikely to strain its carrying capacity.

Mr Griffith reproduces a report from the *Hampshire Herald and Alton Gazette* of 8 June, 1901, written, as he says, 'in a somewhat humorous manner'. Although the point about the inaccessibility of the stations was not entirely unjustified, the writer's mileages are inexplicable, unless he regarded the population of each village as concentrated in the remotest corner of its parish. For instance, most of the inhabitants of Cliddesden were within a mile of their station, and even Bentworth was only one-and-a-half miles off. However, the distances he quotes may well have reflected what the local inhabitants believed them to be, as opposed to what they really were. In any case, the report is well worth reproducing as an indication of the way a light railway would appear to the public:

Opening of the Basingstoke & Alton
Light Railway

———————

A Trip on the First Train

———————

'Quietly and unostentatiously the train service on the new light railway between Basingstoke and Alton was inaugurated on Saturday. It is called a "light" railway because it was constructed under the provisions of the Light Railways Act, and was the first to be sanctioned in Hampshire, but as a matter of fact it is not a light railway, as the term is generally understood. It is of the same gauge as the rest of the LSWR system, and carries the ordinary rolling stock. But yet it is "light" in more ways than one – at any rate at present. It is light as regards the number of trains travelling over it, it is light as regards the loads of the trains, and it is extremely light as regards the station buildings. As we remarked last week, it was generally expected that the opening of the line, for which such a great future had been predicted, and which we were assured was to confer such vast blessings on the community, would be made the occasion of a great demonstration. That this idea seems to have been pretty widespread is evidenced by the fact that last week an enterprising firm of fireworks manufacturers, known the world over, wrote to the engineer of the line, saying that it was usual, on the occasion of the opening of a railway, to include a display of fireworks in the programme, and if such was contemplated on this occasion they would be happy to place their services at the disposal of the authorities. But no fireworks were wanted, for, as one of the company's officials remarked to the writer, "We finish up before dark", in other words the last train for the day ran long before the sun had set. No, this "stupendous business" as the same official called the opening of the line, was not heralded with a fanfare of trumpets, cemented with a public banquet, or crowned with a display of fireworks. The train service began, it inaugurated "the trivial round, the common task" with a modesty thoroughly in keeping with the provision for the requirements of the public which the new line will afford. Trains leave Basingstoke at 9.15 a.m., 12.20 and 5.45 p.m., and return from Alton at 10.25 a.m., 1.55 and 7 p.m. so that if a person arrives at Basingstoke at 11.13 on business, and fails to catch the 12.20 out, there will be no other train available till a quarter to six. Rather a long wait, but then there is the consolation, as someone remarked, that one could walk back quicker.

'The man in the street expects to find the village somewhere near the station. But such little details do not trouble the promoters of railways, who, if the station is somewhere in the parish named – the parish may be a dozen miles in area – are quite content to take the name, which, with common people, is generally associated with the village. And so it has turned out on the Basingstoke and Alton Railway. The three intermediate stations are named Cliddesden, Herriard, and Bentworth and Lasham respectively. But the villages bearing these names are a long way from the stations and not a glimpse of them can be seen from the train. The village of Cliddesden is about a mile-and-a-half from the station, and in fact is almost as near to Basingstoke station, whilst Bentworth village is a couple of miles from the station with the double-barrelled name. Lasham, which takes second place in this double designation, is about half-a-mile from the station, and Herriard is a mile or more from its station. In fact the only houses near any of the stations are the cottages which the railway company have put up for their employees, with a "better-most" one in each place for the station-master. The most imposing objects at each station are the windmills for the purposes of water supply. The station buildings proper are most primitive. They consist of little galvanized iron shanties divided into "booking offices" and "waiting rooms" in neither of which there would be room to swing a cat. There are no signal boxes, and, with the exception of Herriard, no signals. The points are worked by hand-levers on the ground, and the signals at Herriard are manipulated in like manner. One almost expected to find the old-fashioned half-moon signals, but in this respect, at all events, modern ideas have prevailed. At the stations where such innovations are unknown, we get a reminiscence of the dim and distant past by seeing the station-master armed with a couple of flags. Speaking of the station-masters, we may mention that on the new line three old and well-tried servants of the company have been promoted to the charge of the three intermediate stations. These are Inspector Bushnell, of Basingstoke, Inspector Hooper of Woking, and Inspector Pain of Southampton West, who became station-masters at Cliddesden, Herriard and Bentworth respectively.

'And now we must say something about the initial ride over the line on Saturday morning. The train left Basingstoke at 9.15, and it consisted of an engine, two coaches, a guard's van, two trucks of coal, and two road boxes. The coaches and guard's van were all fresh-painted and upholstered. There were a good many passengers, but most of them were "free trippers". The paying passengers did not number many more than half-a-dozen, and these all went for the sake of the novelty. Alderman Powell of Basingstoke, had the distinction of purchasing the first ticket.

'A score or so of people assembled on the platform at Basingstoke to witness the departure, but there was not the least excitement. Mr Scott, the engineer of the line, rode on the engine, and in the train were several officials who made the journey for the purpose of check-ing the times, testing the points, etc. The train started from the siding on the east side of the down platform, and we were soon taking the curve which sweeps round Thornycroft's works, and under the bridge which spans the Salisbury road. From the huts, which are still standing near the bridge, a few men, women and children turned out to give us a parting cheer, whilst a photographer planted his camera on the clearing and possibly got a picture of the train as it emerged from beneath the bridge, or as it proceeded onwards. Cliddesden station was our first port of call. There was a wait of about five minutes, not on account of the number of passengers to be dealt with, for there was none to be set down and not more than three to be taken up, but in order to shunt a road box. As mentioned above, there were two road boxes on the train and two trucks of coal. The coal was for Herriard, and one of the road boxes was for Cliddesden. As Cliddesden was the first stopping place, the most natural thing in the world was to have put that particular road box behind the coal trucks on making up the train at Basingstoke. But this would have been too commonplace for such a "stupendous" occasion, and so the Cliddesden wagon was put in front of those for Herriard, and consequently the coal trucks had to be detached at the platform, then we ran down to the points, shunted the road box into a siding, and eventually backed to the plat-form and again picked up the coal trucks. At length we started again and ran through Winslade, with its little church nestling close to the railway, and, skirting Farleigh and other small parishes, passed through the extensive estate of Mr F.M.E. Jervoise, in the centre of which Herriard station is situate. This is a more pretentious station than either of the other two on the route, for although its "offices" are very little, if any, bigger, there is a double platform, with a relief line of rails. Here there was a longer wait than at Cliddesden. The trucks of coal had to be shunted into the goods yard, but of course the remaining road box was behind them on the train, so that there were more trips up and down the station. The coal, it may be mentioned was consigned by Stephen Phillips & Co. of Basingstoke, and Mr Councillor Phillips, the head of the firm, who was among the passengers, saw the trucks safely deposited in the goods yard. At length we were once more on the move. Hitherto the line had been far from straight, but thence to Alton it is a veritable serpentine character. It is all ins and outs and ups and downs, and this may account for the plentiful supply of boards bearing the injunction, "speed not to exceed ten miles an hour". Either through want of time, or because of the desire to give these boards a spick and span appearance, some of them were not finished. On one the painters were doing the notice, and we noticed that the driver seemed to treat this like the signal which Nelson could not see with his blind eye, for the pace was appreciably quicker over that length. Level crossings abound all the way – there being several highways, numerous crossings from one field to another, and lots of footpaths. Where the crossing is from field to field there are gates at each side bearing the customary injunction, "Shut this gate", but save in one or two cases there is no barrier whatever to the highways, although there are some "grids" to act as deterrents to cattle. However, with trains travelling at ten miles an hour, there is not likely to be much danger to the public.

'It was a delightful morning, and all nature looked fresh and beautiful after the refreshing rains of the previous week. We passed through fields where the fast-growing corn gave promise of a bountiful harvest, through rich pasture lands, and through thickly wooded copses where flowers made a luxuriant carpet. In many places the line runs along the valley with woods sloping down on either side, and in the trees and hedges the birds sang merrily, and here and there a rabbit, frightened by the unusual noise of a train, ran as if for its life. Some women weeding in the cornfields paused for a few minutes and waved their weed-hooks in the air, the cows grazing in the meadows stood still and gazed in blank amazement, while the horses took to their heels. From the few straggling cottages on the side of the line women and children looked out and waved hats and handkerchiefs, and from the woodhouse of one of the cottages a flag was flying. Men and youths, hearing the train coming, left their work and posted themselves on the fence to have a look at the first train on their new line. At Bentworth-Lasham station quite a dozen women and children, in aprons and pinafores, had assembled and cheered as we steamed slowly into the station. Here we dropped two or three passengers and picked up as many more, but as there was no shunting to be done here, not till we came back, the wait was not a long one. Among the passengers picked up at this station was the Rev. W.G. Cazalet, Rector of Bentworth. Away on the hills to the right was Burkham House, the residence of Mr A.F. Jeffreys, M.P., a little further on was Bentworth Lodge, where resides Captain Stephens. Still further on on the same side of the road, but like the other places a good distance off, is Thedden Grange, whilst on the left, up among the hills is Shalden Manor, the residence of Mr J. Gathorne Wood. Adjoining Mr Wood's estate on the north side of the railway is a well-timbered forest sloping down in majestic grandeur to the line. Beyond this we passed the district of Beech, where the people live in bungalows, and then we came to the A.M.B. Hospital Camp,[7] which at present has a very absent-minded appearance. And then by a gentle curve we came on to the Winchester–Guildford line, and running past the hop-fields we pulled up at Alton at twelve minutes past ten, having accomplished the journey of a little over thirteen miles in three minutes less than an hour!

'After all the enthusiasm which the good people of Alton had shown with regard to the new railway, with its promise of a flourishing market, and an almost mushroom-like growth of the town, one expected to see half the towns-people, together with the leading members of the District Council, at the station to greet the first train. But the modesty which characterized the LSWR Company seems to have infected the people of Alton as well, for there were not a score on the platform, and no one raised the cheer which the trippers considered their endurance and pluck deserved. As the train was timed to leave Alton on the return journey at 10.25 there was not time to explore the neighbourhood or even to pay a visit to the nearest hotel, consequently the passengers waited in the vicinity of the station.

'Practically everybody who had made the whole of the initial journey returned on the train to Basingstoke, as well as those who had been picked up at intermediate stations, and in addition there were three or four Altonians who indulged in a ride to Basingstoke. The train left at 10.30, five minutes late, but the return journey was accomplished in less time, there being no long waits. The longest this time was Bentworth-Lasham, where there was an old coach to be picked up from the siding. At Herriard pretty nearly a dozen passengers joined the train, these being principally village women with their market baskets. At a quarter past eleven we arrived safely back at Basingstoke, the entire journey having been accomplished without any mishap, and having been much enjoyed by the passengers.

'On the second train for Alton, which left Basingstoke at 12.20, the Altonians who had come up with us returned, and there were a few other paying passengers, making the total booked on both trains from Basingstoke 19. To this second train was attached a saloon coach, in which rode several of the directors and chief officials of the line, including Colonel the Hon. H.W. Campbell (chairman), Sir Charles Scotter (deputy chairman), Sir Wyndham Portal, D.L., the Rt Hon. W.W.B. Beach, M.P., Mr Spencer Portal, Mr C.J. Owens (general manager) and Mr Sam Fay (traffic superintendent). At Bentworth station these were joined by Mr A.F. Jeffreys, M.P., and Miss Jeffreys, who accompanied them to Alton. From Alton the directors' party returned by a special train to Bentworth station, whence they drove to Burkham House, where they were the guests of Mr A.F. Jeffreys and Mrs Jeffreys at luncheon. Later in the day the special took them back to Basingstoke.'

The report is so full that there is little to add about the line on its opening day. As will be seen from the average speed of about 13 miles per hour, allowing for protracted stops at the three intermediate stations, and the ten miles per hour limit on curves sharper than nine-chains radius, some of the running was quite sprightly, despite a ruling gradient of 1 in 50 and an overall speed limit of 20 miles per hour. The locomotive concerned was No. 203, an 0-4-4 tank locomotive built at Nine Elms in 1891. Although the train was no faster than a motor bus, it was a considerable improvement either on horse transport or on the circuitous rail journey via Winchester, (Journey time was about one hour and fare 1/2d (6p) against about two hours and 3/0½d (15p)).

The only extravagance by present-day standards was the number of

27

staff and the construction of housing for them at the stations. There was a great contrast between the austerity of the corrugated-iron station buildings and the provision of a fully fledged station-master at each stopping place.

In time the service improved, with a separate goods train to reduce the need for the mixed trains. (These were frequently a feature of light railways and apart from the doubtful entertainment value of the shunting operations at each station, were singularly unattractive to passengers.) By 1913, there were six trains each week-day, but the line was closed on Sundays. Attempts were made to reduce costs by introducing steam rail motor-cars, Nos 1 and 2 being tried out on the line in 1904. Somewhat oddly the entire fleet of 15 LSWR rail cars were tried out on the Basingstoke & Alton, but none of them remained there, possibly because of their inability to cope with the steep gradients, and the occasional mixed trains.

The opening of the Meon Valley line in 1903 completed the Basingstoke–Alton–Fareham–Portsmouth route, but no through trains were run, and in the normal course of events the Basingstoke and Alton would have continued as a local line until it lost most of its traffic to the roads. In fact, partly because it was owned by a main line company, it closed at the end of 1916. The main line companies after nearly two-and-a-half years of war were faced with increased traffic and a reduced labour force, and they met the situation by closing lightly used stations and routes, and concentrating their staff where they were most needed. Normally, only staff were moved, but in the case of the Basingstoke and Alton, the track was moved as well, being lifted and taken to France.

Under war conditions, the loss of the railway was accepted, but when, after the war, it became clear that the company had no intention of restoring it, local opinion was incensed. The newly formed Southern Railway decided that this was a commitment they did not wish to honour, as the annual loss before the war had been estimated at £4,000. Powers for abandonment were included in their 1923 Bill, but there was considerable opposition from influential landowners, partly on the grounds that the company had been given the land at very low rates on the understanding that railway service was to be provided. The company saw the way the wind was blowing and withdrew the relevant clause, stating that they would review the position in ten years' time.

Meanwhile the road bed had become weed-infested and the corrugated-iron station buildings had been neglected although the company houses had remained in use. The track was re-laid and the station buildings restored. However, things were not quite as before. For instance, Herriard lost its passing loop so that once a train had left either end of the line, no other train could venture on the 13-mile route until the first one was clear. This time there were no station-masters, the whole line coming under the Basingstoke station-master. One thing which showed no change was the motive power. The first train in 1901 had been hauled by No. 203, and on 18 August, 1924, the locomotive was No. E234 of the same class, built in 1895 at Nine Elms. (The Southern added a prefix E to the numbers of locomotives for which Eastleigh Works were responsible.) The service reverted to the level of 1901 with three trains a day each way, but starting later and finishing earlier. There was no early train to convey the churns of fresh milk to London, although there must have been some milk traffic as a picture of Herriard, taken in the June of 1931, shows churns on the platform.

The fact that there were no trains on Sundays made possible the use of the line for a dramatic crash staged for a film company in 1928. The locomotive was No. A148, a 4-4-0 express locomotive built to the design of James Stirling at Ashford Works in 1889. A weighted steam lorry was placed on a level-crossing, the locomotive and six coaches were set in motion, the driver and firemen jumped clear, and the inevitable and spectacular collision followed. This was filmed and shown throughout the country as part of a film called appropriately enough *The Wrecker*. Breakdown gangs cleared the wreckage and the track was repaired, the remains of the locomotive being sold to Marple & Gillett of Sheffield for scrap.

In rather less than the promised ten years, the accounts of the line were reviewed, and, as a result, the passenger service ended on 12 September, 1932. There was little of the celebration which accompanied later closures. Most of the local inhabitants had already transferred to the roads, and railway enthusiasts were thinner on the ground and less able to pay the fares to be present at the running of last trains. In fact, the last train is reported as leaving Alton at 7.30 p.m. carrying one passenger. This was the end of the line as a through route but the three stations remained open for goods traffic until 1 June, 1936. The track was lifted from the Alton end to Bentworth and Lasham, the goods train operating from Basingstoke.

The filming of *Oh! Mr Porter* took place in 1937, after the final closure of the three stations, using locomotive No. 2 of the KESR, brought from Kent for the occasion. A former LSWR 4-4-0 express locomotive, No. 657, built at Nine Elms in 1895, also took part. The station buildings at

Cliddesden were encased in a tottering structure which represented a mythical Irish station called Buggleskelly. A spurious signal box was placed by the level-crossing and an exciting sequence was filmed between Cliddesden and Basingstoke, where trick photography depicted narrowly averted collisions.

Demolition continued during 1937 until only the two ends of the line were left. They were eventually closed in 1967. At the south end about a quarter-of-a-mile remained between Butt's Junction, Alton and Treloars Hospital which received its coal by rail. It was also provided with a passenger platform but this was never mentioned in the public timetables. At the northern end there was about half-a-mile of track going as far as Thorneycroft's Works at Basingstoke. In 1943 a section of the main road from Basingstoke to Alton at Lasham was diverted to make way for an aerodrome. The new section of road, still distinguishable by its concrete surface and direct alignment, occupied and obliterated about half-a-mile of permanent way.

The railway houses at Herriard and Lasham have been sold, but those at Cliddesden are still let to railway employees. It was frequently the practice to supply water to wayside stations by rail but all the three Basingstoke & Alton stations had their own wells and water tanks, two fed by windpumps, and that at Herriard by an oil engine. All the cottages now have piped water, but the windpump at Cliddesden survived until after the war.

Gradually the relics of the railway are disappearing. The solid concrete platforms survive, and also the station building at Lasham, where a coal merchant continued to use the station yard after the closure of the line. Until recently most of the brick bridges remained, including the underbridge over Worting Road, Basingstoke. However, road improvements have precipitated its demolition, and for the same reason, a bridge at the Alton end has recently gone. Parts of the permanent way, especially where it was level with the adjoining fields have been purchased by the landowners, and returned to the agricultural use from which it was taken, perhaps 50 years earlier. But elsewhere, cuttings and embankments serve as a reminder of the line. A more utilitarian survival are the railway cottages by the stations and the two crossing-keepers' houses. Although the ultimate fate of the line was decided when road transport was mechanized, there is no doubt that neither the traffic between Basingstoke and Alton or that arising from the pleasant countryside in between would ever have supported a railway. But for the LSWR's fear of the Great Western it would probably have never had one.

The Bordon Light Railway

From a legal viewpoint, the Bordon branch was a light railway, but it was always operated in the same manner as a normal branch line. After a short period of 'one engine in steam', tablet working was instituted, and the only visible indications of light railway status were the three ungated level crossings. Nevertheless, the four-and-a-half-mile line was authorized by a Light Railway Order in 1902, and opened in 1905, primarily to serve military establishments at Bordon and Longmoor.[8] Before the Second World War, the station name-board at Bentley advised passengers to 'Change for the Bordon Light Railway'. For the few who took this advise, the normal train service ran as far as the branch terminal, only the occasional special troop train being transferred to the Longmoor Military Railway.

However, a large proportion of the freight traffic was forwarded to the LMR. The branch train which, in latter years, consisted of an M7 class tank locomotive and a push-pull set of two LSWR coaches, left from a down bay platform at Bentley. This was separated from the down through platform by iron railings. Somewhat oddly, no independent third line was provided over the 17 chains to the junction, the branch train using the down main line for this distance. A halt was opened in 1906 to serve the village of Kingsley, and, although sufficient land was obtained to build a station and goods yard, this never materialized. Kingsley was one of the simpler halts, its only adornments being a lamp post, a name-board, a time-table board and a seat. If it rained, waiting passengers became wet. Bordon was more elaborate, with a signal box, station buildings, an engine shed and a length of sidings designed to take any surges of traffic that military requirements might produce, but, in 1927, the signal box was reduced to the status of a ground frame. Closure to passengers came in 1957, and to freight in 1966.

Subsequently, access to the LMR was via the Portsmouth main line at Liss, and the section between Bordon and Oakhanger was closed. Now the sites of both Kingsley and Bordon are occupied by new developments. Although the Bordon branch was a public railway, it always had a military flavour and the site of Bordon station must be haunted by the thousands of soldiers who passed through it in two World Wars.[9]

3

Light Railways in Kent and Sussex

The first light railway in Kent or Sussex was opened in 1897 and, somewhat remarkably, the last, opened in 1927, still carries passenger traffic.

The Hundred of Manhood & Selsey Tramway
(later the West Sussex Railway)

In March 1895, shortly after the opening of the Lee-on-the-Solent Railway, its manager, Mr E.B. Ivatts, produced plans for a line from the LBSCR at Chichester to the nascent resort of Selsey. At the time Selsey was described as a 'pretty and unconventional resort, in great favour with the legal fraternity, and with people who reside there during the season, paterfamilias dividing his time between London and Selsey'. The canal still ran from Chichester to Birdham, and Ivatt's idea was to follow its bank as far as Hunston, with a branch to Birdham. He also suggested that the railway company should buy land at Selsey for re-sale, a proposal of doubtful legality.

In March 1896 Mr Powell of Lewes addressed a private meeting with a new scheme, which won the support of local interests including Mr W.B.B. Freeland of Raper, Freeland & Tyacke, solicitors, and Mr G. Woodbridge, J.P., of Millbanke, Woodbridge, Gruggen & Gauntlet, the Chichester bankers. The company was registered in April 1896 and, not surprisingly, the above persons were appointed solicitors and bankers respectively. Powell & Co. of Lewes acted as land agents, and Mr (later Lt-Col.) Holman Fred Stephens was the engineer.[1]

In February 1897 the contract for constructing the line to Selsey was awarded to Mancktelow Bros of Horsmonden in Kent; two tank locomotives were ordered from Pecketts of Bristol; and some tram-type

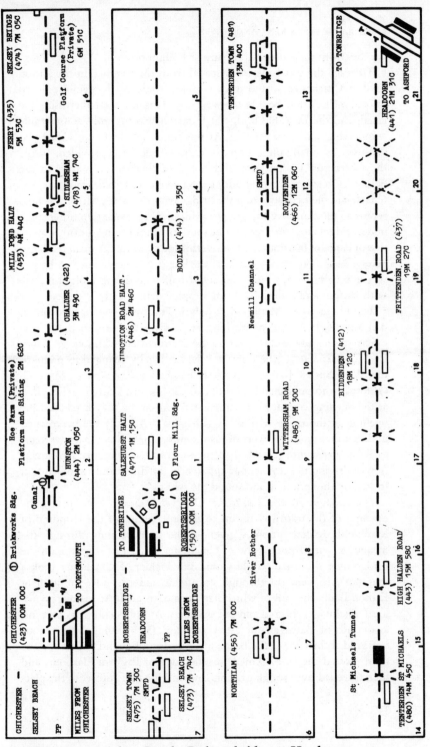

4 **Chichester to Selsey Beach; Robertsbridge to Headcorn**

coaches from the Falcon Company of Loughborough.

To reach the east bank of the canal from the terminal in the station yard at Chichester would have required some costly demolition, so instead the new line kept to the west side. This necessitated crossing the canal, and the movable bridge at Hunston was the only considerable engineering work on the line. At this time the Chichester Canal was still used by small sailing ships, so a drawbridge was provided. While the Chichester Corporation did not give financial assistance to the Selsey Tramway, they did adopt a benevolent attitude, and this was reflected in their constructing the bridge over the canal, which was then rented to the tramway for £2 per annum. There were two other small underbridges crossing streams, one south of Hunston and the other at the side of Pagham Harbour, and an overbridge carrying the main road into Selsey. As the one major work on the line cost the company nothing it was unusually cheap, the seven-and-a-half miles being built complete with stations and rolling stock for a capital debt of only £19,000.

The Hundred of Manhood & Selsey Tramway was opened on 27 August, 1897. As the overbridge at Selsey was unfinished the first official train only went as far as the platform later known as Selsey Bridge. Fortunately, the tramway, which legally changed its name to the West Sussex Railway in 1924, has had a biographer: Mr E.C. Griffiths, who published his history of the line in 1948.[2] He relates that at the opening ceremony at Chichester Station the mayor recalled the opening of the LBSCR station '45 years ago'. (Actually the mayor was underestimating the powers of his memory, for it was in fact, 51 years earlier.) Mr Griffith records that 'the mayor then announced his intention of driving the engine, but apparently the driver only allowed him to step on the footplate and sound the whistle'.

The account in the *Chichester Observer* indicates how much the opening of the tramway meant to the inhabitants of the Hundred of Manhood. A description is given of the train running through the meadows 'with a good view of Chichester' and of its stopping on the bridge over the canal 'while Councillor Fielder of Chichester took a snapshot'. It went on through cornfields and past the windmill at Kipson Bank, the sails of which had been decorated. At various points, local inhabitants cheered and put out flags. At Sidlesham 'Mrs Stevens, an old lady of 86, was an interested spectator'. (She would have been four years old at the time of the Battle of Waterloo.) Beyond Sidlesham, the train crossed the embankment on the edge of Pagham Harbour, and then travelled over rough grazing land and the golf course, to the platform at Selsey Bridge.

The passengers proceeded to a luncheon at Beacon House at which the mayor, presumably having overcome his disappointment at not being allowed to drive the engine, congratulated the company on the economy with which the line had been constructed. He felt that the agriculture of the district might revive – it had suffered from the competition of imported food, facilitated by steamers and overseas railways. He was also delighted that people could go to the seaside at Selsey instead of Bognor whose inhabitants had always been rather 'stand-offish'.

For the first few weeks, the company did not commit itself to arrival times, and in the words of a visitor who travelled on the line a year later, 'I am rather surprised they do so now. It is an over-bold stroke of policy.'[3] Throughout its history, the line was more notable for informality than speed or punctuality. Mr Griffith quotes from the Rev. H.W. Haynes's book on Sidlesham:

'Its playful eccentricities were the delight of the children who went by it to school at Chichester. Morning after morning its engine refused to budge, much time was taken in getting it to start and when at length it did so and "chugged" slowly into Chichester, school had long since started, and the long-suffering mistress had to accept with a smile the frequent excuse for lateness, "The train was late, Miss".'

When running to time, the seven-and-a-half miles were covered in 30 minutes. The frequency of the service varied according to season, from about 12 trains a day each way in the summer to six in the winter. After the First World War, motor buses took away much of the traffic and in the last summer in which trains ran – that of 1934 – there were only seven trains each way.

Although an official distinction was made between stations and halts, with the exception of Chichester and Selsey, all the stopping places looked like halts. Hunston, Chalder, Sidlesham and Selsey Bridge consisted of single platforms with shelters of corrugated iron. The halts at Hoe Farm and Golf Club (near Selsey) lacked shelters and were only intended for persons having business at the farm or playing golf. Together with Mill Pond halt, between Chalder and Sidlesham they were usually omitted from the time-table, although by 1913, Golf Club halt had crept into *Bradshaw*. Tickets were issued on the trains, but staff were provided at Hunston and Selsey to deal with freight traffic. Selsey and Chichester both had gas-works so the terminal stations were illuminated by gas; elsewhere oil lamps prevailed. Water was pumped from a well at Selsey and from a ditch at Hunston. After August 1898, during the summer months, Selsey Town was not the terminal, an extension of half-a-mile to the beach having been opened. This was closed probably in 1904, and not re-opened. Also in 1898 an additional station was opened at the south end of the embankment bordering Pagham Harbour, and was named Ferry after the adjacent Ferry House. The single line had no signals, but there was telephonic communication and occasional use was made of the crossing loop at Sidlesham.

The flat-bottomed track was less substantial than that of the Lee-on-the-Solent line, 41 lbs per yard rail being used on the straight sections and 56 lbs on the curves. As was usual on light railways, the track ballast consisted of gravel, but in this case it contained a proportion of sea shingle. A photograph of a train at Chichester in 1908 shows a jack readily available for re-railing being carried on the footplate of the locomotive. In fact, speeds were such as to make derailment less likely, or, if it occurred, less serious. An unfortunate exception occurred in 1923 when a locomotive jumped the rails near Golf Club halt, the fireman being killed.

In some ways a more dramatic incident was the breaching of the sea wall at Pagham Harbour on 15 December, 1910, which resulted in the flooding of the line between Chalder and Ferry. Normally all the locomotives and rolling stock spent the night at Selsey, but with happy foresight, they had been divided on this occasion, so it was possible to provide a shuttle service with a horse bus linking the two sections. The embankment was rebuilt and raised 12 feet, and while work was in progress, the road connection was maintained between Ferry and Mill Pond halts.

The increase in motor-cars and motor bus competition not only robbed the line of its traffic, but also increased the danger of the ungated crossings. In May 1924, Chichester City Council and West Hampnett Rural District Council requested an inquiry as a result of which the Ministry of Transport decided that at crossings over public roads, trains must stop for the fireman or the guard to advance into the middle of the road armed with a red flag by day or a red lamp by night. Despite these enforced interruptions of the train's progress, the 30-minute schedule was retained.

By 1909, the Lee-on-the-Solent company had persuaded the relevant main line company, the LSWR, to work its line but the West Sussex failed to achieve a similar arrangement with the LBSCR. In fact, until after the First World War, there was no great incentive, for unlike the Lee-on-the-Solent, the West Sussex had a significant agricultural traffic augmented by lobsters and crabs from Selsey.[4] Whereas the Lee-on-the-Solent could only carry Gosport people wishing to visit its seaside terminal for two miles of their journey, the West Sussex carried Chichester people for over seven. But after the First World War, motor buses, motorcars and lorries took the traffic and the railway became bankrupt in 1931, Mr Owen Walker being made receiver and manager. In January 1935, there were hopes that the Southern might have taken over the line; the level-crossing problem was one of the reasons that dissuaded them. So on 19 January the Selsey line went out of business. Mr Griffith quotes from the *Daily Express* of 21 January, 1935:

'The whole staff of a railway line, from superintendent to messenger boy, received their last week's wages and became out of work yesterday. They were the 12 employees of the "Selsey Bumper" – the West Sussex Railway – which ceased to operate today after 38 hectic years of life on the eight-mile run between Chichester and Selsey. Tonight with ex-engine driver George White I toured the old sheds and saw about the strangest collection of railway stock in the world. In a huge corrugated-iron shed with half the roof blown off were three old engines. Outside were some more "engines" – old motor coaches of the famous "tin Lizzie" type, fitted with steel wheels.' (These were the two rail-cars purchased in 1928.) 'Selsey station is a corrugated-iron shed. Further along the line is the Ferry station – a few sleepers tied together for a platform, a small wooden shed for a shelter. There are nine stations along the line, not one of them has a porter or booking office. As we toured round George said, "We've had some strange things happen on this old line in the past two years. Being a single track meant that if there was one breakdown the service was finished for the day. We used to send a boy on a bicycle instead of the train just to tell anyone waiting at the stations that we couldn't be along that day. People used to go for rides just for fun."'

The line was sold to a contractor from Gloucestershire for £3,610. The track was removed and subsequently almost every sign of the line has disappeared. The site of Chichester station has been absorbed into the BR goods yard and that of Selsey Town now consists of rough ground. However, the platforms of Hunston and Chalder, and the abutment of the drawbridge over the Chichester Canal all survive. Two sections of the line are in use as public footpaths, at Hunston and near Sidlesham. (The former also provides a wayleave for an overhead electricity line.) There are some remains at Selsey Beach but these are threatened by an improvement scheme. Although it is remembered by the more senior local residents, visitors to Selsey may be forgiven for being unaware that the West Sussex Railway ever existed. Nevertheless, the amount of freight and the number of passengers it carried before the First World War, show clearly that in its time, it was of service.

The Rother Valley Railway
(later the Kent & East Sussex Railway)

The next light railway to be opened was in the Rother Valley. Like the Hundred of Manhood & Selsey Tramway it changed its name, becoming the Kent & East Sussex Railway in 1904. Whereas the Lee-on-the-Solent Railway and the Selsey Tramway served nascent resorts, the justification for the Rother Valley was less speculative, being based almost entirely on the traffic of a prosperous agricultural district. The prospectus enlarged on this:

'The Valley of the Rother, through which the line passes, consists principally of rich grassland and is an ideal one for a light railway. It is a thickly populated agricultural district which has been greatly handicapped by the absence of facilities for the carriage of goods. The population to be served by the railway numbers about 18,000, at least one half of whom are from six to nine miles from the nearest railway station. The transport of ordinary goods required to feed this large population would alone give this company a considerable income. When the line is opened for traffic, a very large milk trade, it is believed, will be established for the supply of Hastings, Tunbridge Wells and other large markets. Large quantities of hops and fruit are also grown in the surrounding district and would be conveyed over this railway to the markets. Monthly sales of cattle are now held in Robertsbridge. The construction of the line will give access to this market to the farmers and graziers in and around Northiam, Rolvenden and Tenterden with consequent benefit to the company. Two large flour mills, which will be specially served by the company, will also be a source of profit.

A large excursion traffic may also be expected on the line during the

1   Lee-on-the-Solent station on 14 April, 1928. The motor train consisted of an LBSCR 'Terrier' class locomotive and an LSWR saloon coach. The locomotive, then numbered B661, was built at Brighton Works in 1875, and scrapped in 1963. This view shows the typical concrete-faced platform, with the station buildings beyond the train.

2   The last train from Lee-on-the-Solent on 2 October, 1935. This was after the official closure date, and seems to have consisted of empty coal wagons. It was hauled by LBSCR D1 class, No. 2239, built by Nielson in 1881, and scrapped in 1948. The pier, the station buildings and the newly erected Lee Tower are visible in the background.

3   Herriard station on 13 June, 1931. This view shows the station as re-opened after war-time closure, with no passing loop or signals. Visible features include the water tank, the corrugated-iron buildings, the milk churns and the wagons in the siding at the back of the station.

4   Bordon station in use. The 4.47 p.m. motor train from Bentley had arrived on 7 September, 1957. This consisted of LSWR M7 class, No. 30110 built at Nine Elms in 1904, and two SR Maunsell coaches.

1   Lee-on-the-Solent station on 14 April, 1928. The motor train consisted of an LBSCR 'Terrier' class locomotive and an LSWR saloon coach. The locomotive, then numbered B661, was built at Brighton Works in 1875, and scrapped in 1963. This view shows the typical concrete-faced platform, with the station buildings beyond the train.

2   The last train from Lee-on-the-Solent on 2 October, 1935. This was after the official closure date, and seems to have consisted of empty coal wagons. It was hauled by LBSCR D1 class, No. 2239, built by Nielson in 1881, and scrapped in 1948. The pier, the station buildings and the newly erected Lee Tower are visible in the background.

The Last Goods Train
From Lee-on-the-Solent.
Oct: 2. 1935.

3   Herriard station on 13 June, 1931. This view shows the station as re-opened after war-time closure, with no passing loop or signals. Visible features include the water tank, the corrugated-iron buildings, the milk churns and the wagons in the siding at the back of the station.

4   Bordon station in use. The 4.47 p.m. motor train from Bentley had arrived on 7 September, 1957. This consisted of LSWR M7 class, No. 30110 built at Nine Elms in 1904, and two SR Maunsell coaches.

5 Bordon station abandoned. On 4 July, 1971, the line of the platform face and the bases of the steel columns which supported the canopy were still visible. In the right background, the only outstanding relic of the Longmoor Military Railway station was the disused signal box.

6 A typical passenger train of the late 1920s and 1930s on a Col. Stephens railway. A Shefflex rail car traverses an ungated crossing on the main road just north of Ferry station on the West Sussex Railway.

7 The West Sussex Railway today. Remains of the platform face of Hunston station on 15 February, 1975.

8 Engineering works on the Headcorn extension of the KESR. St Michael's tunnel near Tenterden and a cutting illustrate the reason for the extension being expensive by light railway standards. A view taken in the rain on the last day of 1953.

9   Rolvenden on 2 January, 1954, the last day of passenger traffic on the KESR. The passenger station with its characteristic corrugated-iron buildings was virtually unchanged since the opening day in 1900. SER O1 class, No. 31065 was raising steam outside the running shed.

10   Rolvenden on 19 October, 1958. The Locomotive Club of Great Britain's 'Rother Valley Limited' had arrived with 'Terrier' class, No. 32678, built at Brighton in 1880 at one end, and the Brighton Works shunter, No. 377s, built at Brighton in 1878, on the other. Each locomotive had to stop by the water column, and while No. 32678 took water, the five-coach train blocked the level-crossing. By this date, the running shed and station buildings had been demolished, but the lamp room survived.

11   The 10.55 a.m. to Leysdown at Queenborough on 3 December, 1950. Locomotive No. 31705 of the LCDR R1 class was built by Sharp Stewart in 1900, and was scrapped in 1951. Its train consisted of articulated set No. 514 and a van for parcels traffic. At this time Queenborough retained its traditional signalling and gas lighting. This was the last day of traffic on the Sheppey Light Railway.

12   The 10.55 a.m. from Queenborough stopped at Brambledown halt on 3 December, 1950. The crossing gates had been closed against the road, and the train was waiting for the photographer to rejoin it.

13 Hythe, the eastern terminal of the RHDR on 19 August, 1973. This view shows the four-platform station with its overall roof, the original signal cabin, the new colour light signals, and part of the water tank.

14 RHDR No. 10, 'Dr Syn', built by the Yorkshire Engine Co. in 1931, about to leave Hythe on the 2.10 p.m. to New Romney on 19 August, 1973.

15 Shepherd's Well, East Kent Light Railway, on 22 August, 1946, viewed from the embankment which carried the uncompleted northern spur. The passenger station is visible in the middle distance, with a mixed train leaving for Wingham. A coal wagon is being unloaded with the aid of a prop for the side door. This would probably be for locomotives, as the engine shed, visible in the background, lacked a coaling stage. The original flat-bottomed track with weighted point levers is visible in the foreground.

16 Engineering works on the East Kent comparable to those on the Headcorn extension of the KESR. Both had a tunnel but the EKLR Golgotha tunnel was longer, and, as this view of the southern portal shows, was built for double track. Construction through chalk made possible the steep cutting sides, minimizing both the volume of excavation and the width of land required. This view of 20 May, 1967 shows the line relaid with chaired track.

summer months from Hastings and Tunbridge Wells and the South Coast towns to Bodiam Castle, which is a fine old Norman ruin and a favourite object of interest to excursionists from neighbouring towns. As many as 600 people visit this castle in one day. At present, visitors are conveyed to the castle in brakes which drive out from St Leonards and Hastings, the charge for the journey being 4/6d per head. As the company, in conjunction with the South Eastern Railway will be able to convey the visitors for nearly one half of this cost, there is no doubt that a very large proportion of this traffic will fall to this company, and in consequence of the decrease in cost a considerable increase in the number of visitors may be confidently anticipated.'

Although the prospectus was obviously composed with a view to 'selling' the line, its promise was at least partly fulfilled until the coming of motor transport. The engineer was again Mr H.F. Stephens. He estimated receipts of £9,672 and working expenses of £4,368. The balance of £5,304 would pay 4 per cent on the £20,000 debentures which were authorized, leaving £4,504 for a 7½ per cent dividend on the £60,000 ordinary shares. The railway undoubtedly offered faster and cheaper transport than the existing roads. Its claim to serve 18,000 people, however, depended on an estimate of the catchment areas of the stations. The position of existing stations, including the terminal of the SER Hawkhurst branch, made the 18,000 estimate hard to justify. Unfortunately, some of the main sources of revenue, such as excursionists to Bodiam Castle, and fruit and milk for the London and seaside markets, yielded easily to competition from motor transport, but until the advent of the latter, the Rother Valley line carried at least enough traffic to justify its existence.

It was a little too early to obtain its powers under the Light Railways Act of 1896. In 1895 the Tenterden Railway Act had been passed for a line linking the SER Dover line at Headcorn to the Hastings and Ashford line at Appledore. This would have passed through Tenterden, giving it a route to London via Headcorn, but it traversed undulating country and thus had far higher construction costs than a line down the Rother Valley. The Rother Valley (Light) Railway Act received the Royal Assent on 2 July, 1896. It took advantage of the dispensations, mainly concerning signalling and stations which could be granted under the Regulation of Railways Act, 1868. Both the Tenterden Railway and the Rother Valley Railway were about 12 miles long but the easier route and lighter construction of the latter resulted in an authorized capital of

£60,000, which was £75,000 less than that of the Tenterden company. After the passing of the Light Railways Act it was decided to take advantage of it, and Light Railway Order no. 64 was obtained on 8 December, 1899. This required an overall speed limit of 25 miles per hour and specified the use of rails of 60 lbs per yard.

The company also proposed a new line from Cranbrook through Tenterden to Ashford, of which only the Cranbrook to Tenterden section was authorized. This would have had junctions with the SER at Cranbrook and at Ashford and with the first section of the Rother Valley at Tenterden. The ability of the Rother Valley to obtain SER agreement to junctions was perhaps partly explained by the fact that its chairman, Sir Myles Fenton, was a consulting director and the former general manager of the SER company. The only part of the Cranbrook and Tenterden to materialize was the section from Rolvenden to the town of Tenterden, joined to the Rother Valley terminal at Rolvenden by a sharp curve of ten-chains radius.

The East Sussex Light Railways Order of 1901 authorized a branch from the Rother Valley at Northiam to Rye but this scheme was stillborn. Two lines were authorized to the north. Light Railway Order No. 153 of 13 March, 1902 gave powers for the eight-mile extension from Tenterden to the SER at Headcorn which unfortunately for the company, it managed to complete. Order No. 267 of 10 May, 1906 authorized a further ten-mile extension from Headcorn to Maidstone, for which land was purchased, and an especially powerful new locomotive obtained. This was No. 4, 'Hecate', which was of limited value as she was too heavy to run on the original Rother Valley line. Ultimately the land north of Headcorn was resold so in its final form the Kent & East Sussex comprised the original Rother Valley line from Robertsbridge to Rolvenden, the section of the Cranbrook & Tenterden between Rolvenden and Tenterden, and the Tenterden to Headcorn extension. Even after the line had achieved a distinction which fell to few light railways, that of surviving long enough to be nationalized, there was still a difference in the character of the original Rother Valley line and the Headcorn extension.

The terminals of the Rother Valley were characteristically sited. The station for Tenterden was opened in a valley over a mile from the centre of the town. After the extension to the well-placed Tenterden Town station was completed in 1903, the original terminal was renamed Rolvenden, although it was further away from that place than from Tenterden. Engine sheds and carriage sidings were often sited at the end of branch lines, and to these, being an independent company, the Rother Valley added its repair workshops. At the other terminal, the trains used the back of the down platform of the SER Robertsbridge station.

Between the terminals the line followed a valley route, giving low construction costs but leaving it slightly removed from the villages. Of the original three stations Bodiam was half-a-mile from the village centre, Northiam was one-and-a-quarter miles, and the remoteness of the station for Wittersham, two-and-a-quarter miles from the village, was acknowledged by calling it Wittersham Road. By light railway standards, the stations on the Rother Valley were somewhat lavish, with corrugated-iron buildings and platforms with name-boards and oil lamps at all three intermediate stations and at Rolvenden. There were goods sidings at all the original stations, and Northiam had two platforms. In addition to goods facilities at the stations, a siding ran into the mill at Robertsbridge and another served the Bantony Estate at Salehurst.

A proposed station between Robertsbridge and Bodiam presented problems of nomenclature, but as it was situated on the turnpike road from Hawkhurst to Hastings called Junction Road, the slightly evasive title, Junction Road for Hawkhurst, was chosen. (It was four miles from Hawkhurst.) Funds did not run to a building in this case, and when the station was opened about eight months after the others it consisted of only a platform and one siding.

From Robertsbridge to beyond Northiam, while following the valley, the line kept high enough above the bottom to avoid flooding. However, during floods in 1916, the track was not only under water, but had also moved, owing to pressure on the north side. Engine No. 8, on the first train in the morning, was derailed, and came to rest on its left side against a happily placed willow tree.

In order to avoid gradients, Mr Stephens introduced curves of up to 17-chains radius which, because of the overall 25 miles per hour speed limit, did not hamper train speeds. Between Northiam and Wittersham Road, the line had to cross from the south side of the Rother Valley to follow up a tributary, the Newmill Channel, to the terminal. There were 24 bridges over ditches and streams, most of them with spans varying from 12 feet to 40 feet, but that over the Rother was 66 feet long – a Tay Bridge by light railway standards. With curves of up to 17-chains radius and gradients of up to 1 in 70, on what was in any case an easy route to follow, earthworks were kept to a minimum. The highest embankment, 25 feet in height, was that on which the line curved away from the SER at Robertsbridge. Although the Rother Valley soon moved into characteristic light railway style by using very second-hand rolling stock, initially it purchased two new tank locomotives from Hawthorn Leslie of Newcastle. No. 1, named 'Tenterden', spent all its working life on the Kent and East Sussex, but No. 2, 'Northiam', travelled.

In 1949 Mr Lawson Finch published his book on the history of the line, *The Rother Valley, later the Kent & East Sussex Railway.*⁵ By the First World War, Col. Stephens had acquired major interests in a number of light railways, including the Kent & East Sussex, the West Sussex, the East Kent, and the Weston, Clevedon & Portishead. Mr Finch relates that one Sunday morning in 1917 No. 2 set out on the longest run of her career from Rolvenden to Clevedon. There are no details of the route but this would probably have been via Tonbridge, Redhill, Reading, Swindon and Bristol. One may speculate on the reaction of signalmen on the Great Western main line to the sight of the diminutive KESR No. 2 heading west. Although she may well have achieved the highest speeds of her career, it was eight o'clock in the evening before her driver booked off at Bristol. The rest of the journey to Clevedon was completed on the Monday morning.

The next sortie of No. 2 was in 1923 when she was transferred to the East Kent Railway. Compared with her trip to the west, this would have been a modest jaunt, probably via Headcorn, Ashford and Dover. After a few years she returned to the KESR, her next excursion being in 1937 to the already closed Basingstoke & Alton Light Railway. On this occasion her probable route would have been via Tonbridge, Redhill, Guildford, Woking and Basingstoke. (She could not have gone via Alton as the track had already been lifted between Alton and Herriard.) This was not part of an attempt to revive the line, but arose from the belief of Gainsborough Pictures, who were making a film, that the Southern Railway had nothing to offer them which looked quite as antiquated as KESR No. 2. Even so, she was made to look even older, being given an elongated chimney with a serrated top, and named 'Gladstone'. She appeared on cinema screens throughout the country, with Will Hay, Graham Moffat and Moore Marriott in the film *Oh, Mr. Porter.*

No. 3 had a remarkably long life. She was built by the LBSCR at its Brighton Works in 1872, receiving the name 'Poplar'. The Rother Valley bought her in 1901 to help out Nos 1 and 2, and named her 'Bodiam'. She kept going until the 1930s, when she underwent a major refit,

involving replacement of vital parts taken from other ailing members of
Col. Stephens's locomotive collection. Under war-time conditions, in
1943, when everything that would run was needed, No. 3 received a
major overhaul from the Southern Railway.

In 1947, Ealing Studios, perhaps inspired by the earlier success of
KESR No. 2 in films, approached the company for a complete train set –
No. 3 and three vintage four-wheel coaches. Unfortunately the location
of the film, *The Loves of Joanna Godden*, was on Romney Marsh, and, for
the sake of realism, it was necessary for the KESR train to reach the
Southern's New Romney line. Having recently overhauled No. 3
itself, Southern could hardly claim that she was unfit to move on SR
metals, but it did not take this view of the KESR coaches. So No. 3 went
off down the main line from Robertsbridge on her own, through
Hastings and along the Ashford line as far as Appledore, the junction
for the New Romney branch. There she was joined with two former
SER coaches, antique by Southern standards but falling far short of the
antiquity which the KESR could have achieved.

When the KESR was nationalized in 1948, No. 3 became part of the
locomotive stock of British Railways, receiving the number 32670.
(In her LBSCR days, she had been first 70, then 670. If she had become a
Southern engine she would have been 2670.) No. 3 then embarked on
her third career, this time with British Railways. When the KESR was
closed to freight traffic, she was transferred to the Hayling Island branch,
being allocated to Eastleigh shed. With the closure of the Hayling Island
branch, No. 32670 was, after 91 years of service withdrawn in November
1963. However, in April 1964 she was purchased by the Kent & East
Sussex Railway Preservation Society and is now back at Rolvenden.

To go with its initial two new locomotives, 'Tenterden' and
'Northiam' the Rother Valley acquired six new four-wheeled coaches
built by Hurst Nelson of Motherwell. Although the four wheels suggest
something primitive, in fact these were quite comfortable coaches with
automatic vacuum brakes.

This was the new railway which opened for passengers on Monday
2 April, 1900. Mr Lawson Finch[6] quotes from the *Kent Examiner and
Ashford Chronicle* (later incorporated in the *Kent Messenger*) of 6 April:

'Monday last will long be a memorable day in Tenterden, for the
public were then for the first time able to travel from the town by rail.
During the last 50 years project after project has been mooted, and
surveys have been made in every direction, but until the Rother

Valley Railway Company came on the scene every hope had been dashed to the ground. This company started operations in October 1898, and even when the line had been fenced in, few imagined that it would ever be really completed. On Saturday some of the Tenterden folk made up their minds that come what might they would either travel by the first train that left Tenterden or be present at the station to see it start. A bitter north wind blowing and a severe frost did not make a pleasant morning on Monday to tempt the public from their homes at the early hour of 7.30 a.m., at which the first train was timed to start, but nevertheless when this memorable train steamed out of the station, well-filled with passengers, the platform was crowded with a delighted crowd'.

The reporter then gave a list of names, headed by that of the vicar, who was acting in the best tradition of clerical enthusiasm for railways, followed by a selection of the more influential inhabitants of the district. There was a description of the rolling stock, and some comments on the line. The distances stated to separate the stations from the corresponding villages seem a little arbitrary:

'The first station we arrive at is Wittersham which is about one-and-a-half miles from Rolvenden and about the same distance from Wittersham. Both the Tenterden and Wittersham stations are actually in Rolvenden parish, and some of the inhabitants of the latter parish consider they have a grievance having two stations in the parish with other names. Next Northiam is about a quarter mile from Newenden, two miles from Northiam and about three-and-a-half from Beckley. The scenery here is charming and such a spot as picnickers love to find. We come next to Bodiam which is quite close to the lovely Bodiam Castle to which hundreds, and perhaps thousands, of visitors flock every summer. Next stopping place is Robertsbridge where the trains run in side by side with the SER trains.'

The officials showed less disposition for early rising than the local inhabitants. Sir Myles Fenton, the chairman, did not appear until the 2.58 p.m. from Robertsbridge when he travelled to Tenterden and back accompanied by Mr H.F. Stephens, the engineer.

In addition to the above, a rather more racy account came from a correspondent, beginning with the exhortation:

'"Up rouse ye then my merry men, it is our opening day." These were the words which suggested themselves to our minds as we made our way through the long wide-open street with its grassy slopes, in the early morning of a memorable day, for one of the most picturesque towns in the beautiful county of Kent, the inhabitants of which have patiently waited for two score years or more for a railway to connect them with the remaining part of the world.'

He described how:

'The quiet and placid thoroughfare of Rolvenden Road was quickly transformed into a busy scene of traffic, consisting of brakes, buses, cyclists and foot passengers all bent on testing the capabilities of the new railway, or seeing the first passenger train out of Tenterden station. One popular jobmaster carried passengers free to and from the station, to commemorate the event. The scene at the station was all bustle and animation.'

He went on to comment on the rolling stock and concluded:

'The train, both out and home, kept capital time and ran quite smoothly considering the difficulties that had to be overcome in laying down the metals. The officials were attentive and courteous and there seems every reason to predict that the enterprise will be a success, and a boon to the inhabitants of Tenterden and district.'

So indeed it was in the 20 years or so that it had to run before motor transport reached the Rother Valley.

As mentioned above, the Rother Valley was extended on the authorized line of the Cranbrook & Tenterden to a new terminal at Tenterden Town. It was opened on 15 April, 1903. If Rolvenden was the Crewe of the Kent & East Sussex, Tenterden Town was certainly its Euston. The stations to the south were of corrugated iron, those to the north were to be of wood, but Tenterden Town was built of brick. It was provided with a passing loop, sidings and a wind pump to feed, among other things, the water crane. It had an impressive semaphore signal with three arms. And perhaps the most unusual feature for a light railway station, it was easily accessible from the town it served.

But Tenterden, having been released from the relative isolation consequent on lacking a railway, had even better things to come. It will

45

be remembered that the company had obtained powers to extend to Headcorn, and with this in view, changed its name to the Kent & East Sussex Railway in 1904. The extension had no convenient river valley to follow, and this was reflected in its authorized share capital – £115,000 for about eight miles, as compared to the Rother Valley with £60,000 for 12 miles. By 1930, a modest credit balance on a year's working of £66–10s–4d on the original line was more than offset by a loss of £1,725–10s–4d on the Headcorn extension. By present standards, these sums are hardly significant, but in the 1930s they were not acceptable, and, in 1932, the KESR became bankrupt with Mr W.H. Austen, Col. Stephens's successor, acting as manager and receiver for the creditors. While the extension inflicted losses on the KESR it also contributed revenue to the original line by making through traffic possible. Particularly during the Second World War, it was used as an alternative to the main line between Robertsbridge and Tonbridge with its restrictive tunnels.

Despite sharp curves and gradients of 1 in 50, appreciable earthworks were required, and at St Michael's, not only was there a cutting but also a short tunnel. (This was not quite unique for a light railway; the East Kent also boasted a tunnel.) From Tenterden, London via Headcorn was 10 miles nearer than via Robertsbridge, so quite apart from any satisfaction felt by the inhabitants of High Halden, Biddenden and Frittenden at their place-names appearing on station name-boards, Tenterden people should also have been gratified.

The opening on Monday 15 May, 1905 was recorded in the *Ashford Chronicle* of 19 May:

'The long talked of railway from Tenterden to Headcorn has at length been opened to the public. The line was begun by Rigby & Co. in March 1903, and traffic commenced on Monday last. More than 40 years ago it was first mooted that Tenterden should have a railway, and the popular idea always was that the line should be to Headcorn, it being in those days impossible to make the public believe that they could get to London by any other route than via Headcorn.'

The reporter went on to recall the plans for a line from Maidstone to Hastings, reduced by the Tenterden Railway Act of 1895 to the Headcorn, Tenterden and Appledore section. He mentioned that the SER had accepted the powers for the Headcorn and Tenterden section and might have added that, on this account, they guaranteed the payments on the Headcorn extension stock. He welcomed the prospect of further extension to Maidstone and felt that if trade followed the railway, the result would be a material benefit to the Weald of Kent.

His description of the first train to Headcorn rather suggests that Tenterden was not as excited as it had been by its very first train, five years earlier:

'Monday morning saw the opening to the public of the Kent and East Sussex Railway extension from Tenterden to Headcorn, the first train being timed to leave Tenterden at 8.26 and conveying a large number of passengers.

'The first station on the line after leaving Tenterden is High Halden Road, which is situated a little over a mile from High Halden. The next station is Biddenden with a population in 1901 of 1,065, and an area of over 7,000 acres. Frittenden Road is about midway between Biddenden and Headcorn, the latter being the present terminus. The route is a very pretty one, the scenery during the whole journey being particularly pleasing to the eye. The station at Biddenden is close to the old world village, where may still be seen the old Cloth-workers' Hall, now used as residences, and other quaint buildings.'

The paper also carried 'Random Notes of a Man of Kent' who adopted a more romantic approach, seeing Tenterden as a second Maidstone:

'Now that the old town has at last secured a line which connects up with both the South Eastern main line and with the Tonbridge-Hastings branch at Robertsbridge, one hardly knows what to expect. Anything – almost – may happen, in such a case, and we must be prepared to see Tenterden developing in all directions and becoming one of the most go-ahead residential towns in Kent. For that might occur although I am quite aware that no great access of population followed upon the building of the Rother Valley line through the marshes.'

But despite his high hopes for Tenterden, the writer could not resist a mild note of protest at the inconvenience of the connections at Head-corn for anyone wishing to come from Ashford. He deplored 'the necessity of travelling at an unearthly hour (it may not seem so to the early risers of the Weald) or to spending three hours exploring the sights of Headcorn'. But conceded that 'these things are more or less inevitable, of course. I understand that even the railway cannot please everybody, and even suns have spots on them'. In 1905 the railway could fail to please everybody without worrying too much about it, but, nonetheless the connections at Headcorn were improved. However it was not difficult for the first motor buses to win the Ashford to Tenterden traffic.

Sir Herbert Walker, the famous general manager of the Southern Railway, once said that its stations were the shop windows of a railway. Applying this criterion to the stations of the Headcorn extension would suggest that the KESR had more in common with village shops than the glossy chain stores of the High street.

High Halden Road, Biddenden and Frittenden Road all had wooden buildings with canopies giving shelter on brick-faced platforms. They all had goods sidings, and Biddenden had a passing loop. Of particular interest was High Halden's signal, a tall wooden post with two arms slotted into it, probably a 'bargain' purchase from the SER. At Headcorn, the KESR used a separate platform alongside the up platform of the main line, and had its own signal box. When the Southern rebuilt its Headcorn station the KESR acquired a new concrete-faced platform, to the east of the original, complete with shelter. One more stopping place was added to the extension in 1912 when a wooden platform was opened to serve the St Michael's district of Tenterden. On the southern section, a similar platform was provided in 1929 at Salehurst between Robertsbridge and Junction Road.

To operate the extension, more rolling stock was acquired. Reference has already been made to locomotive No. 4 'Hecate', the third and last new locomotive purchased by the KESR. Its usefulness was limited by its weight, being excessive for the line south of Rolvenden, so in 1932 it was traded to the Southern for an ex-London & South Western 0-6-0 saddle tank built in 1876. For the sake of equity, the Southern also sent two spare boilers. No. 5, 'Rolvenden', was another locomotive of the LBSCR 'Terrier' class, built at Brighton in 1872 and purchased in 1905. No. 6 was not a locomotive but an experimental steam rail motor-car, also acquired in 1905. Unfortunately, the experiment proved unsuccessful. The five locomotives kept the KESR running until 1910, when an 0-6-0 of the LSWR 'Ilfracombe Goods' class was obtained. No. 7, 'Rother', was slightly newer than the 'Terriers', having been built by Beyer Peacock of Manchester in 1873. No. 8, 'Ringing Rock' (later 'Hesperus'), an 0-6-0 saddle tank locomotive built in 1876 by Manning Wardle, arrived in 1914 from the Great Western Railway. No. 9,

'Juno', was another 'Ilfracombe Goods' similar to No. 7 and built in the same year.

Of the eight locomotives owned by the company, all were tank engines except No. 7 and No. 9, and all were named after places on the line except 'Hecate', 'Juno' and 'Hesperus'.

By the end of the 1930s the KESR locomotive stock was very run down, and during the war, Southern locomotives, all 0-6-0 or 0-6-0 tank locomotives, were frequently borrowed. Until their sale for scrap in 1941, use was made of petrol-engined rail cars, one pair being purchased in 1923, a second in 1924, and the third from Shefflex in 1930.[7] Following the opening of the extension in 1905 three bogie carriages were purchased from R.Y. Pickering, of which two went to Longmoor in 1910, and one to the East Kent in 1912. This was uncharacteristic – Col. Stephens's lines were more noted for purchasing second-hand coaches than selling new ones. In fact Rolvenden became a Mecca for the connoisseur of vintage rolling stock for both passengers and freight. The LSWR, the North London, the Great Eastern and the Great Western were all represented, but the plum was a royal saloon built by the LSWR for Queen Victoria and the Prince Consort in 1848. It is only fair to add that the locomotives and coaches exhibiting the highest degree of decrepitude were to be found in grass-grown sidings at Rolvenden, and were used only in emergencies.

From 1 January, 1948, the KESR became part of the Southern Region of British Railways. On 4 February, 1948, officials of the Southern Region went on a tour of inspection of this surviving outpost of Col. Stephens's 'old iron empire'. There were four locomotives at Rolvenden, two former KESR and two former Southern, and these were to be inspected by the chief mechanical engineers' department. Of the nine coaches, it was decided that two, Nos 1 and 6, LSWR bogie corridor coaches bought from the Southern in 1945, were usable, with the proviso that they were to be marked, 'To work between Headcorn and Robertsbridge only'. If two more similar coaches were obtained, this was thought to be sufficient for carrying the traffic of the line, and the other seven coaches should be scrapped. The KESR freight stock was also examined, and it was decided that four LBSCR open wagons and two ten-ton brake vans would serve if confined to the KESR line; a cattle truck and another brake van were to be demolished. It was proposed to withdraw the five-ton crane truck, and to look into the possibility of repairing the ten-ton crane. The two road motors, based on Tenterden Town, were to be inspected. At the end of its independent existence, the KESR had a staff of 47 who, the Southern Region noted, had no pension fund and were paid at less than national agreement rates.

Even so, the KESR carried on for five more years. The staff enjoyed improved conditions, and there were improvements in the track. Various types of staff or tablet continued to authorize drivers to occupy the single track sections. Locomotives and coaches now represented only three of the old companies. There were coaches from the SECR and LSWR. Between Rolvenden and Headcorn the locomotives were usually former SECR o-6-o tender engines of the o1 class, while Tenterden to Robertsbridge trains were worked by LBSCR o-6-o tank engines. (Even with the lightly loaded trains, 'Terriers' would have had difficulty with the gradients of the extension line. On the other hand, the o-6-os were too heavy for the Rother Valley section.)

Towards the end of 1953, it was announced that the last passenger trains would run on the KESR on Saturday 4 January, 1954. Because of an aversion to last-day exhibitionism I went down to Headcorn on the last day of 1953. The weather was appropriate – cold, wet and grey. My journey started on the 9.15 a.m. down express from Charing Cross, hauled on that day by No. 30934, 'St Lawrence', a Schools Class locomotive built at Eastleigh works in 1935. The journey was uneventful: out through the London suburbs and over the North Downs to our first stop at Sevenoaks. On to Tonbridge where I changed to the 10.12 stopping train to Canterbury and Ramsgate, hauled by King Arthur class No. 30803, 'Sir Harry le Fise Lake', built at Eastleigh in 1926. There followed a comfortable run through the dank winter countryside, calling at the Kentish wayside stations until we reach Headcorn. The main line train steamed away to the east.

I purchased a monthly return to Tenterden (knowing that the return half would be useless in far less than a month), and crossed the bridge to the Kent and East Sussex platform. The train consisted of one former LSWR corridor brake No. 53165s and a tender engine of venerable appearance – ex-SER Class o1 No. 31065, built at Ashford in 1896, and rebuilt in 1909. I took a photograph, with the rails and sleepers shining in the fine rain. Back in the train, I rejoined my three fellow-passengers – one railwayman, one railway enthusiast and one merely travelling. Looking at my photograph now, I am reminded that the station name-board proclaimed 'Headcorn Junction' in KESR style with white letters on a blue background. The upper quadrant signal of characteristic Southern design operated from the main line box, had been pulled off ready for our departure.

Promptly at 10.55, we moved off, following the line designed so optimistically by Col. Stephens over 50 years earlier, and calling at the three stations which had altered so little since his time, although Bidden-den had acquired electric lighting. At 11.25 we reached Tenterden Town, 53½ miles and 130 minutes from Charing Cross. There was time to photograph the station, and to buy a ticket back to High Halden Road, the first station towards Headcorn. The engine was detached from its coach, drew forward, and then went back on another line, to be coupled up to the opposite end of the coach. The KESR, being designed for tank locomotives, lacked amenities such as turn-tables and so No. 31065 would have to run back to Headcorn tender first, with coal dust, wind and rain blowing down on to the driver and fireman. At 11.32 a.m. I started back to Headcorn, in coach No. s31655 spending its closing years far from the glories of the express runs from Waterloo to Dorset, Devon, and probably Cornwall, which it once made.

At High Halden Road, I noted that one official, a Folkestone man, carried out the duties of porter, signalman, station-master, goods agent, and booking clerk. It was here that I left the train to walk back along the track to Tenterden, and I was joined by my fellow railway enthusiast, a school-master from Hereford. Although we had covered the two miles from High Halden to Tenterden twice already, in order to see a railway it is essential to walk along the track, picking up detail not visible from a railway coach.

For instance, the chairs in which the rails rested bore the initials of the firm which made them and the company for which they were cast. Between High Halden Road and Rolvenden we found chairs marked 'SER', 'SECR', 'LBSCR', 'BR(S)', and – a rarity – 'SECDR 1901'. The oldest dated chair was marked 'SER 1891'. With the possible exception of that marked 'BR(S)', most of the chairs, like the trains, had seen service on various main lines. One other exception to this, found near Rolvenden, was a patent chair designed by Col. Stephens. Another detail, missed from the train, was the only gradient post noticed on the line. This was a wooden post, indicating a transition from 1 in 100 to level, in the cutting north of Tenterden Town. We examined the brickwork of the tunnel at St Michael's while sheltering from the rain and eating sandwiches. The ingenious construction of St Michael's halt from superannuated sleepers could be seen in something approaching comfort as the rain eased off. Tenterden was reached in time to catch the 1.10 p.m. train down the 1 in 50 gradient to Rolvenden.

Here at the 'Crewe' of the system, there were three more coaches.

Two ex-LSWR corridor coaches, No. s2650s and No. s3175s, and a SECR No. s3291s with the 'bird-cage' guard's lookout, so characteristic of that company, projecting above roof line. With these three we had seen the total coaching stock of the line: one coach for each section and two spare. The Rother Valley section was worked by LBSCR 'Terrier' tank engines from St Leonard's shed, and as the locomotive for this section was changed on Thursdays, I was able to see both No. 32678, built at Brighton in 1880, and its replacement, No. 32655 of 1875, also built at Brighton Works. The two-track engine shed and what was left of the workshops, which in Col. Stephens's days had performed such miracles of resuscitation, were still intact.

Unlike the memorable signal at High Halden Road, the Rolvenden home signal had been purchased new from Evans, O'Donnell & Co. of Westminster and Chippenham. A carping thought was that, however well Rolvenden reflected times past, by 1953 nationalization had pushed it into comparative tidiness, and that if a visit on 31 December, 1953 was rewarding, one in 1933 would have been sheer delight.

In failing light, we walked back up the track to Tenterden to catch the 4.35 p.m. on to Robertsbridge. Even from a distance we could see the platform bathed in its post-war electric light. Soon we were seated in another ex-LSWR corridor coach for what was to be my last journey on the KESR, behind No. 32655. After re-passing Rolvenden, we came to Wittersham Road, dim in the light of oil lamps. Down the valley we went, in gathering darkness, until looking at the window showed nothing except one's own reflection. And on to the main line junction at the other end of the line – Robertsbridge. I left the KESR train at the back of the down platform, and booked through to Tonbridge. Robertsbridge must have been almost the only main line station to have a poster-board, headed 'K&ESR'. It was very quiet on the up platform so the sound of the approaching train could be heard from a long way off. The level-crossing gates opened and a porter came over from the down side. The train came into view, the position of the oil lamps on the front of the locomotive indicating that it was on its way from Hastings to Charing Cross. The number was visible in the station lights and No. 30925, 'Cheltenham', took me back to London.

When the rest of the line was closed, the section from Robertsbridge to Tenterden remained open for goods traffic until 12 June, 1961. During this time, four special trains carried passengers on the line. First in April 1958, the Branch Line Society hired a train, followed in October 1958 by the Locomotive Club of Great Britain. The third, sponsored by Mr G.R. Lockie and the Ramblers' Association, ran in October 1959, and last of all, another Locomotive Club of Great Britain special made an appearance on 11 June, 1961. This was its 'South Eastern Limited', which on the same day visited the Hawkhurst branch. The seven-coach train was the longest of any of the specials, and despite the efforts of two 'Terrier' class locomotives, Nos 32662 and 32670, one at each end of the train, it stalled on the climb from Rolvenden to Tenterden. These must have been some of the most heavily loaded passenger trains the KESR had ever seen. (The numbers they carried might have been approached during the hop-picking season.)

After 1961 for a few years a P Class ex-SECR locomotive worked at Robertsbridge between the main line and its owners' premises, Hodson's Mill. It was named 'Pride of Sussex'. By this time the Kent & East Sussex Railway Preservation Society had been formed to resuscitate the line. At the time of writing the track is still down and the Rother Valley stations, except Rolvenden and Wittersham Road, are still intact. At Rolvenden, the society has assembled an impressive collection of locomotives and coaches, including an ex-GWR diesel rail car. At the moment, the future of the scheme is uncertain as in 1967 Mrs Castle, when Minister of Transport, refused to grant an Order for re-opening the line as the trains would interrupt road traffic. However, members of the society hope to get this decision reversed, and work goes on at Rolvenden repairing and restoring the rolling stock which, it is hoped, will one day be running between Tenterden and Robertsbridge.[8]

The Sheppey Light Railway

The Sheppey Light Railway was authorized by Light Railway Order No. 43 of 3 May, 1899. It was a speculative line, ostensibly justified by existing potential traffic, but built in the hope that Leysdown would become a popular resort and residential centre. This hope was reflected clearly in the original plans for a line, which showed a trailing connection with the LCDR Sheerness branch at Queenborough and ran directly across the marshes and low-lying fields to Leysdown. An article by Mr C.R. Heney appearing in the *Railway Magazine* in November 1906 quotes Sir Edwin Arnold on the subject of Leysdown:[9]

'A wilderness between two rivers of the wildest and freshest marsh meadows to be found anywhere. It is, if capitalists only understood

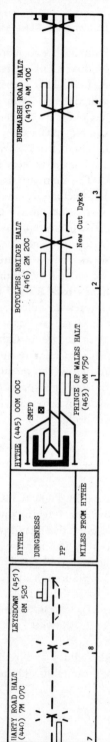
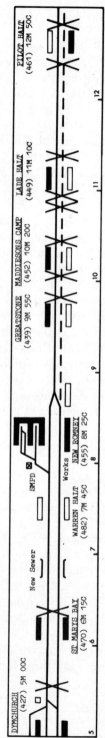
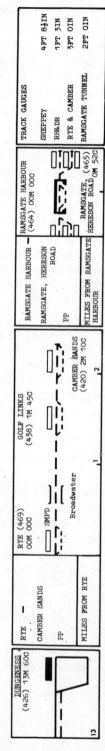

5 Queenborough to Leysdown; Hythe to Dungeness; Rye to Camber Sands; Ramsgate Harbour to Ramsgate, Hereson Road

their business a playground more spacious, free and various than any other great city could command. A great railway company already runs its trains through thousands of silent and unpeopled solitudes which only await enterprise, imagination and financial genius to make an earthly paradise out of these now desolate wastes.'

Mr Heney noted new golf links at Leysdown and felt that 'it would not be rash to hazard the opinion that a residential district such as Westcliff-on-Sea in Essex will some day be established with a frequent service of express trains for business men'. In fact, none of the places hopefully approached by the Lee-on-the-Solent, the Selsey, or the Sheppey lines respectively has justified the hopes of the railway promoters; far from becoming Bournemouths they have failed even to grow to modest Tankertons.

The promoters' draft order, presented to the Light Railway Commissioners, was fairly conventional in character. Initially, there were to be four directors, three of them from the Light Railways Syndicate. There were the usual time limits of three years for the compulsory purchase powers for the land, and five for the completion of the line. Clause 28 was for power to have stopping places without platforms. The maximum axle load was to be 15 tons, and the speed 35 miles per hour with a ten-mile-per-hour limit over the ungated level-crossings. Capital was fixed at £60,000 with powers for the LCDR to subscribe, and there were powers to borrow an extra £20,000. The maximum passenger fares were the usual ones – 3d per mile first class, 2d, second class, and 1d per mile third class.

The schedule contained various engineering details. The track was to be laid with 64 lbs rail, with check rails provided on curves above nine-chains radius. The only signals were to be at passing places. Warning posts were to be provided to remind engine-drivers of ungated level-crossings. The stopping places were not to be provided with platforms, but the lowest step on the coaches was to be not more than 16 inches above the ground. Trains with not more than three coaches carrying passengers would not have continuous brakes, i.e., brakes on each coach which could be operated remotely by the engine-driver or guard.

The commission reported on these proposals. It referred to the 'novel proposal by the ingenious young engineer of this line, Mr H.F. Stephens, that no train not exceeding three passenger vehicles carrying passengers need be provided with continuous brakes'. The commission felt that as the locomotives and coaches would presumably be fitted with continuous brakes in any case, it would not recommend this clause. Instead of a 35-mile-per-hour speed limit, it suggested the usual 25-mile-per-hour. It found the estimate of £1,900 per mile for 64 lbs rails rather high, and the total cost of £43,852, including 68¾ acres of land at £60 per acre somewhat expensive. Because of this the commission questioned the capital of £60,000: 'The capital fixed by these promoters always seems to be excessive, and in this case it seems more excessive than usual'.

The enquiry was held at the town hall in Queenborough on 29 April, 1898. The practice of holding a local enquiry at the nearest convenient centre to the railway was obligatory under the 1896 Act, and was certainly cheaper and probably more democratic than the parliamentary committees which considered railway Acts of Parliament. The commissioners who came down to Queenborough were the Earl of Jersey, Mr Fitzgerald and Colonel Boughey. The proceedings began with statements by Mr H.C. Gillan and Mr E.W.I. Peterson, the solicitors for the Sheppey company.

Mr Gillan stated that in response to requests from local interests, they had decided to divert the line to the north so that it could come within a mile of Sheerness and half-a-mile of Minster, re-joining the original alignment at Eastchurch. This would increase the length of the line from seven-and-threequarter to eight-and-a-half miles. He referred to the benefit of the line to agriculture, which was suffering from increased competition from imported food. He also elaborated on the future development of Leysdown, including a possible railway hotel, but the chairman intimated that he proposed to advise against giving the company powers to build it. (When one considers the relation of a light railway station to a normal station, it is interesting to speculate on the possible character of a light railway hotel, compared to, say, Charing Cross Hotel. Perhaps the wooden shack style of the 'hotel' provided at Port Victoria is an indication.)

Mr Peterson followed to describe the diversion to serve Sheerness and Minster. Mr W.J. Penney of the Sheerness Chamber of Commerce felt that the diversion did not go far enough. He wanted the western end of the line diverted from Queenborough, and directed along the middle of the road through Sheerness High Street and on to the LCDR station outside the dockyard. This would obviously benefit the town and would also be convenient for passengers using the SER route via Port Victoria who crossed by the ferry to Sheerness. However, it was clear that this was quite inconsistent with the aim of making Leysdown easily accessible from London. In the event, Mr Penney's request was partly met by the construction of an electric tramway from the light railway station at Sheerness East, to the LCDR Dockyard station. The tramway opened in 1903 and closed in 1917.

Next, the engineer, Mr H.F. Stephens, described the line in detail, including the proposed sites for the stations. Only one farmer, Mr Goodwin, the tenant of Harp's Farm, objected to the railway, as the line would bisect his land, but promises of an occupation level-crossing and compensation satisfied him. Mr Hallett told the commissioners of his plans for developing Leysdown. Mr Copus, of the Colne Valley & Halstead Railway in Essex gave evidence of potential traffic, estimating annual revenue at between £9,000 and £10,000. This broke down as follows: goods (mainly agricultural plus domestic coal) £3,000; bricks and tiles (for building developments) £1,600; parcels £200, ordinary passengers £2,000, excursionists (at reduced fares) £1,200, miscellaneous £200.

The commissioners were sufficiently favourably impressed, and at the end of the day the chairman stated that they would recommend the President of the Board of Trade to make an appropriate Light Railway Order. However, in their report they confirmed their view that the maximum speed should be 25 miles per hour, but accepted Mr Stephens's suggestion for exemption from continuous brakes.

The promoters responded by pointing out that the Lambourn Valley Railway was allowed 25 miles per hour with 50 lbs rails, so surely they could run at 30 miles per hour with 64 lbs rails. They also asked for their deposit to be reduced to £2,000, and the limit on the amount of interest they could pay to shareholders out of capital during the construction period to be raised from £3,500 to £4,500.

The ensuing negotiations took more time, and it was 13 months later, in May 1899, when the Order finally appeared. The speed limit remained at 25 miles per hour, the weight limit was 14 tons per axle, and the line was to be fenced. Little time was wasted in awarding the contract, which went to Mr W. Rigby, and the line was opened on 1 August, 1901.

It was typical of light railway design in that although its summit was a little less than 100 feet above sea level, and the Isle of Sheppey was no more than gently undulating, the earthworks were so slight that the ruling gradient was 1 in 70, and the profile of the line resembled a deflated switchback. There were no bridges, but a number of level-crossings of which eight were on public roads. Stations were provided at Sheerness East, Minster-on-Sea, Eastchurch and Leysdown. The buildings were all of corrugated iron, possessing a strong affinity to Col. Stephens's designs for the Rother Valley line. Each included an office for the man in charge, lavatory accommodation and a waiting-room. Mr Heney, in his article of 1906, described the waiting-rooms as 'lined with match-boarding, containing seats and a small coal stove for the passengers' comfort in the winter months'. Considerable use was made of superannuated material from main line railways including sleepers to support the front of the platforms. In fact, these rotted fairly rapidly, and were replaced by concrete. Wooden trellis fencing at the back of the platforms for the same reason was replaced by iron railings. As it was hoped to gain considerable revenue from agriculture, all the stations were provided with sidings, and in most cases with cattle pens and wharves for loading livestock. In addition, short sidings to hold up to three wagons each were provided for farm traffic at Brambledown and Grove between Minster and Eastchurch, and at Holford and Harty Road between Eastchurch and the terminus.

While goods wagons worked through, passengers had to change at Queenborough, but by 1906, of the seven weekday trains five had London connections. The best time ever possible between London and Leysdown – one hour and 50 minutes – could be achieved by using the Flushing Boat Express between Victoria and Queenborough before the First World War. Comparable places such as Tankerton and Herne Bay were reached so much more conveniently that Leysdown's chances of attracting commuters were negligible.

Nevertheless, residential development with the emphasis on retired people was possible, and a large estate was laid out at Leysdown and a Marine Parade constructed. Another hope came from Minster where the Land Company of London acquired an estate which it divided into plots. In 1902 a new station was opened to serve it, about half-a-mile to the west of Minster station. This was named East Minster, presumably to avoid confusion with Westminster. It consisted of a platform with no buildings, except a somewhat primitive shelter. At regular intervals special trains ran down from London, through to Minster, where plots were sold off to willing passengers. Inspection of the estate today would suggest that of the passengers, usually numbering about 150, not many were willing. Perhaps as a reflection of doubts about the effectiveness of the Sheppey Light Railway, powers were sought to construct a pier at Minster 7000 feet long at which the London to Margate steamers could have called at all states of the tide, but this failed to materialize. Nevertheless, the SECR, which had leased the line, were sufficiently hopeful by

1905 to buy it.

An article in the *Railway Magazine* in 1901 called the Sheppey 'a useful little line for opening out a district which could not yield sufficient traffic for an ordinary standard line'.[10] Every attempt was made to reduce costs, and to increase revenue. The four farm sidings were designed to stimulate freight traffic. When a rail motor-car was introduced in 1905 at two of them – Brambledown and Harty Road – wooden platforms were added. These consisted of old sleepers laid on posts, as compared to the station platforms which were solid with a wooden face alongside the track. The wooden faces of the station platforms had to be replaced with concrete, but the only alteration made to the halts was the addition of simple shelters.

For freight traffic and for relieving the rail motor-car, the SECR purchased one of the Brighton company's 'Terrier' class tank engines, a type eminently suitable for light railways. No. 654, 'Waddon', had been built in Brighton in 1875, and was bought for £670 in September 1904. It was May 1905 before she became fully operational on the Sheppey railway, where she was well liked by the train crews. The SECR renumbered her No. 751, and while she had no official name, she was known locally as 'Little Tich'. (Little Tich was the name used by the music hall entertainer Harry Relph, who came from Kent.) Early in 1910 she was replaced by a new SECR class tank, No. 27, and, in 1912, the rail cars were withdrawn from Sheppey.

Between 1918 and 1939 the passenger service was maintained by an 0-4-4 tank engine, usually of the LCDR R1 class, with a train consisting of two of the bodies of the steam rail motor-cars. Most agricultural traffic went over to road transport, but a new source of traffic was the R.A.F. Station at Eastchurch. The estate at Minster grew very slowly, developing a strange landscape of odd huts and bungalows, isolated in expanses of waste land, and divided into squares by concrete or dirt roads. Leysdown was no better, with the stress on even less substantial residences, many of them used only at weekends. Holiday-makers and day-excursionists increased but brought little traffic to the railway, their characteristic means of transport being old cars or motor-cycle combinations. A hotel for 1200 guests was projected but failed to materialize. In 1938, Southern Railway officials visited Leysdown, and in view of the many campers on the foreshore decided to investigate the possibility of following the precedent of the LMSR at Rhyl, and setting up a holiday camp. After the end of the Second World War, the RAF station became an open Borstal, and it was clear that neither Minster nor Leysdown were going to support a railway. The last day on which trains ran for the public was Saturday 2 December, 1950.

I intended to go down to Sheppey during the preceding week, but unfortunately I was unable to visit the line until its last day. The weather was flat, grey and dry. In many cases, the journey to a light railway was made by a sequence of main line express, local train and, finally, light railway. My visit to Sheppey began on a semi-fast electric train to Gillingham, which at the time was the outer limit of Southern electrification. There I joined a Kent coast express for the run through the orchard country to Sittingbourne. The express came in late behind King Arthur class No. 30793, 'Sir Ontzlake', built at Eastleigh in 1926. At Sittingbourne, I crossed the platform for the Sheerness branch train, which consisted of a SECR class 0-4-4 tank locomotive hauling SECR compartment stock.

In 1950, railway closures were not the attraction they later became, and only about ten railway enthusiasts were making the journey on the 10.55 a.m. from Queenborough to Leysdown. When I arrived most of them were watching the engine of the Leysdown train taking water at the water crane which used to stand beyond the end of the platform. In the early days of the line, locomotives had been able to get water at Leysdown, the tank being fed by a windpump over a well. However, for some years, locomotives watered only at Queenborough, and in 1950 I noticed that the column of the water crane was still painted with white bands to help engine-men to find it during the darkness of the war-time blackout. (Incidentally the gas lamp-posts on the platform had been treated in the same way.) The locomotive was No. 31705 – an 0-4-4 tank locomotive of the R1 class, built by Sharp Stewart & Co. in 1900. I was pleased to see that the train consisted of two of the coach portions of steam rail cars Nos 1 and 2, resurrected as a two-coach articulated Set No. 514. (One of the coaches was number s3561s and the other s976s.) This and Set No. 513 were the only articulated stock on the Southern. (Three bogies supported two coaches, the ends of both coaches resting on the bogie in the middle.) For parcels traffic a four-wheel van No. s1353s had been added.

We left on time to branch off on a 14-chain curve across the flat marsh-land, with its well-filled ditches serving as field boundaries. This part of the line was level, and after the initial sharp curve, direct. Sheerness East, the first of the Sheppey Light Railway stations was quiet but looked cared-for. The sheds of the Sheerness electric tramcar under-taking were still there, but in use as a bus garage. Although the line did not cross the 50 feet contour till beyond East Minster-on-Sea, the direct alignment and lack of earthworks produced gradients of 1 in 89 up, 1 in 170 down, 1 in 75 up, and 1 in 100 down, in fairly rapid succession. East Minster-on-Sea, with its background of high hopes, having changed so little since its opening day in 1902, looked as sad as the winter fields. From here, through Minster to Brambledown halt was the 'mountain' section of the Sheppey Light, climbing at 1 in 70 and 1 in 75 to the summit west of Brambledown, and then descending on a similar gradient. The ungated level-crossings were provided with cattle grids, and we conformed to regulations by giving a warning whistle and reducing speed to something like 10 miles per hour. Most of the gated crossings were near stations, and the gates were operated by station staff, but where this was not the case, the train had to stop for the opening and shutting of gates by the train crew. My photograph at Brambledown halt was taken from the roadway with the crossing gates open ready for the train, which was standing alongside the wooden platform with the driver looking out from his cab, waiting for me to re-join the train.

At Eastchurch, some of the inmates from the local Borstal were on the platform, and the warder who was escorting them was worried at the appearance of my camera. Fortunately they left before the train started, so I was able to photograph the platform and buildings as we pulled away for Harty Road halt. Looking at the picture again and seeing the white bands painted on the posts which supported the canopy, reminds me of the war-time blackout and of the RAF personnel who would have arrived or departed from the corrugated-iron building during the war period.

On that December day, we went on across the low fields above the marsh, all carefully fenced off from the railway as required by the Order of 1899. Leysdown in winter had the rather forlorn air of a resort out of season, but even more than is usual. The gaily striped awning covering a 'Dodgem Car Arena' seemed out of place and there were no people in sight. No. 31705 ran round its train, and the small band of railway enthusiasts photographed it, all knowing that it would be the last time they would see a train at Leysdown. We departed for Queenborough at 11.36 leaving the more determined enthusiasts to travel by the very last train in the darkness of the early evening. I went back to London thinking how remote the busy electrified line seemed from the single line in Sheppey whose last day this was.

It is probably a mistake to go back anywhere, and it was not until the end of January 1969, just over 18 years later that I went back to Sheppey by motor-car. Strips of land once occupied by the Sheppey Light Railway had been sold back to the farmers, and much of the remainder was too overgrown for walking. So I visited the parts of it which I had photographed on its last day, to see if anything had survived.

At Sheerness East, the concrete-faced platform was still standing, and although the buildings had gone, the site still retained a railway atmosphere. But East Minster-on-Sea had gone without leaving a visible trace. I drove on through the villages of Minster and Eastchurch to the site of Harty Road halt. Here an overgrown strip of land indicated the line of the railway, but there was no sign of the wooden platform or the farm siding. Because the concrete-faced platform at Sheerness East had survived, I wondered if that at Leysdown would be there to see. There was no difficulty in finding the station site. In January it was a sad expanse of empty car park, but doubtless in the summer it could contain far more cars and coaches than the sum total of its daily trains.

A January impression is inevitably limited, but it looked as though Leysdown had done a little better since losing its trains than when it had them. There was something slightly symbolic in land being used as a car park instead of a train terminus. I made my way back by Brambledown halt and stood in the road at the point where I had photographed the Leysdown train, 18 years earlier, with the engine-driver waiting for me to re-join the train. At first I thought there was nothing left except the houses in the background. Only as I was about to record that Brambledown halt had gone without a trace did I notice the concrete post from which the level-crossing gate had been hung, almost covered with vegetation. It was not much to find, but it was something.

In a way, the Sheppey was one of the more successful light railways, showing sufficient promise to be taken up by a main line company. But at best, its economic condition was marginal, and although it served Sheppey, it is very doubtful if at any time during the 50 years of its existence, it was of any benefit to railway shareholders.

The Romney, Hythe & Dymchurch Railway

The Romney, Hythe & Dymchurch is one of the few railways in the south of England whose opening I can remember. Even then, only indirectly, from my father's account of his visit with the Institute of Transport in 1927. Memory is strengthened by the booklet about the line which he brought home for me at the time.[11]

The RHDR has always been a very special line, owing its survival, not its geographical position, but to its unusual character. However, before the mechanization of road transport, the gap in the railway network between the SER station at New Romney and its line at Hythe was tempting enough to persuade the main line company to apply for a Light Railway Order in 1899. In fact, neither the SER nor the LCDR themselves built any lines which made use of the 1896 Light Railways Act, and their 1899 application was withdrawn in favour of normal powers granted under the SE and LCD Railways Act of 1900. The inhabitants of Romney Marsh waited hopefully, but in the 1905 edition of his novel *Kipps*, H.G. Wells wrote: 'The light railway concession along the coast is happily in the South Eastern Railway Company's keeping and the peace of the marsh is kept inviolate'.

By the early 1920s, a considerable amount of experience had been accumulated about the working of passenger railways with a track gauge as little as 15 inches. Sir Arthur Heywood had carried invited passengers on his Duffield Bank line from 1874; this had been followed in 1896 by the Eaton Hall Railway; and in 1910 by the Sand Hutton Railway. Three 15-inch-gauge passenger-carrying lines of significant length survive: the Ravenglass & Eskdale in Cumberland, narrowed to 15-inch gauge in 1915; the Fairbourne Railway in Merioneth, narrowed in 1916; and the RHDR, opened in 1927. Captain J.E.P. Howey and his friend, Count Zborowski, both well-known as racing motorists, had been so impressed with the Ravenglass & Eskdale line that they decided to construct something similar for the south of England, preferably in an area favoured by holiday-makers. Romney Marsh was sufficiently flat to minimize construction costs, and Sir Herbert Walker, general manager of the newly formed Southern Railway, was quite prepared to relinquish any prior claims to the route his company might have inherited from the SER.

Application for a Light Railway Order was made in November 1925, constructional work by direct labour began in January 1926, and Light Railway Order No. 472 was granted in May 1926. This was for eight-and-a-quarter miles of double line from a terminal alongside the Royal Military Canal at Hythe passing Dymchurch to a terminal near the end of a Southern branch line, roughly mid-way between New Romney and Littlestone-on-Sea. The estimated cost at about £2,500 per mile was £18,264. (£30,000 per mile would have been the approximate cost of an 'average' double track railway at this time.) Somewhat exceptionally, the RHDR did not find it necessary for its capital to be increased over the

£33,000 authorized by its Light Railway Order, mainly thanks to informal capital subsidies from Captain Howey.

While signalling and interlocking were provided at Hythe, Dymchurch and New Romney, the RHDR was not required to have locks on its facing points, turn-tables for its locomotives, gates on its level-crossings, or toilets and other amenities at its stations. However, as the locomotives were all equipped with tenders, and tender-first running at 30 miles per hour is uncomfortable, turn-tables were installed at Hythe, Dymchurch and New Romney, contrary to usual light railway practice. Subsequently, that at Dymchurch has been removed, while a large second-hand turn-table, obtained from the Lynton & Barnstaple Railway after its closure in 1935, has been provided at New Romney. The Hythe turn-table has also been renewed. But the level-crossings, while equipped with cattle-guards, have no gates, and with the increase of road traffic the ritual of whistling, and speed-reduction to five miles per hour has become more onerous.

The RHDR has had numerous stopping places, but only a few have been provided with buildings sufficient to justify their being called stations. They have varied from the patch of hard-standing plus notice-board, which served as Lade halt for some years after the Second World War, to the overall roof, signals, toilets and refreshment rooms of New Romney.

While earthworks were minimal, drainage ditches had to be crossed at a number of points. The most impressive of the bridges was that over the new sewer between St Mary's Bay and New Romney with a span of 56 feet and a width of 12 ft 10 in. to take the double track. The insertion of curves on either side reduced, but did not eliminate, a degree of skewness. It was constructed by Theakstons of Crewe in time for the Duke of York, later King George VI, to drive a train over it on 5 August, 1926, when visiting a boys' holiday-camp at Jesson. The other bridges were of a sufficiently limited span to consist of steel joists on concrete abutments, and were considerably cheaper than the Duke of York's bridge.

Money was also saved on track because the locomotives weighed only 5 tons 6 cwt, with an extra 1 ton 15 cwt for tenders, compared with the 28 tons 5 cwt of that mainstay of the light railway, the 'Terrier' class tank engine. Rail of 24 lbs per yard could be used instead of the 60 lbs which was frequently used on standard-gauge lines. It was laid on shingle which was readily available.

The locomotives were designed by Henry Greenly, and were based on the Pacific class designed by Sir Nigel Gresley for the GNR and the LNER. They were built by Davey, Paxman Ltd of Colchester, and cost about £1,600 each. This was dearer than s second-hand 'Terrier', but then a second-hand 'Terrier', at least in 1927, would not have attracted pleasure-riders. Initially, the passenger stock consisted of 60 four-wheeled coaches, open at the sides but with roofs, giving accommodation not unlike that provided for third-class passengers in the early days of the main lines. However, what is unacceptable for a long winter's journey may be pleasant enough for a pleasure ride on a summer's day.

The official opening by Earl Beauchamp, Lord Warden of the Cinque Ports, took place on 16 July, 1927, about 18 months after the start of constructional work, the comparatively rapid completion of just under eight-and-a-half miles of double line limiting the period during which investment was unbalanced by revenue.

Consideration was given to an extension from the Hythe terminal to Sandling Junction on the Folkestone main line, which was almost as near, better served, and more accessible than the Southern's Hythe station on the Sandgate branch. However, it was decided that the money would be better spent extending the line from New Romney as far as Greatstone over the marsh, and then over the shingle to Dungeness. The section over the shingle must have been one of the cheapest passenger-carrying railways ever built, the sleepers being laid directly on the shingle, bound with a little sand and clay where necessary.

Work was already well-advanced when the extension of five-and-three-quarter miles was authorized by Light Railway Order No. 485 of 12 July, 1928. The capital of £15,225 coincided with the engineer's estimate of the cost of the line, leaving nothing for extra expenses. Even allowing for the cheapness of the land, this suggests that the powers to raise capital under the original Order had proved more than sufficient. The double-track line was opened in 1928. Instead of a conventional terminal, at Dungeness a loop was provided, thus avoiding the need for reversal.

While the extension was level, and had no engineering works of significance, it was far more speculative than the original line, for south of Greatstone, the shingle wastes were almost uninhabited. There was a signal station for ships, a lighthouse, a coastguard station, and some isolated public houses, one of which, 'The Pilot' was aptly named, as pilots joined London-bound vessels off Dungeness. Originally, New Romney was designed as a terminus and the change of plan did involve the RHDR in re-arrangements at their southern terminal, which will be described later. Highly varied building development ensued between Greatstone and Dungeness, including a holiday camp. It was sufficient to persuade the Southern Railway in 1937 to divert their New Romney branch to the east so that for about three-and-a-half miles it ran almost parallel and roughly quarter-of-a-mile inland from the RHDR. New SR stations at Lydd-on-Sea and Greatstone competed with the five stopping places on the narrow-gauge line; the very infrequent Southern Railway service to its Dungeness station was withdrawn at the same time.

The RHDR had always aspired to give all the services provided by more conventional railways, and there were exchange sidings for freight traffic at New Romney. In fact, even by the late 1920s, road transport had developed so far as to preclude the growth of freight on the RHDR, but, for a few years, shingle traffic from the Dungeness extension was of significance. Somewhat oddly, cars and buses did little to harm the RHDR, as they tended to feed it with pleasure-riders.

After the fall of France, Romney Marsh and Dungeness were obviously in danger from invasion, and in June 1940 the RHDR was requisitioned. An armoured mobile anti-aircraft train was constructed, while the line continued to transport troops stationed along its length. One would give much for a photograph of a troop-train on the RHDR, bringing in soldiers from the shingle wastes of Dungeness to the comforts of Hythe. In 1944 it was decided to lay pipelines under the Channel to carry petroleum to France, and one ran from near Dungeness to Boulogne. Sections of the pipeline were assembled at New Romney station and then conveyed by the extension line. This was the section which suffered the greatest usage, but when the line was de-requisitioned in January 1946, repair work, in which prisoners-of-war took part, was concentrated on the Hythe to New Romney section.

In March 1946, the Mayor of New Romney performed a re-opening ceremony for the original line, although some trains appear to have run over the extension as far as Maddieson's Holiday Camp. With new rails almost unobtainable, it was decided to single the extension line, and after the completion of this work during the hard winter of 1946/1947 the entire line was re-opened by the film stars Laurel and Hardy in March 1947. (The succession of official openers is an interesting one, from the Lord Warden of the Cinque Ports through the Mayor of New Romney to famous American comedians.)

Since that time, changes in the RHDR have been matters of detail. There have been purchases of new coaches, and the nine steam locomotives, supplied between November 1925 and May 1931, all received new superheated boilers between 1956 and 1964. Some interesting vintage rolling stock and a petrol-engined locomotive were obtained from the Duke of Westminster in 1947, when he sold his Eaton Hall Railway. In 1965 a useful quantity of second-hand material, including colour light signals, rails, points and sleepers, was obtained from the Ramsgate Tunnel Railway.

Many of the more conventional light railways were associated with Col. H.F. Stephens, but the RHDR owed a comparable debt to Captain J.E.P. Howey, who, far from being an 'absentee landlord', lived at 'Red Tiles', a bungalow only a stone's throw from the locomotive shed at New Romney. Captain Howey died in 1963. Mr S.H. Collins, who now has a controlling interest in the RHDR, has moved into 'Red Tiles' and the company continues to benefit from vigorous management.[12]

As trains from Hythe to Dungeness are called 'down trains', a run over the line may well begin at the former terminus. Alterations were made to the front of Hythe station in 1967, and notices proclaim the 'World's Smallest Public Railway'. Beyond the façade there has been little change, the four platform tracks and the overall roof being essentially as built in 1927. However, the signals operated from the cabin situated on the down side, are now colour light instead of semaphore. Facilities for taking coal and water are provided, but as Hythe water is hard, its use is avoided as far as possible. For this reason most of the steam locomotives are fitted with larger tenders to enable them to run from New Romney to Hythe and back without taking water.

For about the first three-quarters-of-a-mile the line runs between the Royal Military Canal and the back gardens of houses on the main road. Then a double curve saved construction costs by decreasing the degree of skewness of the Prince of Wales overbridge carrying the Hythe to Lympe road. (The Duke of York's bridge was named after the Duke who had driven a train over it, but the Prince of Wales bridge took its name from a nearby inn.) Further saving was achieved by making a shallow cutting for the railway on either side of the bridge, the spoil from which provided material for the approach ramps which carry the road. Like all light railways, the RHDR was prepared to carry passengers from almost anywhere, and a halt, consisting of hard-standing and a notice-board was provided near the 'Prince of Wales'. By 1928 it was disused.

Another, more gentle curve takes the railway round some gravel workings at Palmarsh and a sewage works, and then it takes a virtually direct line across the marsh to New Romney, interrupted only by the curves to reduce the skewness of the Duke of York's bridge and that of the overbridge carrying the main road from Hythe to New Romney. The next level-crossing was less than half-a-mile from the hamlet at Botolph's Bridge, and the halt at this point, two-and-a-quarter miles from Hythe, was in use until 1939. The one-and-three-quarter miles of level track between Botolph's Bridge and Burmarsh Road, crosses the 'New Cut' Dyke and the Willop Sewer but no roads, and here trains may run at up to 30 miles per hour. Although the halt at Burmarsh Road has also been closed, it did survive until 1948. Strips of concrete on either side of the track indicate its site. Beyond Burmarsh Road, the houses of Dymchurch appear on the down side, and the station is entered cautiously, over a level-crossing protected by a flag-man, and a bridge over a drainage ditch.

Originally, the bridge carried a footpath leading to the station, in this respect resembling Charing Cross railway bridge in London. This has now disappeared. But Dymchurch remains one of the three places named in the title of the railway and retains a station with such refinements as an overall roof and a foot-bridge across the tracks for passengers. It has, however, lost its turn-table and signal-box, the colour light signals being operated from the station office. A bay platform survives on the down side, but is rarely used. It is only a mile across the marsh to the next station at St Mary's Bay. From the point of view of facilities, St Mary's Bay occupies an intermediate position between the quite elaborate stations and the minimal halts. It has concrete strips on either side of the line, and a shelter on the up side with an office adjoining, which is opened at peak periods. Tracing St Mary's Bay in RHDR documents can be confusing as at various times before 1939 it appeared as Jesson or Holiday Camp.

The section on to New Romney includes the Duke of York's bridge over the new sewer and the overbridge, consisting of twin arches approached through cuttings, which carries the main road from Hythe to Rye. Despite curves on either side, the degree of skewness combined with the width of the road makes these appear almost as short tunnels, 49 ft 6 in. in length. Warren halt, adjoining the main road, was closed in 1928.

New Romney, just over eight-and-a-quarter miles from Hythe, has always been the headquarters of the system. There is a signal-box with a 24-lever frame, now equipped with colour light signals. Here are situated the locomotive sheds on the down side, and the carriage sheds on both sides of the line. The main station buildings face on to a forecourt adjoining Littlestone Road, and a large car park is provided. In fact this, combined with the construction of a tower in 1926 to draw attention to it, savours of London Transport rather than of normal light railway practice. There are high-level terminal and low-level through platforms, the high-level being the originals built on a level with Littlestone Road before the extension to Dungeness. The Southern extended its siding across Littlestone Road, the main traffic in latter days being coal for the RHDR locomotives. However, to avoid an RHDR level-crossing, it was decided that instead of an end-on junction, the extension would branch off short of the terminal platforms and tunnel under the road. A shallow cutting ran alongside the original station occupying the site of the western terminal platform, and reached by modest gradients 1 in 288 at the north end, and 1 in 230 at the south. Initially only a down low-level platform was provided in the main station, the new up platform being located in the cutting on the opposite side of the road, adjoining the Southern's station, to which it was linked by a footbridge. Space was left on the opposite side of the tracks for a down platform, but this was never opened. Presumably the case for platforms adjoining the Southern station was to give improved inter-change facilities, but, by 1930, a new up platform had been squeezed into the cutting north of the road, and the isolated platform south of the road was abandoned. Its site is indicated by the red-brick building which survives near the end of the concrete retaining wall. As the Southern station was closed in 1967, it is perhaps fortunate that the RHDR did not pursue their plans to get nearer to it. A characteristic RHDR overall roof was built over the low-level station, and amenities, such as refreshment-rooms and a model railway layout have been opened to attract pleasure-riders. Like St Mary's Bay, New Romney has had more than one name, appearing as Littlestone from 1928 until 1940.

As mentioned above, after the Second World War the extension to Dungeness was singled, and the two tracks converge opposite the build-ing which stood on the ephemeral up platform of 1928, south of the Littlestone Road overbridge. (Like the bridge which carries the main road further north, this consists of twin ferro-concrete arches, long enough to resemble short tunnels. The amount of excavation required was reduced by raising the road by two feet.) The RHDR runs close beside the site of the Southern for about half-a-mile, then diverges to run roughly parallel, but just behind the road and the beach. The first RHDR station, built at the request of an estate company, is at Greatstone, and falls into the same intermediate category as St Mary's Bay. Until 1971 it had a shelter and booking office which was open at busy times.

Originally it had platforms on both sides of the double track and a lever frame in the booking office, but all this has disappeared.

Here the line leaves the grass of the marshes for the barren shingle of Dungeness. Beyond the line of chalets and bungalows which border the road, fishing boats are drawn up onto the beach. A source of revenue is Maddieson's Holiday Camp opened at the same time as the line in 1928. This is very much a minimal station, with hard-standing on either side of the track, but it has a very large station name-board which includes the name of the railway company, a list of the places served and the times of the principal trains. One of the eight ungated level-crossings on the extension adjoins the station. For a while after the Second World War, Lade and Pilot were without buildings but in 1968 both were equipped with concrete shelters. In the early days of the line there was a request-stop near the Britannia Inn.

Dungeness looks even less like a railway station than anywhere else on the line – almost as though its refreshment facilities took precedence over its trains. Whereas Dymchurch, with its overall roof, is essentially a station, Dungeness could easily be a golf club-house. Features of interest in its early days included a wind pump for water supply and a typical RHDR bracketed signal, but these have both gone. When the line was singled, Dungeness was unaffected, with its single platform on a terminal loop. In the summer, in times past, passengers who left the trains visited the old light-house or the life-boat station, while a minority were attracted by the unique natural history of this unusual shingle habitat. In recent years, the scene has changed fundamentally with the construction of the great nuclear power-station. But the RHDR relies as much on its own attractions as those of the places which it serves.

The RHDR differs considerably from the other light railways which have been described. It now carries passengers only, freight never contributing significantly to its revenue. It is the only light railway with refreshment and toilet facilities and car-parks at its four main stations – Hythe, Dymchurch, New Romney and Dungeness. There is no question that a conventional railway linking these places would have been closed; it is the special character of the RHDR which must be credited with its survival.

The narrow gauge and the topography of the district traversed, together with Captain Howey's contribution, kept its capital investment surprisingly low. The only relatively expensive items were the specially designed and built locomotives, but their unique attractions leave no doubt as to their being wise investments. One problem is the seasonal nature of the traffic: a service is usually provided from late spring until September with a peak period in late July and August. The labour problem is met by maintaining a permanent staff of about 20, including six engine-drivers, who are employed on maintenance work in the winter. The 20 permanent employees are augmented in the summer by about 30 temporaries. With the ever-increasing attraction of steam locomotives, the future of the RHDR would seem to be assured.

KENT & EAST SUSSEX RAILWAY.

Any unauthorised person removing this lable from the Vehicle to which it has been attached, will render himself liable to Criminal Prosecution.

NOT TO GO

Defects................ ....

....

Examined by..... . ... Station

Date......... ....193.........

4
East Kent Light Railways

The East Kent was essentially different from any of the other lines that have been described, for its basis was the hope that east Kent would become a major industrial area. In 1911, when the first Light Railway Order was obtained, a note in *Railway Magazine* referred to the nascent coal-field as being of:

'Sufficient extent and richness to convert Kent – even all the southern Home Counties – into a second Lancashire. The principal colliery upon which reliance is in the first instance placed is that of Tilmanstone where an extensive power-station has just been constructed, together with a contractor's line, which at one end connects with the SECR at Shepherd's Well and with the colliery at the other.'[1]

This was the beginning of what might have become an extensive system of light railways, authorized by a series of Light Railway Orders obtained between 1911 and 1931. In fact, the four collieries that proved successful did not precipitate the industrialization of east Kent, and the agricultural and passenger traffic of the district was insufficient to support the railway.

The East Kent fully justified the use of 'Railways' in its title for it proposed 40 of them. The following table summarizes the results:

Rail-way No.	Date of application	No. of Light Railway Order	Date	Mileage authorized		Mileage constructed		Notes
				Miles	Chains	Miles	Chains	
1	1910	361	1911	10	20	9	61.7	Shepherd's Well to Richborough
2	1910	361	1911	5	72.5	5	34.2	Wingham to Eastry
3	1910	Not authorized						

Railway No.	Date of application	Authorized No. of Light Railway Order	Date	Mileage authorized Miles	Chains	Mileage constructed Miles	Chains	Notes
4	1910	361	1911	2	31.5	2	22.5	Guilford Colliery branch
5	1910	361	1911	—	60	—	69	Tilmanstone Colliery to Eythorne
6	1910	Not authorized						
7	1910	Not authorized						
8	1910	361	1911	—	18	—	18	Spur from Guilford branch to Eythorne
9	1910	361	1911	—	10	—	19	Richborough Castle siding
10	1910	361	1911	—	21.5	—	35	Incompleted northern spur at Shepherd's Well
11	1910	367	1911	4	33.6	—	—	Eythorne to Mongeham
12	1910	367	1911	2	34	—	—	Guilford to Maydensole
13	1910	367	1911	2	72.5	—	—	Guilford to Stonehall
14	1910	367	1911	—	52.5	—	36.5	Woodnesborough Colliery branch
15	1911	382	1912	3	52	—	—	Wickhambreux Colliery branch
16	1911	382	1912	1	50	—	—	Ripple Colliery
17	1912	Not authorized						
18	1913	426	1920	4	66.5	—	—	Woodnesborough to Snowdown
19	1913	426	1920	2	49	—	—	Mongeham to Deal
20	1913	426	1920	—	21	—	—	Deal Spur
21	1913	Not authorized						
22	1913	426	1920	3	76	—	—	Wickhambreux to Canterbury
23	1913	426	1920	7	14.5	—	—	Guilford to Drellingore branch

Rail-way No.	Date of applica-tion	Authorized No. of Light Railway Order	Date	Mileage authorized		Mileage constructed		Notes
				Miles	Chains	Miles	Chains	
24	1913	426	1920	—	73	—	—	Stonehall to Drellingore line
25	1913	Not authorized						
26	1913	426	1920	—	46.5	—	—	Northbourne branch
27	1913	426	1920	—	70	—	—	Spur to Wingham Colliery
28	1913	426	1920	—	20	—	11	Spur to Richboro Old Wharf
29	1928	Not authorized						
30	1928	Not authorized						
31	1928	Not authorized						
32	1928	Not authorized						
33	1928	493	1931	2	0	—	—	Wingham to Wickhambreux cut-off line
34	1928	Not authorized						Junction from Rlwy. No. 1 to SECR near Sandwich
35	1928	Not authorized						Spur to above
36	1928	Not authorized						Junction from Rlwy No. 15 to SECR near Chislet
37	1928	493	1931	4	0	—	—	Improved version of Rlwy No. 11
38	1928	Not authorized						Tilmanstone Colliery to main line north of Elvington
39	1928	Not authorized						
40	1928	Not authorized						Extension of Richborough Castle siding

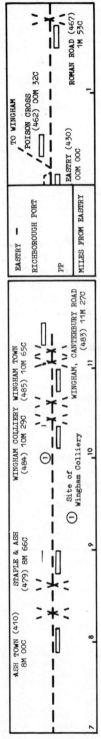
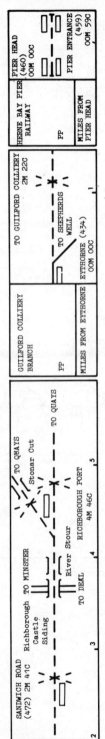

6 Shepherd's Well to Wingham, Canterbury Road; Eastry to Richborough Port; Guilford Colliery Branch; Herne Bay Pier Railway; Aquarium, Brighton to Black Rock; Paston Place, Brighton to Rottingdean

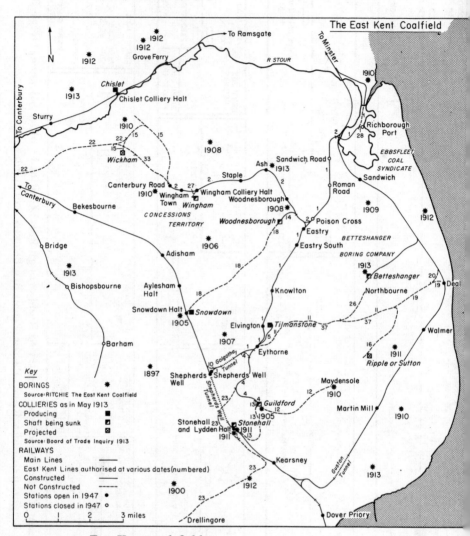

The East Kent Coalfield

7   East Kent coal-field

The remark 'not authorized' is a little misleading, as in some cases the company abandoned its plans for lines before the commissioners adjudicated on them. However, there is no doubt about the general trend of development: nearly all the construction that materialized was authorized by the first Order, No. 361 of 1911. This reflects only too clearly that the only colliery to achieve significant production on the East Kent railway was Tilmanstone, and that Richborough as a Kentish Cardiff was a non-starter.

As the development of the railway was so inextricably linked with that of the coal-field, to explain the former it is necessary to refer to the latter. On the Continent, concealed coal-fields were already being exploited in the 1850s, but in Britain the mineral wealth of the exposed coal-fields reduced the incentive to seek elsewhere. Geologists drew attention to the possibilities in Kent, but capitalists took little interest. In 1855 Godwin-Austen read a paper to the Geological Society entitled, 'Possible Extension of the Coal Measures beneath the South East Part of England'. Thirty-five years later, in 1890, the eminent geologist, Whitaker, was regretting that, 'As a geologist I must decline to be in any way bound by the lamentable failure, or one may say, heartrending absence of commercial enterprise amongst my fellow Englishmen'.

However, if he had been alive to write again 35 years later, he might have conceded that the financial rewards from Kentish coal hardly merited more than a luke-warm approach. Between 1872 and 1875, a boring was made at Battle in Sussex under the aegis of a Sub-Wealden Committee of the British Association, but this failed to strike coal. In fact, the circumstances under which the first successful boring was made can only be described as fortuitous.

Since the time of the Napoleonic Wars, proposals to tunnel under the Channel have shown varying degrees of promise. By the late 1870s construction was in progress, but, at the instance of the Board of Trade and mainly for strategic reasons, they were suspended in 1882. The workings remained accessible from the entrance near the Shakespeare Cliff at Dover. In 1886 Boyd Dawkins was advocating the use of the site for a boring, and in 1890, in an article for the *Journal of the Society of Arts*, Whitaker made the same point, with a reference to Sir Edward Watkin, who was chairman of both the South Eastern Railway, and the Channel Tunnel Company.

'Without wishing to touch on a subject so provocative as the Channel Tunnel is, I cannot but say that it would be useful if Sir E. Watkins's well-known weakness for tunnelling could be turned, for a time at least, from a horizontal to a vertical direction, so that a shaft might be at once sunk at Dover.'

In fact, in the same year, the engineer in charge, Francis Brady, was given permission to bore, and struck coal about 1,100 feet below the surface. In quality it resembled Welsh coal, and it was associated with iron ore. There was, however, no dynamic exploitation of the discovery, and it was six years before a company was formed to sink a shaft. Although the coal was there, Dover Colliery was so prone to flooding as to be uneconomic, its total production being concentrated in 1912 when, 22 years after coal had been found, enough of it to fill 12 ten-ton wagons was brought to the pithead. In his book on the Kent coal-field, A.E. Ritchie stated that this was 'the only real consignment of coal that has ever been made from Shakespeare Cliff Colliery'.[2]

The importance of the Dover Colliery lay in the stimulus it gave to exploration elsewhere. Continental capital was active, especially in the north and east of the coal-field, but the largest single group was financed in Britain, and the various companies were referred to collectively as the 'Kent Coal Concessions' or merely the 'Concessions group'. Their activities occurred in two phases, in both of which a leading figure was Mr Arthur Burr. So important was his role that companies of the first phase were sometimes referred to as the 'old Burr group' and those which formed part of 'Kent Coal Concessions' as the 'new Burr group'. Although the various companies tended to have slightly different functions, their proliferation was accelerated by Mr Burr's habit of rescuing a company which was moribund by creating a new company to take it over. By 1909 he was running short of names, and had to resort to such titles as 'Extended Extensions Ltd'. Despite the somewhat rickety character of this highly complicated organization, it was responsible for some 47,677 feet of boring and it is to it that most of the credit for the exploration of the coal-field must be given.

There is no indication that Mr Burr originally intended railways to be included among the enterprises of his group, and there were no applications for powers to construct them until 1910, nine years after the registration of the first of the 'Concessions group' companies. The sinking of borings did not make very heavy demands on transport, and, in any case, was of too temporary a nature to justify railway construction. But for a colliery, railway communication was essential, and Mr Burr decided that it should come even before the sinking of the shafts.

However, at both Tilmanstone and Guilford Collieries, construction had begun in advance of railway connection. Especially in the case of Guilford, which could only be reached by way of a narrow unmetalled lane, transport difficulties had delayed the work considerably. Moreover, the company had to face heavy claims for compensation from the highway authorities. During the winter months, Guilford Colliery became virtually inaccessible to heavy equipment, and it was decided to concentrate all activity at Tilmanstone until the railway reached Guilford.

In the *Kent Coal-field*, Ritchie summarizes the situation by saying that:

'The lack of direct railway communication was a severe handicap during a great part of the constructional period, adding materially to the cost of the work and resulting in heavy claims from the local authorities for extraordinary traffic.'

At a Railway Inquiry in 1912, Mr Burr's son, Dr Malcolm Burr, confirmed the decision of the Concessions group to build railways in advance of mines, and this had a considerable influence on the development of the East Kent Light Railways. It would be attractive to attribute all the difficulties to the lack of railways, but it is only fair to say that financial difficulties, reflected in the complexities of the Concessions group, were also significant.

Although the East Kent Light Railways began as a unit of the Burr group, it became increasingly separated from the colliery undertakings. A sign of its increasing independence was its promotion of lines to serve collieries being developed by other concerns. For instance, lines were proposed to the collieries at Chislet, Snowdown and Betteshanger. Chislet and Snowdown were on the SECR and Betteshanger had only to construct a short branch to reach it. However, in other parts of Britain, collieries sometimes welcomed connections with two railway companies as they could play one off against the other. This situation might have arisen if Richborough had rapidly developed a coal export trade, and the East Kent line had reached it in time, but while its only outlet was on to the SECR at Shepherd's Well, its scope for competing with a company which it had to depend on for forwarding its traffic was clearly limited.

In the event, Tilmanstone was the only productive colliery which the East Kent reached, and its only appreciable source of income was the revenue obtained by hauling its coal over the two-and-a-half miles to the main line at Shepherd's Well. Even this traffic was threatened when the colliery, after its separation from the Concessions group, escaped from the East Kent railway's monopoly by constructing its own aerial cableway to Dover Harbour. Fortunately from a railway point of view, this was only of value for shipments by sea, and after the Second World War when virtually the entire output of Tilmanstone was consumed in south-east England, the cableway was disused and all its traffic reverted to the East Kent railway. At the present time, this is the only traffic on the only surviving section of the East Kent, so that the initial association with the coal industry is perpetuated.

Railways Authorized by Order No. 361 of 1911

The first constructional work consisted of a contractor's line, linking Tilmanstone to the SECR at Shepherd's Well. This was already planned when the East Kent presented its proposals to the Light Railway Commissioners. While the main promoters were the Kent Coal Concessions, the names of the East Kent Colliery Co., the East Kent Contract & Financial Co., the Extended Extensions Co., Snowdown Colliery Ltd, South Eastern Coalfield Extension Ltd, Fonçage Syndicate Ltd, and Sondage Syndicate Ltd, also appeared in supporting roles. The Contract & Financial Co. having no money, undertook to finance the line, and owing to its inability to acquire money, substantially delayed construction.

The local inquiry was held at the County Hotel, Canterbury, on 20 October, 1910. Originally ten lines had been proposed, the two main lines forming a letter Y with extremities near Canterbury, at Richborough Port and at Shepherd's Well. All were transfer points: at Richborough, to water transport, and at the other two places to the SECR. The main junction and hub of the system was to be at Eastry. It may be surprising that the decision was taken to concentrate traffic for export on Richborough which, even after the construction of the military port during the First World War, lacked the capacity of Dover. One reason was the fear that the Admiralty, which had constructed the outer harbour at Dover, would inhibit commercial development. This was far more of a possibility in 1910 than it was to be after the First World War. In fact after the war, the commercial development of Dover was more vigorous than that of Richborough, which was leased to Pearson & Dorman Long. From a strictly railway viewpoint, traffic to Richborough would use the East Kent railway throughout, whereas shipments via

Dover would complete their journey over the SECR.

There was no doubt about the desire of the Dover Harbour Board to attract coal traffic to its eastern arm in the period between the wars. It culminated in the Dover Harbour Act of 1933, which empowered the board to construct a railway from the Dover and Deal line just east of Old Park Road, tunnelling under the chalk to reach the harbour's eastern arm. Mainly because of the decline in coal exports, the powers were never used and coal shipments either used the tramway which ran along The Promenade, or the aerial cableway from Tilmanstone Colliery.

Apart from a period of intense activity during the First World War, when the new wharf and the train-ferry terminal were constructed, Richborough Port, like so many other hopes of the East Kent, has never developed. At later dates, perhaps because of concern at a lack of enthusiasm on the part of Pearsons & Dorman Long for the East Kent railway other possibilities were considered. These included a dock system on the site of the golf links at Deal, and a long jetty between Reculver and Birchington. Branches of the East Kent railway would have served these new developments, but all the established ports, like Dover, were already served by the SECR. These included Whitstable, Faversham, and Queenborough on the Isle of Sheppey. Sandwich was of very limited capacity and, like Ramsgate, lacked rail access to the quays. Most of the output of the Kent coal-field was used in London and Kent, but occasional shipments between the wars were made from Dover and from Queenborough.

With the advantage of hindsight it is easy to see that the orientation of the East Kent railways was misguided, but this was certainly not apparent in the optimistic atmosphere of 1910. The Light Railway Commissioners who went down to Canterbury were the Hon. Gathorne-Hardy, Col. Boughey and Mr H.A. Steward. The East Kent Railway No. 1, from exchange sidings with the SECR at Shepherd's Well to Richborough Port was authorized as proposed, and was ultimately constructed. Railway No. 2 ran from exchange sidings to the east of Canterbury West station, and, serving proposed collieries at Wingham and Woodnesborough, joined No. 1 at Eastry, the junction being arranged to give through running to Richborough.

There were a number of objectors. The SECR felt that there was no need for the No. 2 line to go beyond Wingham, and proposed that it should be diverted to join its line at Adisham about six miles south-east of Canterbury. It objected to any direct junctions, and the Board of

Trade agreed that certainly a facing junction with the down main line at Shepherd's Well was undesirable, but felt that connections through interchange sidings should be authorized in all cases. In view of further objections from the War Office, the Ecclesiastical Commissioners, and others, Railway No. 2 was cut back to Wingham and reduced in length from just over 11 miles to just under six. No. 3 was a spur at Eastry to form a triangle, and gave direct running between Shepherd's Well and Wingham but this was withdrawn. No. 4 was a branch, nearly two miles in length, joining Guilford Colliery to the main No. 1 line at Eythorne, with the junction facing Shepherd's Well. No. 8 was a spur to form a triangle junction at Eythorne and give direct running to Richborough. Betteshanger Colliery near Northbourne was to be joined to Eythorne by Railway No. 5, a three-mile branch, but this was cut back to the three-quarters-of-a-mile which reached Tilmanstone Colliery. No. 6 Railway, a branch from Wingham to a proposed colliery at Goodnestone was deleted as it was far more convenient to serve the latter from the SECR main line. With it went No. 7, the spur which would have made Wingham a triangular junction. No. 9, although only a short line, might have been important as it would have joined the East Kent to the SECR near Richborough Castle. No. 10 was the necessary spur to complete a triangle at Shepherd's Well.

The case for the promoters was stated by Mr Talbot who referred to the 'intolerable pressure' on the local roads, which were being repaired at the expense of the colliery companies. As evidence of impending development, he cited the successful Waldershare and Fredville borings of 1906 and 1907 and the Snowdown, Tilmanstone and Guilford collieries already under construction. Work was about to start on another three mines and already over 1,100 persons were being employed. He pointed out that the parties who had come to oppose the draft Order, including Dover Rural District Council, the Commissioners of Sewers, and six landowners, were only concerned with details, and not against the line in general. For the engineering of any light railway, the choice of Mr (later Lt-Col.) H.F. Stephens was an obvious one, and the detailed design of the East Kent was his work. It was of course, a far more extensive scheme than for instance, the Sheppey Light Railway, and included provisions for electrifying the line, using power generated at Tilmanstone Colliery.

On the question of speed, when the Light Railway Order finally appeared, the commissioners were seen to have slightly demurred from Col. Stephens's requests. They reduced the maximum speed from 30 to 25 miles per hour and, on gradients of 1 in 50 or over, the reduction was from 25 to 20 miles per hour, with 15 miles per hour for over 1 in 40. On curves less than nine-chains radius or within 200 yards of ungated level-crossings, the commissioners substituted ten miles per hour for the 15 miles per hour requested. The operating conditions which were to prevail on the East Kent, and the fact that, in the absence of speedometers, the observation of limits depended on the engine-driver's sense of speed, made it unlikely that these five-miles-per-hour reductions were of great significance. Perhaps surprisingly, the minimum weight for the flat-bottomed rails which was given as 60 lbs per yard in the draft Order, appears as 58 lbs in the final Order.

The two outstanding engineering works on the East Kent were both on the No. 1 Railway: the Golgotha Tunnel between Shepherd's Well and Eythorne, and the bridge over the River Stour at Richborough. Although commercial navigation of the Stour up to Fordwich had virtually ceased, it was still thought necessary to allow both for navigation and drainage, so a movable bridge leaving a clear waterway of 30 feet wide was specified.

Many of Col. Stephens's proposals were already familiar to light railway passengers, such as platforms or steps on the coaches being authorized as alternatives, and the freedom of the company to decide whether or not stations were to be provided with shelters and conveninces. The draft Order stated that no turn-tables needed to be provided, but when tender locomotives ran tender-first, a 30-miles-per-hour speed limit would apply. However, as the commissioners imposed a general speed limit of 25 miles per hour this was not important.

Unparalled optimism, which went as far as boasts of extensions to London, accompanied the promotion of the East Kent, and, for much of the route, land was purchased for double track, although a single line was laid. Perhaps dazzled by predictions of heavy traffic, the commissioners required gates on the level-crossing at Woodnesborough; and at Eythorne and Ash, the substitution of bridges for crossings. The original title was the East Kent (Mineral) Light Railway, but in view of other possible sources of traffic, the '(Mineral)' was dropped from the name.

At the inquiry, Mr H.W. Plumptre drew attention to the benefits to agriculture, especially in the fruit-growing districts between Eastry and Wingham. In contrast to say, the Sheppey Light, on which passenger revenue was an important factor, especially as it failed to reach Canterbury, the East Kent always accepted the fact that passenger traffic would depend on the collieries, and more particularly would arise from miners going to the pits. After hearing the local views the commissioners returned to London and in the following year, on 19 June, Light Railway Order No. 361 authorized almost all of the East Kent which was ever constructed.

Railways Authorized by Order No. 367 of 1911

As the plans that followed had such limited results, they are of less practical interest. Notice of the plans for Railways 11 to 14 was given in November 1910, the month following the inquiry in Canterbury. No. 11 was designed to tap developments near Mongeham. No. 12 was an extension of the Guilford branch to Maydensole, No. 13 linked Guilford to the intended colliery at Stonehall, and No. 14 was a short branch to Woodnesborough. Partly because all the lines were directly linked to the development of the coal-field and there was virtually no opposition, the plans were authorized with unusual rapidity. The public inquiry was held in Dover in February 1911, and in September, Light Railway Order No. 367 appeared, only three months after No. 361.

Railways Authorized by Order No. 382 of 1912

By November, the East Kent was back for the third time, with two more lines, No. 15 to Stodmarsh and Wickhambreux, and No. 16 to Ripple. The inquiry was held at the Bell Hotel, Sandwich on 15 March, 1912. At this stage Mr Crundall, who spoke for the promoters, felt that it was necessary to convince the commissioners that the East Kent was capable of building the lines entrusted to it, and he referred to the temporary line between Shepherd's Well and Tilmanstone Colliery already in operation, while the excavation of Golgotha Tunnel for the permanent line was proceeding. He stressed the way in which Railway No. 15 followed a 'very circuitous route in order to avoid doing more injury than was absolutely necessary to the property of the landowners'. Other witnesses included Mr Stephens, who stated that his choice of alignment was determined by the 'configuration of the country and the desires of the landowners', and Dr Malcolm Burr who said that 'our difficulties are vanishing away before us'. Again there was little delay, Light Railway Order No. 382 for Railways Nos 15 and 16 appearing on

8 November, 1912.

Railways Authorized by Order No. 426 of 1920

The fourth time of asking was initiated by two applications, Railway No. 17 being applied for in May 1912 and Nos 18 to 28 in May 1913. There were also two inquiries, both held at Dover, the first in July 1913, and the second in July 1914. At the first inquiry it was stated that Snowdown and Tilmanstone Collieries were in production and that work was in progress at Wingham, Woodnesborough, Guilford and Stonehall. Sites had been selected near Ripple and near Wickhambreux. As for the railway, it was complete from Shepherd's Well to Wingham Colliery, and as far as the future site of Poison Cross station towards Richborough, together with the branch to Guilford Colliery. Local papers began to record progress.

For instance in July 1913, the *Kentish Gazette* reported that Snowdown and Tilmanstone were each raising about 900 tons of coal per week, and that Guilford would be in production within the next few months. Stonehall, Wingham and Woodnesborough should follow during the next two years.

The *Dover Express* in its issue of 26 July, 1913 interviewed Dr Malcolm Burr who thought that in a short time production would reach 2,000 tons a day, and in three years would be running at between 10,000 and 15,000 tons per day. There is some discrepancy between the report on the progress of railway construction with that given at the inquiry. Although completion of the line between Shepherd's Well and Wingham was confirmed, it was described as 'a temporary line'. Eastry to Sandwich Road was in an 'advanced condition', but the branch to Guilford Colliery was not begun. (Other evidence suggests that despite this statement, the Guilford branch was in use.) The line beyond Wingham Colliery was 'in course of construction'.

In the case of the East Kent, the distinction between temporary and permanent way would not be as striking as on a main line, and this probably contributed to the contradictory statements made about the completion dates of lines.

The acquisition of the Pickering coach from the KESR in 1912 indicates the possibility of passenger traffic; by 1914 the EKLR had four passenger coaches. But if the provision of an advertised passenger service is taken as the mark of formal completion, then the Shepherd's Well to

Wingham section was finished by 16 October 1916.

The outbreak of war in August 1914 delayed progress, and, although eight of the 12 lines proposed in 1913 and 1914 were eventually authorized, the relevant order was not made until 1920. No. 17 was one of the casualties, being withdrawn by agreement with the Betteshanger Boring Company. No. 18 ran from Woodnesborough to a point near Snowdown Colliery, and was opposed by the Adisham Colliery Co., and also by a landowner, Mr Plumptre. Because of this, the commissioners delayed their decision until their second inquiry in 1914, when Mr Burr explained its importance. He stated that Snowdown was producing 1,000 tons per week, and was the site for a possible coal by-product plant and for a central railway marshalling yard. Railway No. 18 would link it to the East Kent system and thus to the Port of Richborough. No. 19 consisted of a branch from No. 16 to a terminal near the SECR at Deal, with a spur line, No. 20, providing for the interchange of traffic.

There were objections from a Mr Elliott, whose orchard would be spoiled, from Deal Corporation over a road-crossing and from the owner of Hull Place whose opposition was withdrawn following an offer to deviate the line. The owner of Sholden Court anticipated damage to his tennis courts. But despite the objections, Railways Nos 19 and 20 were authorized, as a route to convey miners living in Deal to and from the coal-field, and to serve possible port developments.

No. 22 was the extension from Wickhambreux to a junction with the SECR at Canterbury, almost on the line of the route proposed in 1910, and if this had been built, it would certainly have strengthened the position of the company for a few more years. It was just over four miles in length and the cost, estimated at £36,622, was considerably less than half that of the most expensive of the East Kent promotions. The latter was No. 23, which followed a tortuous course from its junction with the Guilford Colliery branch over seven-and-a-quarter miles of downland to Drellingore at an estimated cost of £92,296.[3] Despite careful adjustment to what Col. Stephens called 'the configuration of the country' with steep gradients and sharp curves, it still proved necessary to include two tunnels in the plans. No. 24 was a steeply graded spur with a reverse curve of eight-and-a-half-chains radius which joined No. 23 to Stonehall Colliery. A brick-works at Northbourne, near Betteshanger Colliery, was to be served by No. 26, a branch from the Deal line. No. 27 was to have been a short spur at Wingham Colliery, and No. 28 joined the East Kent to the Richborough tramway system of Pearsons & Dorman Long.

17   Mixed train on the East Kent approaching Eythorne from Shepherd's Well in
September 1921. The train consisted of the Pickering bogie coach, obtained from the
KESR in 1912, and wagons working through from the main line. It was hauled by
locomotive No. 2, 'Walton Park', built by Hudswell Clarke in 1908, moved from
Col. Stephens's Shropshire & Montgomeryshire Railway to the EKLR in 1916, and sold
for scrap in 1943.

18   Eythorne Junction in October 1954. The 'main' line to Wingham has been lifted,
but the branch to Tilmanstone Colliery remains in use. In the foreground is a typical
ungated crossing with cattle guards, and in the background, the headstocks of
Tilmanstone Colliery.

19 Knowlton, a wayside station on the EKLR on 15 August, 1956. The platform was surfaced with cinders and its face consisted of old sleepers. Passengers were offered seating and shelter but there was no name-board. (It was perhaps not replaced after wartime removal.) The original flat-bottomed track was visible.

20 The site of the EKLR and Knowlton station viewed from the south on 28 January, 1969.

21   The bridges carrying the EKLR over the railway from Minster to Deal and the River Stour, on 14 April, 1947. The railway is visible in the foreground, but the river is concealed. The EKLR was not permitted to carry passengers over the river bridge, so mixed trains to Richborough left their coaches at Sandwich Road.

22   The unopened station at Richborough in 1937. It consisted of the usual ash-covered platform with railings, a bench, two lamp posts and a name-board marked 'Richboro Port'. In the foreground, the edge of the main A258 road is visible, with a track of the Richborough Port lines beyond. The level-crossing between this track and the EKLR was at the east end of the platform, and was provided with gates which were closed when an EKLR train was crossing.

23 Aquarium Station, Volk's Electric Railway on 25 July, 1955. Car No. 6, probably built in 1901, was about to depart. The driver having released his brake, was turning the controller fixed under the roof.

24 The car, 'Pioneer', seen from the Banjo Groyne at Brighton on 28 November, 1896, the ceremonial opening day of the BRSER. The tide being out, part of the outer track is visible. Details, including the lifebuoys and life-boat, marked 'Pioneer Brighton', are visible, and the mayor appears to be inspecting the controller, which is covered by a white sheet. The car is alongside the Brighton terminal pier.

25 View from the Banjo Pier showing the BRSER car approaching the Brighton terminal. The track is submerged but the poles supporting the overhead wire are visible. The driver in his nautical uniform is at the controller with the 'ship's bell' almost over his head.

26 The 1.45 p.m. from Golf Links on arrival at Rye on 18 July, 1914. The entire coaching stock of the RCT is in use, hauled by the 2-4-0 tank locomotive 'Victoria', purchased from Bagnalls in 1897. The conductor-guard appears to be shepherding a group of children on an outing.

27 Golf Links station on the RCT on 20 June, 1950. The corrugated iron building testifies to the identity of the engineer, Col. H. F. Stephens. The wartime concreting of a section of the track bed is visible.

28 The Pier Head terminal of the Herne Bay Pier Railway before the First World War. This was the period of electric traction, with the live rail in the conduit, offset between the rails. At this time there were no platforms, and the line was never fenced off. The octagonal restaurant is in the background.

29 The Sandgate Hill
terminal of the Sandgate
steep-grade railway,
before the First World
War. The view shows
both the cable-hauled
cars, which, partly
because of the variations
in gradient, were operated
independently and not
balanced against each
other.

30 The Devil's Dyke
steep grade railway from
the Poynings end about
1900. Although the two
cars were connected to
opposite ends of the same
cable, and therefore
always moved at the
same time and passed half
way up the incline, the
tracks did not converge
above and below the
passing place.

31 The site of the
Devil's Dyke steep-grade
railway in May 1975.
There are clear indications
of the track bed and of
the terminal at the upper
end.

32 An 0-6-0 of 1934
running light on the
Hastings Miniature
Railway on 7 April,
1974. The locomotive
modelled on the 'Royal
Scot' stands outside the
workshops.

During the First World War, Richborough was taken over by the War Office, and it is possible that if the East Kent had been sufficiently advanced, some of the war traffic would have come its way. In the event, the existing tramway system was much extended, but the interchange sidings were with the SECR Deal branch, south of Minster. As most of its powers expired after five years in 1917, the East Kent had to apply for their renewal. By this time the ten-and-a-quarter miles from Shepherd's Well to Wingham were open to goods and the less demanding type of passenger; and four miles of the Richborough line were open for goods only. A fresh submission was made for the lines applied for just before the war, and on 21 August, 1920, Light Railway Order No. 426 confirmed the powers to construct Railways Nos 18, 19, 20, 22, 23, 24, 26 and 28. No. 27 had been withdrawn when it became clear that Wingham Colliery was a doubtful starter.

The period of the war divides two phases in the development of the Kent coal-field and its associated railway. The Burrs, father and son, resigned from the network of companies with which they were associated in 1914, and after the war, the various collieries and the East Kent Railway followed more independent policies. Lack of funds bedevilled both the mines and the railway, and it was 1925 before the Richborough line was ready for passenger traffic. But this was not authorized to cross the bridge over the Stour, so the mixed train, which conveyed a passenger coach as far as Sandwich Road twice daily, left it there while the goods vehicles went on to Richborough. Also in 1925, a halt was opened at Eastry South. The land for the Deal branch was marked out but there was never enough money to complete it.

Railways Authorized by Order No. 493 of 1931

The position changed dramatically in 1927 when the Southern Railway was authorized to invest £300,000 in the East Kent. First fruits of its interest was a fifth application for the renewal of powers for old lines and for some new lines which were either improved versions of existing authorized routes or short but useful spurs and connections. The improvements were No. 33, which cut off the extremely circuitous route between Wingham and Wickhambreux, and No. 37 which provided for an improved alignment for part of the Deal branch. After a great deal of discussion, Sir Herbert Walker, general manager of the Southern, 'advised' the East Kent to withdraw its application for all the lines asked for in 1928 except Nos 33 and 37, and these were the only two which appear on the East Kent's last Light Railway Order, No. 493 of 27 March, 1931.

The inquiry, the fifth and last for the East Kent, was held at the County Hotel, Canterbury on 19 April, 1928, with Mr A.D. Erskine as chairman, supported by Mr T.L. Paterson of the Ministry of Transport. One of the results of the application was a most valuable report on what had actually been constructed by January 1928.

The lines were considered in numerical order starting with No. 1 from Shepherd's Well to Richborough. Of the ten miles 20 chains authorized, nine miles 62 chains had been constructed, but because of passenger traffic not going over the Stour bridge, only eight miles seven chains were open to passengers. The half mile of line not constructed was accounted for partly by the stopping short of the SECR at Shepherd's Well, and partly by the curtailment of lines at Richborough. Railway No. 28 to connect with the Richborough Port tramway, controlled by Pearson & Dorman Long, was described as 'under construction' and provided an alternative access to the port. It was noted that the bridge over the Stour had not been constructed in conformity with the authorizing Order. Instead of an opening span giving an 11-feet clearance at high tide, the bridge had been constructed with a fixed span resting on temporary wooden piers. The height was given as 24 ft 8 in., but it is not clear if this was above water level at high tide.

Of the five miles 72 chains of No. 2 Railway from Eastry to Canterbury Road, Wingham, five miles 34 chains had been constructed, all of which were open for goods and passengers. Instead of the authorized junction at Eastry facing Richborough, an unauthorized junction facing Shepherd's Well had been made just north of one of the few underbridges on the line. This explained the discrepancy between authorized mileage and mileage constructed. The company began work to complete the authorized alignment at Eastry in 1926 but it was interrupted by the General Strike, and had not been resumed.

The Guilford Colliery branch was open for goods traffic, with a junction at Eythorne facing Richborough, but the company was completing the authorized triangular junction to give a direct run to Shepherd's Well. The Tilmanstone Colliery branch, No. 5 on the original Light Railway Order, was also open to goods traffic but the report noted that it was on a 'different alignment to that shown in the deposited plans and was probably outside the limits of deviation'.[4]

No. 9 railway was the spur to the SECR at Richborough, and although no junction had been made, 19 chains had been constructed instead of the ten chains authorized. However it was only used as a goods siding and the extra nine chains fell within the limits of deviation. Railway No. 10 was the northern spur of the triangular junction at Shepherd's Well, and 35 chains, consisting of embankment and cutting, had been completed, but could only be used as a siding as the end did not join the SECR. Instead there was a short spur from the No. 1 line, branching off just short of the terminal platform on a sharp curve to join the SECR sidings. This was constructed by agreement with the main line company and was within the limits of deviation.

The report summarized the company's performance in building the lines allotted to it by Light Railway Order No. 361 by stating that most of Nos 1 and 2 were open to goods and passenger traffic, and that Nos 4, 5, 9 and 10 were available for goods. But at both Eastry and Eythorne, one side of the triangular junction was incomplete, and although all the required land was purchased, an extension of time for completion was requested.

As for the lines authorized by the second Order, No. 367, the company wished to abandon No. 13 as it had become clear that there would be no colliery at Stonehall. No. 14 was the Woodnesborough Colliery branch and although the pit failed to materialize, the branch, 36 chains in length, served a brick-works. On the four-and-a-half mile Deal branch, by 1928 the company had acquired just under two miles of land and had undertaken construction work on one mile. It wished to purchase another half mile of land on the original alignment, but for most of the route wished to re-locate the line.

The two lines of the third Order, No. 382 of 1912, were both to collieries which failed to materialize, but the powers for the line to Wickhambreux were revived. It was felt that of the lines authorized by the 1920 Order, it was worth retaining powers for Nos 18, 19, 20, 22, 23, 24, 26 and 28. Of these, 11 chains of No. 28 were complete as far as the unopened Richborough Port station, and 16 chains of land were purchased for No. 19, which formed part of the Deal branch. Nothing at all had been done on any of the others. The report summarized the position as follows:

Open to passengers and freight	13½ miles
Open to freight only	6 miles
Fenced or under construction	4 miles
Total land purchased	23½ miles

Mileage abandoned   15½ miles
Mileage pending   17 miles

Having summarized the constructional achievements of the company, the report considered its new proposals. Of the lines finally authorized, No. 33, the Wingham to Wickhambreux cut-off, was remarkable for its cheapness. The estimate was £9,278, and this was achieved by introducing a ruling gradient of 1 in 15, curves of 20-chains radius and four level-crossings. No. 37, the re-aligned Deal branch, had a ruling gradient of 1 in 60, but to obtain this there were banks up to 28 feet high, cuttings 42 feet deep, and a tunnel 88 yards long. The other lines consisted of a connection to the north of Tilmanstone Colliery to enable trains to run direct to Richborough, a branch to join the Southern Railway at Deal, and a line from Wingham to the Southern near Chislet Colliery.

Perhaps the most obscure of the lines was No. 40, an extension of the Richborough Castle siding which ran parallel to the Southern without joining it. Pearsons & Dorman Long suggested that its only function would be to cut off land purchased for coal-mining from the main line railway. The EKLR stated that it had been laid out in agreement with the Southern, but then proceeded to abandon it.

Pearson & Dorman Long outlined the position at Richborough Port, explaining that when they leased it from the War Department in 1925, the agreement included provision for the East Kent to construct a line, and have wharfage accommodation on the Stour. However, they were completely opposed to the East Kent which they regarded as quite unable to honour its commitments. They felt that 'nothing more should be done to establish in the locality a concern which is financially unstable'. Moreover, they found the routes proposed 'of no practical use to the localities' and a hindrance to the development of the coal-field. Downs Collieries Ltd took the view that collieries would prefer to build their own branches to the nearest point on the Southern, and that passenger traffic was better conveyed by motor bus. This last view was not entirely disputed by the East Kent Railway, who sought power to run its own buses. Needless to say this clause was opposed by a small army of road passenger operators ranging from the East Kent Road Car Co. to the Gravesend & Northfleet Electric Tramways.

The extension to Canterbury included a bridge over the Stour, and this was objected to by both Canterbury Corporation and the Kent County Council as being so small as to hold back the water and cause flooding. Mr Selby of Sandwich stated that in December 1927, flooding had been caused by the existing road bridge at Sturry. In view of complaints about the East Kent's 'illegal' bridge at Richborough, he demonstrated that as for interference with drainage, it compared very favourably with other bridges over the Stour. He referred to the road bridge at Pluck's Gutter, and pointed out that permission had been given to fix the swing-bridge on the Dover and Deal railway line in 1919, and that this had been rebuilt as a fixed bridge about 1924. In particular, he mentioned the bridge built by Pearsons in 1897 which carried its tramway from the gravel pit and concrete works at Stonar to the SER at Richborough, and had a clear span of only 27 ft 5 in. (Probably this was permitted as being temporary, and built in connection with the essential construction of the harbour of refuge at Dover.) The lowest bridge, that at Sandwich had an opening span of 29 ft 6 in. with 15-foot arches on either side, compared with the East Kent's temporary bridge of 40-feet span. In addition to crossing the river, the Canterbury extension had a level crossing near the city and this aroused the objections of both Canterbury Corporation and the East Kent Road Car Co., although it was suggested that the latter was not entitled to object.

At the inquiry, Mr Bury appeared for the EKLR, and began by stressing its constructional achievements despite the handicap of two railway strikes, two coal strikes, a General Strike, and four years of war. As stated in the report, the company had made some progress with about 23½ miles of its authorized mileage of 56. The Southern had invested in the line, and provided three out of the five directors, namely Sir George Courthorpe, Sir Francis Dent and Lt-Col. G.S. Szlumper, and this should counter any accusations of financial instability or irresponsibility. He defended the illegal bridge at Richborough by comparison with Pearson's fixed bridge, only half-a-mile upstream and with an appreciably narrower span. As to the service provided, he felt that it would not be 'many years before one train an hour was in full swing'. (In fact the service was reduced to two trains a day.)

Presumably because it was unable to find any support from the collieries, the railway company sought it from agriculture. A fruit-potato- and corn-grower, who farmed 105 acres at Weddington near Ash, claimed to dispatch 350 tons of produce by the railway. Moreover, when his broccoli was ready for the market, for a period he had filled one train a day. Another supporter made regular use of Richborough Castle Siding.

Evidently the inquiry's chairman, Mr Erskine, was not entirely satisfied, as he delayed his verdict pending a further meeting at the Ministry of Transport in Whitehall on 29 June, 1928. Mr Bury again appeared for the promoters, while the objectors were whittled down to the Town Clerk and Surveyor of Canterbury and Mr Cash for Pearson & Dorman Long. Mr Cash stated that agreement had been reached for the railway to have the exclusive use of both the old and new wharves at Rich-borough. After drawing attention to some mistakes in the estimates, Mr Erskine closed the inquiry and proceeded to compose his notes to the Minister of Transport.

He found that the most serious objections were those of the City of Canterbury to Railway No. 22, because of its level-crossings and the possibility of its interfering with drainage. On this and some other lines, he recommended the substitution of bridges for level-crossings. He had considered Railway No. 28 which had not been extended over the Sandwich to Ramsgate main road. If this were completed across the road to the old wharf it would make the fourth level-crossing within 2,360 yards. (The other three were the tramway crossing, 110 yards to the north; the crossing by the 'Red Lion' 933 yards on; and the Weather-less crossing at 1,320 yards). He noticed that under section 43 of the Sandwich Port and Haven Act of 1925, railway use of the crossings was confined to the hours from 9 p.m. to 9 a.m., but still felt that the fourth crossing was unnecessary.

In due course, the Minister stated that he was prepared to make an Order reviving the powers for Railways Nos 11, 15, 19, 20 and 22, with extensions of time for the completion of No. 2 (at Eastry) and Nos 4, 8, 9 and 10. (Most of these were already virtually complete.) He was also ready to authorize Railways Nos 33 to 39, and to 'legalize' the bridge over the River Stour. However, before the Order was made, Col. Stephens wrote in his capacity of engineer and general manager to state that on the 'advice' of Sir Herbert Walker, general manager of the Southern, the East Kent wished to drop Railways Nos 34, 35, 36, 38 and 39. So that when the fifth and last Light Railway Order, No. 493 of 27 March, 1931 finally appeared, the only new developments were the cut-off from Wingham to Wickhambreux for the Canterbury extension, and the improved alignment for the Deal branch.

Subsequent Developments of the East Kent Railways

The hopes of the East Kent had been based on the development of a number of collieries with coal exports through Richborough. In the event, Tilmanstone, owned by the East Kent Colliery Co. was the only pit on the East Kent railway that proved in any degree successful, and very little of its coal was for shipment by sea. The East Kent Colliery Company was finally taken over by Mr R. Tilden-Smith, and most of its capital written off. As the East Kent railway provided the only means of dispatching coal from its colliery, and this was the railway company's main source of income, it made as much revenue as possible from it. To counter this, Mr Tilden-Smith finally obtained powers to construct the aerial cableway to the eastern arm of Dover Harbour, where the harbour board constructed large concrete hoppers to store the coal. This was completed in 1930, but during the years of trade depression, the demand for coal exports was so low that the cableway was little used. Its importance to the East Kent railway was that it ended the latter's monopoly of Tilmanstone Colliery traffic, and it virtually ended any hopes for the development of the Port of Richborough.

If a year had to be chosen for the zenith of the East Kent, it might well be 1928. This was the year in which it was bolstered up by the interest of the Southern Railway, and in which the fortunes of the coal-field seemed to take an upward turn. (Snowdown Colliery which had been closed since 1921, was re-opened; and production from Betteshanger was becoming significant.) But for the trade depression, and the switch from coal to oil, and from rail to road traffic, the East Kent might have begun to fulfil its promises. In the event, Tilmanstone Colliery just carried it through the 1930s and the Second World War.

Freight tonnage for 1927 was 222,320, and while much agricultural traffic was lost to the roads, this was more than offset by the growth of coal for the home market. In 1935 the East Kent conveyed 240,796 tons of coal, 7,048 tons of general freight, and 2,118 tons of minerals other than coal. Three hundred and thirty-six head of livestock were carried, but passengers had already left for the roads. The 4,588 ordinary-fare passenger journeys and 24,957 workmen's-fare journeys of 1927 had slumped to 838 by 1935. The workmen's traffic consisted of colliers, mainly from Canterbury and Dover, who used the East Kent between Shepherd's Well and Tilmanstone. While the extension to Canterbury might have increased the workmen's traffic, the Southern, which by this time was in an influential position had two good reasons for a lack of enthusiasm. It would have lost revenue to and from Shepherd's Well, and, perhaps more significantly, after the 1930 Road Traffic Act it held a substantial share-holding interest in the East Kent Road Car Co.

Quite apart from the East Kent failing to run where people wanted to go, its trains could hardly be rated as attractive to the ordinary passenger. The outstanding item in its collection of coaches, and the only vehicle to ride on bogies, was the Pickering-built vestibule car, acquired in 1912, whose use expedited the issue and collection of tickets by the guard on the train. The rest of the passenger stock consisted of four-wheel and six-wheel coaches which their previous owners – the LSWR, the North London, and the SECR – must have been only too glad to sell. Mr R. Job of the National Coal Board mentioned in a letter his recollections of the morning workmen's train from Shepherd's Well up to the colliery:

'This was rather an amusing service; in fact I rode on it at times when the last carriage jostled off the rails and became disconnected, whilst the rest of the train chuffed off happily along to the colliery leaving a carriage-load of disgruntled men and boys behind. As my wages were then only 2s (10p) per day, I did not of course, lose much. There is little wonder, however, joking apart, that the service was not continued, for the maintenance of the line was shocking and of the rolling stock was worse than shocking'.

Apart from the miners' train, East Kent passenger traffic was handled by mixed trains, though unappreciative passengers might have described them as freight trains with a passenger coach next to the engine. It is however only fair to quote from an article by Charles F. Klapper and H.F.G. Dalston in the *Railway Magazine* for March 1937 in which they wrote that 'The writers' journeys have invariably been most comfortable.[5] Under war-time conditions, to enable the passenger service to be retained, two venerable bogie coaches were obtained from the Southern.

When a Labour Government, pledged to nationalize the railways, was elected in 1945, the East Kent hung on, hoping that its value for compensation would be enhanced if even one decrepit train per day was able to reach Wingham over the weed-infested track. In fact, the compensation paid was nominal, but on 1 January, 1948, the East Kent became part of British Railways, Southern Region.

After an inspection by Southern officials, whose reactions were predictable, closure to passenger traffic followed on 1 November, 1948. As far as can be ascertained, no traffic had gone through to Richborough Port for some years and from 1 January, 1950 the Richborough branch was formally abandoned. The final closure on the Wingham line took place on 1 March, 1951, after which the only wheels to pass over the track were those of the demolition trains. The line between Shepherd's Well and Tilmanstone Colliery was retained with its newly acquired standard-chaired track and, at the time of writing, continues to carry on appreciable amount of coal traffic. Out of the 56 route miles to which the East Kent aspired, this two-and-a-half miles is all that remains.

East Kent Rolling Stock

In connection with the reasons for the loss of passenger traffic, the character of the coaches has already been mentioned. The East Kent also owned 36 open wagons, two box vans, three timber wagons and a brake van. The condition of these was comparable to that of the passenger stock, and it is perhaps understandable that the Southern would not permit them to run on its own line. Therefore, most of the goods and mineral traffic were moved in the rolling stock of other companies. But the East Kent did undertake its own haulage with a collection of locomotives as remarkable as its carriages and wagons. If anything, each successive purchase was of greater historical interest.

The first locomotive, used during construction and in the early days of the line, was an 0-6-0 saddle tank, originally built by Fox Walker & Co. of Bristol in 1875. She was No. 2 of the Whitland & Cardigan Railway, and, after absorption by the Great Western, No. 1386 of that company. She was rebuilt at Swindon in 1896, and reached the East Kent in 1911. Like all East Kent locomotives, she suffered extinction by slow decay rather than demolition, but in 1937 was reported as 'recently scrapped'.

For the official opening and start of advertised passenger services in 1916, another 0-6-0 saddle tank was purchased, and this was the second newest locomotive ever possessed by the East Kent. No. 2 had been built by Hudswell Clarke as recently as 1908 for the Weston, Clevedon & Portishead Railway, when she acquired the name 'Walton Park'. She moved to another section of the Col. Stephen's empire, the Shropshire & Montgomeryshire, before transfer to the East Kent. No. 2 remained on the line until 1943 when she was sold to Thomas Ward & Co. for scrap. During the rest of the First World War, the slow development of traffic and the shortage of locomotives discouraged the East Kent from further acquisitions.

However, in 1918, a veteran of the LSWR came to Shepherd's Well.

This was one of W.G. Beattie's 'Ilfracombe Goods' class, designed to operate over the steeply graded line between that resort and Barnstaple. Built by Beyer Peacock in 1880, LSWR No. 394 had actually been derailed on the Ilfracombe line on 24 December, 1890, owing to excessive speed. She retained her LSWR livery, and with her magnificent stove-pipe chimney and pierced splashers, her appearance must have given much pleasure to the small boys of Wingham and the other places along the line. She was the first tender engine acquired by the East Kent, and was referred to as No. 3. By the end of the 1920s, her performance had deteriorated, and she became increasingly unreliable up to the date of her withdrawal in August 1933. She was not scrapped at once, but decayed on a siding at Shepherd's Well until her remains went to the breakers in March 1935.

No. 4 was the newest engine ever to run on the East Kent, having been built for the Inland Waterways and Docks Department by Kerr Stewart in 1917. She was an 0-6-0 side tank locomotive of considerably greater power than her three predecessors, and, after her acquisition in 1919, she was used mainly to haul coal trains from Tilmanstone to Shepherd's Well. She continued in use throughout the life of the East Kent, and on nationalization, was allotted the BR number 30948. However, by this time her economic life had ended, and she was scrapped in 1949.

The second purchase of 1919 – 4-4-2 well tank locomotive No. 488 – has the distinction of being the only East Kent locomotive still in operation in 1972. Built to William Adams's design by Neilsons for the LSWR in 1885, by the First World War, No. 488 was approaching the end of a normal locomotive life-cycle, and in 1917 was sold to the Ministry of Munitions at the war-inflated price of £2,104. The East Kent managed to get her in April 1919 for £900. Her mileage on the East Kent was moderate, but she was repaired for the last time in 1937. In March 1939, in true East Kent style, she was 'laid aside', and remained stationary all through the war years, in case the need for her should be great enough to justify the cost of repair. Meanwhile, for a branch on the borders of Dorset and Devon, the Southern had found that the best engines were the Adams 4-4-2 well tanks. It had two, but in the summer, they were both needed to operate the service, and there was no spare engine. So East Kent No. 5 was sold to the Southern for £800, and in March 1946, seven years after being laid aside, she left Shepherd's Well for Eastleigh Works. There she was repaired, mainly with parts taken from less fortunate members of her class, and in August 1946 began a new career as Southern No. 3488. She was used on the tortuous branch line between Axminster and Lyme Regis, and after nationalization became No. 30583. By 1961 it was found that 2-6-2 tanks of LMSR Class 2 were suitable for the Lyme Regis branch, and this was the end of the Adams tanks, except for No. 30583. She was purchased by the Bluebell Railway and is still steaming between Sheffield Park and Horsted Keynes. It would have been possible to attempt to restore her East Kent livery, but her first and longest service of 32 years was with the LSWR, so, appropriately enough, she now bears the latter's livery.

With these five locomotives, the East Kent kept going until 1923 when the promise of increasing traffic combined with the increasing debility of the existing locomotives, encouraged the directors to allow Col. Stephens to make another purchase. From the newly formed Southern Railway he obtained the SER O class 0-6-0 No. 372. This had been built to the design of the SER locomotive superintendent, James Stirling, by Sharp Stewart in 1891. Many of this class were rebuilt to Class O1, but No. 372 was sold to the East Kent in 1923 in her original condition, with domeless boiler and curves between the roof and sides of the cab. In 1932 she went back to Ashford Works and was fitted with a second-hand O1 pattern boiler. Usually rebuilding from Class O to O1 included the replacement of the somewhat inadequate curved cab by a squared version, but East Kent funds did not run to such luxuries as increased weather protection for engine-men, and East Kent No. 6 retained her original cab until she was finally withdrawn by British Railways in February 1949, after nationalization. KESR No. 2, 'Northiam', was lent to the East Kent and remained until about 1929. By 1925, however, enough funds had been accumulated to buy another second-hand engine and what became No. 7 was bought from the Southern for £380. This was a former LSWR 0-6-0 saddle tank No. 0127, built to W.G. Beattie's design by Bayer Peacock in 1882. Delivery was made in January 1926, No. 0127 running from Eastleigh Works where she had been repaired, via Brighton, Hastings, Robertsbridge, Rolvenden, Headcorn, Ashford and Dover to Shepherd's Well. The most convenient route would have been from Hastings via Rye to Ashford, so the diversion via the KESR, where some days were spent at Rolvenden shed, was presumably in accordance with some plan of Col. Stephens. No. 0127 was renumbered No. 7 and spent most of her time with No. 4, working the coal traffic from Tilmanstone to Shepherd's Well. She received a major overhaul at Shepherd's Well in 1936, and, in the last years before she was 'laid aside', frequently worked on the mixed trains to Wingham. Perhaps on account of the post-war demand for scrap metal, her period of decay was very short by East Kent standards, for she was withdrawn in June 1945, condemned in October of the same year, and cut up at Ashford Works in March 1946. Another loan from the KESR from 1917 to 1918 was the 0-8-0 side tank 'Hecate', but this powerful machine proved rather too heavy for the colliery sidings.

The purchase of No. 8 followed in 1928 when a second SER 0-6-0 of the O class was purchased. Like East Kent No. 6 she had been built by Sharp Stewart in 1891, but never achieved re-boilering, being withdrawn by the East Kent in 1935.

For a reason which has not been ascertained, the replacement for No. 2 was first numbered 100 but became No. 2 after the demise of the original No. 2, 'Walton Park'. No. 100 had been built by Sharp Stewart in 1893 as SER No. 383, and had been rebuilt from the O to O1 class in 1908. The East Kent bought her for £850, and she proved a sound investment. After nationalization she became BR No. 31383, received heavy repairs in 1949, and was not withdrawn until 1951. In fact, she outlived the last of the East Kent purchases, which was another O1, built as O class No. 371 by Sharp Stewart in 1891 and rebuilt in 1909. By the time the East Kent bought the latter in 1944 for £1,125 she had become Southern No. 1371 and she was not renumbered. Although she survived long enough to be nationalized, she did not receive a BR number, and was withdrawn at the beginning of 1949.

British Railways decided that the O1 class engines were the best for working the East Kent, and four of them were allocated to Dover shed for work on the colliery lines and also on the harbour lines at Dover. No. 31258 of 1894 lasted until 1961, while No. 31425, No. 31430 and No. 31434, all built in 1897, were withdrawn in 1959. Now the surviving section of the line between Tilmanstone and Shepherd's Well is worked by diesel locomotives. Judged in terms of performance, the engine-men of the East Kent had little to boast of; any smart running would probably have brought them off their track. Their achievement, and that of the engineering staff at Shepherd's Well, was that they managed to keep the traffic moving with such a venerable and delicate collection of locomotive power.

Such were the locomotives; the passenger services were equally unconventional. The peak period was from 1925 until 1928. On the Wingham line there were three trains a day, and on Saturday evenings a train which normally terminated at Eastry worked through to Wingham. In addition there were three miners' trains into Tilmanstone Colliery yard. Twice daily, a passenger coach was trundled to and fro along the Richborough branch as far as Sandwich Road. By 1937, the miners were travelling by road, the Richborough branch had lost its limited service, and only two trains a day served the line to Wingham. They left Shepherd's Well at 7.30 a.m. and 4.45 p.m. returning from Canterbury Road, Wingham at 8.40 a.m. and 6.10 p.m. respectively. This lasted until the withdrawal of passenger services in 1948, after which freight traffic was carried until 1951.

The East Kent from 1945 Onwards

I made my first pilgrimage to see what the East Kent looked like during a weekend leave in February 1945. It began with a typical war-time journey from Sheerness to Canterbury. There was a SECR H class tank on the Sheerness branch line to Sittingbourne, a 'King Arthur' on the Kent coast express to Faversham, and a SECR L class on the stopping train to Canterbury and Dover. It was a grey, wintry Saturday, growing dark by the time I reached Canterbury. There was time for tea and the securing of a bed before a visit to an inevitably crowded cinema. Although I knew that it was unlikely that there would be any movement on the East Kent on a Sunday, in the days following the invasion of Europe anything might happen, and I did entertain some faint hopes of seeing an East Kent locomotive in steam. So on Sunday morning, I boarded a bus of the East Kent Road Car Co., and asked a slightly puzzled conductress for a single to Wingham Station. She knew what I meant but hastened to assure me that she had never seen a train there. This I interpreted as meaning 'hardly ever', but all the same, realized that my chances of riding on the East Kent railway were very slight.

I was put down at the level-crossing on the Canterbury side of Wingham, and the East Kent bus disappeared down the road, on its way to Sandwich. There was the platform, significantly enough on the Canterbury side of the road, with the empty cutting curving away in the general direction of the city. There were a few wagons, looking very immobile, and no sign of life, and so, deprived of the opportunity of riding on the line, I decided that at least I would walk it.

Writing many years later, I very much regret that I failed to make more detailed notes of this, my first visit, because my recollections are inevitably mixed with the impressions of later visits. To some extent, this was the result of a reluctance to incur the suspicious looks which anybody taking notes of railways during the war years was likely to receive. At a time when interest in railways was regarded as at least, highly abnormal, anybody perambulating the East Kent on a winter Sunday, would invite curiosity which was unlikely to be allayed by wearing a naval uniform. My only guide was the first edition of *The Col. Stephen's Railways*, which I had kept and cherished since I purchased it for one shilling in 1937.[6]

The first half-mile consisted of what was clearly an up gradient, at first on an embankment. Crossing over the road leading into Wingham from the south, I came into Wingham Town station. Its name had led me to expect a distinctly urban station, with solid buildings and resident staff who might challenge me. On the contrary, Wingham Town resembled most of the East Kent intermediate stations, with a single platform adorned with a wooden shelter. Although I remember that no station name was visible, I cannot recall whether, to satisfy wartime regulations, the name-board had been removed or merely obscured.

While my recollections of Wingham Town in 1945 are vague, I have a photograph, taken in September 1921, which is more informative. It shows the platform with ballast and ashes filling the spaces between the side of the cutting and the brick face. The wooden shelter is there, together with a name-board and a bench. According to the *Railway Clearing House Handbook of Stations*, in addition to passengers, Wingham Town could handle livestock, but there is no sign of a cattle pen in the photograph. Although the station was not officially open in 1921, there is a single passenger coach alongside the platform, with a saddle tank locomotive, looking like No. 2, running round it. The guard-shunter is standing in the foreground by a turnout operated by a weighted lever. It is tempting to think that No. 2 had worked through on the mixed train from Shepherd's Well, putting down freight vans and wagons on the way, and had come on to Wingham Town station to run round on to the other end of the passenger coach before returning to Shepherd's Well. (There were no facilities for running round at Wingham Colliery.) Perhaps the photographer had been a passenger on the train, who had been allowed to enjoy an unauthorized ride to Wingham Town provided that he promised not to leave the officially unopened station.

Beyond Wingham Town came another ungated crossing, a down gradient and an embankment, before Wingham Colliery station was reached. This was a single platform for passengers only, and again, I have no clear recollection of the way it looked on that February day. What I do remember very well is my perplexity at not being able to see

Wingham Colliery. The headstock of a pit can usually be seen from some distance, and I prided myself on being able to recognize mines or even the sites of them without difficulty. In fact, the boring at Wingham was a short distance away from the railway, but did not advance enough to leave more than the kind of signs which require a fairly intensive search for recognition. The name 'Wingham Colliery' for the platform was just an example of East Kent optimism. In retrospect, it is remarkable that the village of Wingham (the use of the word 'town' was again East Kent wishful thinking) should have been provided with three stations. Admittedly only Canterbury Road handled freight, but even the provision of three separate passenger platforms added something to the East Kent's capital debt.

My last visit to Wingham was at the end of January 1969 when, for all that was left, the East Kent might never have existed. The cutting beyond the end of the line had been filled in, and the site of Canterbury Road Station was under cultivation. There was something left of the embankment going off towards Wingham Town, but even this had been partly removed. The sites of the Town and Colliery stations were identified by fragments of fencing, signs of ashes from the platforms, and a concentration of thorn and blackberry bushes.

Having skirted the buildings of Wingham, the East Kent followed a tributary stream of the Little Stour along a valley towards Woodnesborough. This was fruit-growing country with intensively cultivated farms, the lack of hedges and field boundaries giving the country an open appearance. Col. Stephens's design avoided engineering works almost completely, and, needless to say, any concentrations of buildings.

It was about a mile-and-a-half from Wingham Colliery to the next station, which being about three-quarters-of-a-mile from Staple and a mile from Ash, was called Staple and Ash. By East Kent standards, this was a main station, with a passing loop. In addition to the usual platform and shelter, it had facilities for all kinds of traffic, including livestock, horses and carriages. A windpump, which was still erect in 1945, provided water. Another three-quarters-of-a-mile further on was Ash Town, which consisted of one platform. There was no point in providing any more, as the only access was by a field-path from the near-by village, and only pedestrian passengers could reach the station.

The East Kent had had high hopes for its fruit traffic, and put in two sidings for the use of large farms – Poulton Farm Siding to the west of Ash Town Station, and Moat Farm Siding to the east. While so many details of my 1945 visit have been forgotten, I do recollect both the farm sidings, probably because they had vans in them, and this was the first rolling stock I had seen since leaving Canterbury Road, Wingham. What they were taking to or from the farms in February is enigmatic; fertilizer seems most likely.

Approaching Woodnesborough, I met another line walker approaching from the opposite direction, and was relieved when he abstained from curiosity about my activities, and confined himself to a comment on the temperature. Woodnesborough Station was about three-quarters-of-a-mile from the village by a level-crossing which, despite Board of Trade wishes to the contrary, was ungated. It was virtually identical to Staple and Ash, with a platform, bench and shelter on one side of the line, and provision for freight traffic on the other. At the Shepherd's Well end of the platform there was a water tank of moderate dimensions, mounted on massive timbers which looked as though they might have been left over from the bridge over the Stour at Richborough. Tank engines usually stopped there for water.

Beyond Woodnesborough, at the far end of a short cutting, was the half-mile branch to the colliery. Like Wingham, this had proved abortive but luckily for the East Kent, a brick-works on the same site had proved successful. This was still operating in 1969, although it lost its rail connection in 1951.

At this point, there was a marked change in the character of the country from the light soils of the fruit-growing zone to the great estates and large farms of the chalk country. Its undulations presented difficulties for the East Kent but Col. Stephens managed to follow a dry valley for most of the way from Eastry to Eythorne, and although earthworks were unavoidable, only short lengths of bank and cutting proved necessary. As explained above, Eastry was designed to have a well-spaced triangular junction. The southern arm was withdrawn on account of the opposition of Lord Desborough, but the northern arm, giving a direct run from the Wingham and Woodnesborough collieries to Richborough Port was authorized. However, pending its completion, a sharply curved unauthorized line was constructed, performing the function of the southern spur, but branching off just north of an under-bridge, whereas the smoothly graded curve originally planned would have necessitated a second underbridge. Work was started on the northern spur but was never completed.

One recollection from 1945 is of surprise at finding a signal post with two lower quadrant semaphore arms, one mounted above the other, indicating whether the road was set for Wingham or for Richborough.

There was a passing loop which, with the junction, was controlled by a small frame characteristically located in a corrugated-iron shed. With the passenger service to Sandwich Road never exceeding two trains per day, Eastry was described in the time-tables as the station for Sandwich, which was about three miles away.

But I also remember Eastry as the point at which I had to decide which line to follow. It was five-and-three-quarter miles to Shepherd's Well and two-and-a-half to Sandwich Road. Although it was still only the middle of the afternoon, the temperature was dropping, and I knew that by five o'clock it would be growing dark. To my retrospective regret, I played safe and took the Richborough line. It was only half-a-mile to Poison Cross station. (The residents of a nearby mediaeval ecclesiastical institution are said to have died by poisoning.) From Eastry down to the edge of the marshes at Great Poulder's Farm, the line traversed fruit-growing country, and this may have accounted for the presence of vans at Poison Cross. There had, of course, been no passenger service on the Richborough line since 1928. The passenger facilities had been even more sparse than those on the Wingham line, the only accommodation apart from the platform itself being one bench. An interesting economy was achieved by forming the platform faces from wooden posts supporting sheets of corrugated iron. Roman Road, Woodnesborough, consisted of a single platform, but Sandwich Road had both platform and siding.

That was the end of my first visit to the East Kent. I walked back along the main road past an impressive windmill, in gathering darkness with a threat of snow in the air. Train services on Sunday evenings in 1945 were often better than the published time-tables suggested, and by war-time standards, my return journey to Sheerness was not a difficult one. I had failed to see the end part of the Richborough line, and the main line from Eastry to Shepherd's Well.

In fact it was 9 May, 1956 before I visited what was left of the Richborough line. After the grey February of my first visit, my notebook records that 9 May was a 'fine, sunny morning'. I went down to Ashford on the 9.15 from Charing Cross behind Schools Class No. 30934, 'St. Lawrence'. Despite three permanent way restrictions, we reached Ashford at 10.35, dead on time. The 10.45 to Ramsgate was waiting with a 2-6-4 tank locomotive whose number I omitted to record. I do remember the pleasant run, down the valley of the Stour to Canterbury and on to Minster.

There I left the train, and, armed with the track permit that I had by then acquired, set off along the line to Richborough. My first intention was to find what was left of the marshalling yard and train-ferry dock constructed for the heavy traffic of the First World War, and, to my considerable surprise much of this was still in position. This brought me to the new wharf from which the East Kent had so confidently anticipated a coal export traffic, comparable to that of South Wales or the North East coast. In 1956 there were hopes of reviving maritime trade from the new wharf, but these were to prove unjustified. I followed the port lines, which were in surprisingly good condition, crossing Stonar cut by a bridge parallel to that carrying the main road. The exchange sidings between the port lines and the East Kent were situated on the west side of the road about half-a-mile south of Stonar cut. In addition to the three siding roads, the East Kent had constructed a station, consisting of ashes and ballast supported by a timber face and backed by a fence of timber posts and metal rails. The furniture consisted of a wooden bench, two posts from which oil lamps could have been hung, and a name-board lettered 'Richboro Port'. It was at right angles to the main road and separated from it by the track of the port line to the war-time ammunition works.

All East Kent stations were used sparingly but Richboro Port was the only one which never had a passenger. With the aid of a photographer of 1937, I was able to find the site of the station, for although everything else had gone, ballast and ashes in the unmistakable form of a railway platform still survived. (They were still there in the spring of 1969.) I made my way through the site of the sidings, which were completely overgrown, to find what was left of the bridge over the River Stour. Immediately to the west, the East Kent had passed over the Deal branch of the SER, and the narrow strip of land between river and railway was crossed by an embankment. There has been little change between 1956 and the present day. The red brick piers which carried the metal spans over the SER are still in position, and the earthworks are complete. However the metal spans over both railway and river were removed some time between 1947 and 1954, as also were the 'temporary' piers of the wooden bridge.

The final objective of my 1956 visit was the Richborough Castle siding, built to serve Richborough Farm and some ballast pits, with the possibility of extension to join the main line. At least until 1937 there had been a cattle grid where the siding stopped short of a minor road, but this had gone by 1956. I walked along the road, back to Sandwich this time, to return to London via Dover.

The following description of the section from Eastry to Eythorne and Guilford belongs to January 1969, and that from Shepherd's Well to Tilmanstone Colliery to March 1968. Characteristically, my visit of January 1969 was made by private car. My first objective was the site of Eastry South, opened in 1925, the 'zenith' year of the East Kent. It was better placed to serve Eastry than the station at the junction, and was provided with both a platform and a goods siding. However, by 1969 all had been erased.

Going south, the chalk cutting near Knowlton was well-preserved; only in parts was its use as a convenient receptacle for rubbish being exploited. Knowlton once consisted of the usual East Kent platform of ballast topped with ashes, plus shelter, a bench and a name-board. In 1969, the line of the railway was still distinct, but nothing remained of the station. About three-quarters-of-a-mile further south was the point at which the Tilmanstone Colliery sidings would have joined the main line for coal traffic bound for Richborough, but as the traffic failed to materialize, so did the junction. Elvington halt was originally known as Tilmanstone Colliery halt and was of conventional appearance, the platform being faced with bricks. Like Knowlton, it had no goods siding, and again like Knowlton, the site was clearly defined in 1969.

Eythorne was the most important intermediate station on the East Kent, being the junction for both the Tilmanstone and the Guilford Colliery lines. Not only did it have a longer platform, but instead of the usual simple shelter, a brick-built waiting room and office was provided. After passenger traffic finished in 1948, the platform was shortened, but the brick building survived. By 1954, BR had re-laid the main running line, which ran alongside the platform, with chaired track, but the parallel siding line retained its East Kent flat-bottomed rails. An East Kent iron trespass notice, dated March 1946, survived at the road crossing. In January 1969, the notice had gone, the siding had been lifted and the platform erased, and only the main line to Shepherd's Well and the branch to Tilmanstone Colliery remained in use. The alignment of the track towards Eastry and to Guilford Colliery was so overgrown with thorn as to be impassable. The earthworks of the Guilford branch could be made out at several points, and a number of the buildings of the abortive colliery were still intact. But any influence the branch had on the very pleasant scenery had been virtually eliminated.

Oddly enough, my last coverage of the line from Shepherd's Well to Tilmanstone Colliery was by special train. This was the 'Invicta Rail Tour', run by the Locomotive Club of Great Britain on 3 March, 1968.

We arrived at Shepherd's Well about 1.15 p.m., having travelled down from Blackfriars via the Gravesend West branch. There was never direct running on to the East Kent, and we were drawn back into the exchange sidings. Neither of the arms of the triangular junction by which the East Kent would have joined the main line were completed and it was possible to compare their respective condition.[5]

The southern arm, which would have given a through run to Dover, was always separated from the main line by an unexcavated strip of chalk, and the East Kent terminal platform adjoined it, as near as possible to the main line station. It had a shelter and waiting-room and two less likely refinements – a starting signal and a porter's trolley. By 1968 the platform was indicated by a faceless mound, but the track was still in use as a siding. The embankment and cutting, constructed for the northern arm, were trackless, and the sidings which had remained on the site of the engine shed at least until 1955 had been lifted.

With a diesel locomotive on each end of our main line train, we traversed the tortuous curve between the exchange siding and the East Kent proper. At this point I was called for lunch, and thus acquired the possibly unique experience of lunching in a restaurant car on the East Kent main line. We climbed to Golgotha Tunnel, which with its steep-sided approach cuttings, was built for double track. However the Col. Stephens sense of economy prevailed to the extent of not removing all the chalk from under the arch so that at one end of the tunnel there was only room for a single track. On through Eythorne it was not surprising that our passage excited the curiosity of the local inhabitants. We stopped in the sidings of Tilmanstone Colliery, and I contemplated the distinction between the wine served in our restaurant car and the cans of tea carried by the miners who would have covered the same route in the ramshackle early morning trains of the East Kent. We returned to Shepherd's Well and the electrified speed of the main line.

So in 1969, all that was left of the East Kent was worked as a long siding. Some stations, like Canterbury Road, Wingham, had been erased; others like Richboro Port survived as mounds, only to be recognized by the initiated. It was a project which went almost completely wrong, but incidentally provided a useful service for a few years for a very few people.

5

Independent Railways Open to the Public

Strictly, any line on which the rolling stock runs on rails could be called a railway. However, in cases where the rails were laid down along a public road, the term tramway was usually preferred, although one line which was partly on its own right of way, partly in the road, and partly alongside it, was called the Portsdown and Horndean Light Railway. In this chapter, railway is taken to apply to tracks which do not share a right of way with a public road.

None of these railways was owned by main line companies, and none was connected to the main line. Because of this, there was no strong case for the adoption of standard gauge, and the lines described vary between the extremes of ten-and-a-quarter inches and 18 feet.[1] Signalling systems ranged from the sophisticated colour lights of Volk's Electric Railway to the non-existent. Passenger stations showed a comparable variety. Motive power included steam locomotives, hydraulic and electric power and diesel engines.

All the lines depended almost exclusively on passenger traffic. They were all short, the longest, the Brighton & Rottingdean Seashore Electric Railway having a mileage of two-and-three-quarters. Most of them were constructed at seaside resorts, and the few that were opened inland, relied heavily on pleasure traffic. The survival rate has been appreciably higher than that of the light railways. The five lines with mileage of about one or over are listed in Appendix Two and the remainder, the steep grade railways and pleasure lines, appear in Appendix Four.

Volk's Electric Railway

The first electric railway in Britain was opened at Brighton on 4 August, 1883. Initially, it ran along the top of the beach for about quarter-of-a-mile from a point almost opposite the Aquarium to the Old Chain Pier. Undoubtedly most of the passengers who used the line in 1883 would have been more attracted by the sensation of movement by electric power than by the prospect of conveyance. The generating plant consisted of a Crossley gas engine and a Siemen's dynamo producing a 50-volt supply.

Such was the success of the line that in 1884 it was rebuilt to a wider gauge – 2 ft 9 in. instead of two feet – and extended to the Banjo Groyne near Paston Place. It then ran for about three-quarters-of-a-mile, and, while many of its passengers were pleasure-riders, it did fulfil a definite transport function. A regular service at very frequent intervals was provided, both winter and summer, until 1940. The line was almost level except at the point where it dipped steeply down to pass under the Chain Pier. In 1896, a severe storm damaged the pier so badly that it was subsequently demolished.

Another event of 1896 was the construction of what was, in effect, an extension of Volk's Electric Railway from a pier on the far side of the Banjo Groyne to Rottingdean. This unusual line, the Brighton & Rottingdean Seashore Electric Railway, which is described below, was closed in 1901, and by way of compensation, the Corporation allowed Volk to extend the original line for about half-a-mile to Black Rock. Banjo Groyne was crossed by a level-crossing and, for a while, after the opening, cars stopped on either side, and passengers had to walk across the groyne. The service continued to be provided by single cars running at frequent intervals rather than trains. A minor change was the opening of a new terminal at Aquarium, about 200 yards east of the original; also at Black Rock, to coincide with the opening of a new bathing pool. In 1938 the Brighton Corporation (Transport) Act placed the Brighton Beach Railway on the Statute Book and also gave the Corporation power to take it over. This they did on 1 April, 1940, but in July 1940, under the threat of invasion, the beaches were closed and the railway ceased to operate.

During the war, the condition of the line deteriorated steadily, and the decision to re-open it came as a pleasant surprise. New island platforms were provided at Children's Playground, just west of the car sheds at Paston Place, and at Black Rock; and a redundant tram shelter was erected at Aquarium. The seven best cars were restored and the line re-opened in time for the 1948 summer season.

The tradition of all-the-year-round operation was ended in the winter of 1952/1953, and after the experiment of weekend operation in 1953/

1954, the line has been closed each year from the end of September until Easter. In 1964, experiments were carried out with the operation of two cars coupled together, and subsequently the long tradition of single-car operation was broken. Perhaps significantly, in 1960 the Corporation transferred the line from the Transport Committee to the Entertainments and Publicity Committee, thus recognizing the fact that most passengers were pleasure-riders. Very wisely, the committee decided not to operate modern-style cars, but have resuscitated the veteran rolling stock, supplementing it with two cars of similar appearance from the Southend Pier Railway. In 1963 the eightieth anniversary of the line was celebrated, and one may hope for even greater celebrations in 1983.

The Brighton & Rottingdean Seashore Electric Railway

The extension of Volk's railway to Rottingdean could have been carried out, either by climbing to the top of the cliffs or by constructing a viaduct or embankment along the top of the beach. Instead, Volk decided to build his line on the chalk bed rock, out to sea beyond the shingle beach. It consisted of a double line of 2 ft 8½ in. gauge, the tracks being set 18 feet apart. The rails were supported on five feet by three feet concrete blocks fixed in the chalk at three-feet intervals.

The line extended from a pier alongside the Banjo Groyne for two-and-three-quarter miles to Rottingdean, and in places was 100 yards out from the shore. At high tide the rails were under 15 feet of water. The only car to operate on the line was called 'Pioneer', and, in his definitive article on the Brighton & Rottingdean, Alan Jackson wrote: 'Looking at it one came to the inescapable conclusion that its ancestors were respectively an open-top tram-car, a pleasure yacht and a seaside pier'.[2] First, in order to be above water at all states of the tide, the car had four braced 'legs', 23 feet long. This part was evocative of a seaside pier. Above was mounted a deck with a saloon surmounted by a knife-board seat. Poles carried electrified wires at the landward side of the track, and the car had tram-type trolley poles at one side. The electric motors were on the deck driving two of the wheels through bevel gearing. (For much of the time, the wheels were under water.) The 'Pioneer' was driven by a motor man operating a trap-type controller, but wearing a seafarer's uniform. The 'pleasure yacht' atmosphere was strong in the saloon with its padded seat, carpets and electrolier. In the summer, an awning could be erected over the upper deck. Other marine features were the lifebelts, a ship's bell, a flag and a life-boat.

Considerably more capital was needed for this than for the earlier line, and an Act of Parliament was passed in 1893 authorizing a nominal share capital of £20,000 plus £5,000 in loans. These amounts were increased by £8,000 and £2,000 by a second Act of 1896. The Brighton & Rottingdean was opened to the public at the end of November 1896. It had terminal piers adjoining the Banjo Groyne and at Rotting-dean, and an intermediate landing place at Ovingdean. In its early days, 'The Daddy Long Legs' caught the public imagination, and there were plans for similar ines across the Channel. However, one of the Brighton & Rottingdean's main drawbacks was the slow speed of the car. When the tide was out, eight miles per hour was sometimes attained, but at high tide this was much reduced. The original intention to use the line as a regular transport service was, therefore, not pursued, and curious passengers were merely taken out some distance from the Banjo Groyne and then returned without being landed anywhere.

The storm of December 1896, which destroyed the Chain Pier, damaged both the car and the piers, and the line was not re-opened until July 1897. The gale damage had cost so much to repair that there was little chance of obtaining a second car, or increasing the power of the generating equipment and the motors on the 'Pioneer'.

Another problem was the track: although it was sited beyond the beach, there was a tendency for sections of it to disappear below sand and shingle. In the event, the issue was decided by Brighton Corporation's plan to construct groynes which would have necessitated the re-alignment of the tracks further out to sea. There was no possibility of doing this, and, in 1901, this unusual line was closed.

After the 'Pioneer' came to rest she was lashed to the intermediate landing place at Ovingdean, and was still there in 1909. Mr Jackson records that the car, the three piers and the rails were sold to scrap-merchants shortly afterwards, and sent to Germany. Needless to say, the concrete blocks were not removed and many of these are still to be seen at low tide.

Although it may be argued whether the 'Pioneer' was a mobile pier, a marine tram-car or a yacht-on-wheels, the Act of Parliament was for the Brighton & Rottingdean Seashore Electric Railway, and this is sufficient reason to include it with other railways with which it had so little in common.

The Rye & Camber Tramway

At the beginning of this chapter, it was explained that sometimes lines which followed roads were called light railways; conversly the Rye & Camber, which followed its own right-of-way across the marshes, was called a tramway. Unlike the Romney, Hythe & Dymchurch, it was never a member of the Railway Clearing House, and it never possessed any statutory powers. One of its functions was to carry golfers from Rye to the golf course at Camber, but it also conveyed passengers to Camber Sands and to Rye Harbour. Compared with most railways it was unusually successful, and, in its early days, dividends of $7\frac{1}{2}$ per cent were not unknown. This was not so much on account of its traffic, although 18,000 tickets were sold during the first six months of operation, but rather the result of its low capital cost. The Rye & Camber Tramways Company was registered in June 1895 with a capital of £2,300. For this the company obtained just over one-and-a-half miles of three-foot-gauge single track, designed by Col. H.F. Stephens, and opened on 13 July, 1895. The two stations were provided with low platforms and modest buildings of corrugated iron; at the Rye end there were sheds, also of corrugated iron, for the locomotives and coaches.

Initially, the company purchased one 2-4-0 tank locomotive and one passenger coach from Bagnalls. This was an open car, very similar to those being constructed for the metre-gauge departmental railways in France at the same time, accommodating first- and second-class passengers. In 1897 a second 2-4-0 tank locomotive was purchased and named 'Victoria'. A second coach for third class only was built locally at the Rother Iron Works in Rye in 1896. Traffic was always operated by one locomotive in steam, and with this arrangement no signals were required. A picture taken by Mr Henry Casserley at Rye in 1931 shows some small wagons at the back of the locomotive shed. These may have been used for carrying stores, but they were also used, with improvised seating, to carry passengers on busy summer days. Fare collection took place on the train by a conductor/guard who, at busy times, must have been kept very fully employed. When the line was opened the first class fares were 4d single and 6d return, and the second class 2d single and 4d return.

In 1908, the line was extended for about half-a-mile to a new terminus in the middle of the sand dunes. There were a few houses at Camber, but the railway stopped short of the road, and the naming of the station as Camber Sands, underlined the fact that it was intended to take people to the sands and the beach. At the same time the original terminal had its name changed from Rye Harbour to Golf Links. This was a realistic re-naming as the settlement which had grown up alongside Rye Harbour was on the west side of the water, while the Rye & Camber's station was on the east side. (The SER had constructed a long siding down to the west side, but never provided a passenger service.)

The Rye & Camber was an early convert from steam traction, purchasing in 1925 a strange-looking machine with a petrol motor (often compared to a king-size lawn-mower), and selling a year later one of its steam locomotives. The second was sold in 1937, after which the line would appear to have had no spare motive power. Another economy was conversion to third class only, the original car losing the cushioned luxury of its first-class section.

The road to Camber went round by East Guldeford and was sufficiently indirect to ensure steady passenger traffic for the railway at least until the 1920s. But inevitably, the motor bus and the private car eroded its traffic, and although, even in the late 1930s an hourly service was provided from 10 a.m. until 6.15 p.m., receipts were falling steadily. The line was closed at the outbreak of war in September 1939.

A Service Department took it over in 1940, but had no use for it as a railway. A section of the permanent way between the Halfway House request stop and Golf Links station was converted into a road by the simple process of concreting strips on either side of the rails, and, in some places, between them as well. In this way, road vehicles gained access to the east side of Rye Harbour, and to an Army complex of Nissen huts. The rails were not removed, and after the war, in 1945, the rusting track was returned to its owners. Volk's Railway was revived, but the Rye & Camber remained unused, and in due course, the rails were removed. In 1946, Rye Corporation purchased the land once occupied by the tramway.

Reference has already been made to the visit of Mr Casserley to the line in 1931. He almost certainly would have arrived at the SER Rye station of 1851, and then walked out of the town, over the river bridge, to the Rye & Camber terminus. Some attempt was made to compensate for its out-of-town site by proclamation of the destination of the rail service. On the end of the corrugated-iron building which faced the road, a notice advertised 'Tram to Camber-on-Sea', while, on the sloping roof of the station, even larger white letters appeared. These were big enough to be seen from the town and read 'Tram Station'. Mr Casserley's photographs also show the iron railings with which the line was fenced. These provided a contrast to the usual wooden rail and post. Points were operated by weighted levers and there were no signals.

I made my most recent visit to the site of the Rye & Camber in the early evening of 24 March, 1967. The corrugated-iron buildings had disappeared, leaving no trace above the ground. There was however, something left of the iron fencing, and it was possible to follow the line for about the first half-mile to the point where it crossed a drainage ditch. When Mr Alan Jackson visited the line on 20 June, 1950, the bridge was virtually intact, with wooden beams spanning the gap between the concrete abutments, and the rails still in position. Seventeen years later, the abutments remained but were carrying what appeared to be a water main. The next section of the line was partly obliterated by excvations for gravel, but it was rejoined at Halfway House. From here to Golf Links station the war-time concrete survived and in some places the rails were embedded in it. Golf Links station, semi-derelict in 1950, had been converted into a store, and part of the platform face removed. However, surviving pieces of track left no doubt as to its former function.

I followed the course of the extension of 1908 along the embankment, but there was no sign at all of Camber Sands station. Whereas the original two stations had concrete-faced platforms and corrugated-iron buildings, Camber Sands was of timber throughout, and in a position of such isolation among the sand dunes as to make it difficult to locate the site. The best relic of the line is certainly Golf Links station and it is the section from here to Halfway House that is particularly recommended to the visitor.

The most evocative photograph I know of the line was taken by the late Mr Ken Nunn on 18 June, 1914, when he was at Rye shortly after the arrival of the 1.45 train from Golf Links. This consisted of 'Victoria' and the two coaches. The side of the locomotive cab is closed with what looks like canvas, which in June seems strange. The smoke from the locomotive is being blown by a fairly strong wind, but it does not appear to have been raining. Protection against blown sand might have been necessary at Camber but hardly at Rye. The first of the two coaches is the original longer one, which, at least until August 1959, survived in a field at East Guldeford. The guard/conductor is shepherding what appears to be a children's outing into line before permitting them to board the train, and something of the excitement they felt at the prospect of the train ride and the joys of sand and sea has been caught by the photographer.

The Rye & Camber must have given pleasure to many people, especially children, during the 44 years of its existence, but it could not compete with motor transport.

The Herne Bay Pier Railway

By the 1830s, steamer services to the principal seaside resorts within reach of London were well-established. Places with gently shelving shores, such as Southend or Herne Bay, because the water retreated so far at low tide, required long piers if steamers were to come alongside the pier-heads. For instance by 1846, Southend Pier had been extended to one-and-a-quarter miles. Distances of this order led to the provision of railways on piers, initially for the conveyance of luggage in hand-propelled trucks. Exposure to wind was doubtlessly one of the reasons why sail propulsion was used when possible. In 1890, following major rebuilding, Southend had one of the first lines to be worked by electricity, thus enabling it to vie with Brighton in matters of advanced transport technology.

A few of the piers in the parts of Southern England covered by the present volume were long enough to be rail-served. At Herne Bay, a pier, 3,640 feet in length, was opened in 1832.[3] The single line of narrow-gauge track was opened for the conveyance of luggage, but appears to have carried passengers as well from 1833. Propulsion was by wind if available, otherwise by hand. Unfortunately, neither Herne Bay nor its pier developed with the rapidity anticipated. After the opening of the direct railway line in 1861, the route by steamer and pier suffered strong competition, and the last steamer called in 1862. Attack by teredo worms weakened the structure of the pier and it was closed in 1864.

A new and much shorter iron structure replaced the original pier in 1873, but could not be reached at all states of the tide. It was not until 1898 that the first pier was truly replaced, by a structure 3,920 feet long. An electric railway line used in the construction work was opened for passenger traffic in April 1899. Rolling stock consisted of a powered car, two former horse tram-cars purchased from Bristol in 1901, and a luggage truck. The pier company obtained its revenue from steamers, railway passengers and pedestrians, together with the rents from the owners of various shops and coin machines.[4] Unfortunately, revenue was reduced by a dishonest general manager. This led to bankruptcy, and in 1909, the pier with its railway was purchased by Herne Bay Urban

District Council. Operations continued until the outbreak of the First World War when the pleasure steamers were requisitioned for mine-sweeping, the railway ceased to operate and the rolling stock was sold for scrap.

During the post-war recovery period it was decided to restore the service, but instead of an electrified line, a petrol-electric car was delivered in 1925. It did not prove satisfactory and, in 1934, a car, with its electric motor driven by batteries was delivered. The earlier car had its machinery removed, and at times when traffic was heavy, operated as a control trailer. Between the wars, despite the advent of motor coach competition, the pleasure steamers still carried a good summer traffic which was augmented by passengers merely traversing the length of the pier. The outbreak of the Second World War ended this, and unlike its Southend counterpart, the Herne Bay Pier Railway closed down and was not re-opened.

Whereas pier railways such as those at Hythe (Hampshire), Ryde, and Southend had a reserved right-of-way, fenced-off from the rest of the pier, the track at Herne Bay was not separated. The stations consisted of nothing more than low platforms, added in the 1930s, and with only one powered car running on a 3 ft 4½ in.-gauge single line, there was no signalling. Over the years, six forms of motive power were used – manual, sails, electricity from a live rail in a conduit, a petrol-electric motor and a battery-electric motor. A steam miniature railway operated on the pier for two seasons after 1945. In view of its close relationship to steamers using the pier, there is little doubt that their withdrawal sealed the fate of the Herne Bay Pier Railway.

Other Railways on Piers and Jetties

In some cases, the rails on piers formed part of the main line system. For instance, at Dover both the Admiralty and the Prince of Wales Piers carried standard-gauge track for boat trains.[5] That on the Prince of Wales Pier has been disused for many years, but the Admiralty Pier was re-placed by Dover Marine station. At Margate, it is necessary to distinguish between the stone pier (really a jetty) which protects the harbour, and the iron jetty (really a pier) which served the life-boat station and passenger steamers. The jetty was provided with a narrow-gauge track for baggage trolleys.[6] In 1948 a ten-and-a-quarter-inch-gauge was opened with a steam locomotive to run on the pier, but this was a pleasure line rather than a pier railway. At the end of the 1963 season, the track was removed to be relaid on the jetty, ready for use in the 1964 season. There was a change in locomotive power from steam to diesel, and in function, as in its new position the line could carry both pleasure-riders and steamer passengers. The rolling stock suffered severely in a fire at the end of 1964, but has been rebuilt.

The Ramsgate Tunnel Railway

The Ramsgate Tunnel Railway consisted of just under three-quarters-of-a-mile (1,144 yards) of two-foot-gauge single track of which 780 yards was laid in an abandoned main line tunnel. When the LCDR reached Ramsgate in 1863, it opened a station alongside the beach and harbour in a much more favourable position than the SER station at the back of the town. However, to reach this advantageous site a tunnel, 1,124 yards long with a 1 in 75 gradient, was necessary.

After the union of the SE & LCD, various schemes for the rationalization of the lines in Thanet were considered, but it was not until the Southern Railway had been formed in 1923, that any work was completed. The Southern built a new, Ramsgate station, which was even further from the sea than the SER terminus it replaced, and connected the SER with the LCDR by a link line which joined the LCDR in the cutting just north of the Ramsgate Tunnel. In 1926, the new line was brought into use and the old stations and the tunnel were closed. The site of Ramsgate Harbour station was purchased by Thanet Amusements Ltd which provided a fun-fair, refreshment facilities and a small zoo, using parts of the station building.

The company considered possible uses for the abandoned tunnel and finally decided to utilize part of it for an electric railway, terminating at Hereson Road in the Dumpton Park district of Ramsgate. It was hoped that the line would have both a transport function, as a useful link between Dumpton Park and the harbour and sea front, and would also carry pleasure-riders. To attract the latter, for about the first quarter-of-a-mile of the old tunnel, some of the space on either side of the single track was used to erect illuminated tableaux. To reach the terminal in Hereson Road, a new tunnel, eight feet high, six feet wide and about 260 yards long was excavated through the chalk. As this was built to take a single track of narrow gauge as compared to double-track standard gauge, the point at which the train left the old tunnel for the new was very apparent. Another contrast was that of gradient, the old tunnel being inclined at 1 in 75, and the new, at 1 in 15.

The new railway was opened on August Bank Holiday, 1936. It was a wet day, and contemporary pictures taken at Dumpton Park show rain-coated passengers on the wooden platforms doubtlessly looking forward to the protection afforded by the tunnel. There were two trains, each consisting of four cars, the end cars being motored. Electricity at 400 volts D.C. was supplied from a rotary converter situated just inside the tunnel at the seaward end, and was fed on to a tramway-type overhead wire. At first, one of the trains had driving positions on its two-trailer cars, so that at slack periods it could be divided into two two-car trains, and subsequently the second train was adapted for division. As most of the journey was in the tunnel, although the cars had roofs, they were open-sided, and had no doors. There was no provision for parcels traffic, and no class distinction.

In 1937, 1938 and 1939, the line was open from Whitsun until September, most of its patrons being summer visitors. (Local inhabitants were not lured away from the buses.) Trains left the terminals simultaneously, signalled by colour lights, and crossing on a passing loop. Closure in 1939 was for six years, the tunnel being used as an air-raid shelter during the Second World War.

The Tunnel railway was re-opened for the 1946 season, and some minor changes were made before its final closure. In 1948 the rotary converter was replaced by a mercury arc rectifier. By the time I visited the line in 1954, the tableux were looking decidedly worn, and they were subsequently removed. Owing to a cliff fall, the line did not open for the 1957 season, and at this time one of the two tracks was removed from each of the stations, while concrete platforms replaced wood. Journey time remained at four-and-a-half minutes, giving an average speed of ten miles per hour, this depending partly on the 1 in 75 and 1 in 15 gradients faced in one direction.

Final closure came at the end of the 1965 season, the last trains running on Sunday, 26 September. As mentioned above, some parts of the railway are now in use on the Romney, Hythe & Dymchurch line.

Steep-Grade Railways for Passengers

Cable-worked inclined planes were not common in the south of England. Reference is made elsewhere to those which formed part of the original Canterbury and Whitstable Railway and to the much steeper line serving the chalk-pit and lime-works at Offham, near Lewes.[7] An interesting development was the use of inclined planes to convey passengers up cliff faces at seaside resorts. This is one kind of railway on which cable haulage still prevails, normal adhesion between wheel and rail being quite inadequate. Rolling stock consists of single cars rather than trains, while, being self-contained, there is no need for steep-grade railways to adopt the standard gauge. Gradients and lengths vary, but as the lines are intended for people requiring vertical rather than horizontal transport, gradients are as steep as 1 in 1.28, while lengths have not exceeded the 840 feet of the Devil's Dyke line. Although these lines are approaching the function of escalators or vertical lifts, because they consist of cars running on rails, they have a place in any account of railways.

The first passenger-carrying steep-grade railway of this type in Britain was opened at Scarborough in 1874, and it was 11 years later, on 16 September, 1885 that a line was opened in the south. This consisted of two tracks of 5 ft 10 in. gauge ascending Leas Cliff at Folkestone. The car bodies were kept in a horizontal position by resting on triangular underframes, which provided housing for water tanks. There was one car on each inclined track connected by a cable passing round a drum at the top of the incline. When a car reached the top its tank was filled with water, and when it stopped at the bottom, its tank was emptied. The additional weight of water ensured that when the brakes were released the descending car would pull its ascending neighbour to the upper terminus. The cars held 18 people, and traffic was so heavy that on busy summer days they proved insufficient to carry the traffic.

Therefore, in 1890 a second pair of tracks was added on the east side of the original pair, making a four-track steep-graded railway. However, the new tracks were of a different gauge, 4 ft 10 in. instead of 5 ft 10 in., and the car bodies, instead of being horizontal, sloped, their floors consisting of a series of steps. The Leas Cliff Lift still operates during the summer season, although for most of the time only two cars are in use.

In the following year, the West Hill Lift was opened in Hastings. Like the Folkstone line, it was promoted by an independent company. In other respects, it differed, the most interesting being that instead of running up a steeply inclined cliff face, it passed through a brick-lined tunnel, formed partly by a natural cave. The gauge was six feet, and the line was 500 feet long, with a 1 in 3 gradient. The normal arrangement of cables was provided, but instead of using water tanks on the cars, motive power was applied to the drum, initially by a Crossley 40-horse-power gas engine, which was later replaced by a Tangye 32-horse-power diesel. The West Hill Lift was purchased by the local authority in 1947.

The third line to open in the south again differed in detail. This was completed at Sandgate, near Folkestone in 1893, running from the lower end of Sandgate Hill to a point near the Martello Tower at the end of Leas Cliff.

Whereas all the other lines had a uniform gradient, because of crossing over Radnor Cliff Crescent, the Sandgate Hill Lift consisted of 403 feet at 1 in 4.75 broken into by 267½ feet at 1 in 7.04. For this reason, the descending car would not have exerted a steady pull on its ascending neighbour, and so the two cars were operated individually, each being connected to a water tank which descended a shaft instead of being attached to another car. The line closed officially in 1918, but signs remain of embankment, of cutting and of the abutments which supported the bridge over Radnor Cliff Crescent.

The last of the nineteenth-century steep-grade railways ascended not a cliff but the scarp face of the South Downs at Devil's Dyke, near Brighton. It was associated with the development of Devil's Dyke as a pleasure resort. After the opening of the standard-gauge branch line up the dip slope from Hove in 1887 Mr J.H. Hubbard purchased the area, opening a hotel with restaurant and bars and a small funfair. In 1894 he initiated the construction of a cableway across a ravine, which was owned and operated by the Telpher Cable & Cliff Railway Syndicate Ltd. This was an extension of the funfair as much as a transport facility.

However, Hubbard's next idea not only utilized railway track but also had a definite transport function. The village of Poynings lay at the foot of the downs, about four miles from the railway station on the main line at Hassocks, but less than one mile from the Dyke station. However, the mile included a climb of about 480 feet, and the new steep-grade railway carried passengers up 395 feet of this ascent. It was also hoped to carry farm produce, plus visitors to the Dyke who might wish to descend to the village. Hubbard leased the necessary land to the Pyramidical Syndicate of London, which became responsible for the railway.

It is of interest that it was constructed by Courtney & Burkett, engineers and yacht builders from nearby Southwick. Yacht builders frequently use cable-operated inclines to lift boats out of the water, and it is presumed that the company's experience with boats encouraged it to tender for a railway using similar techniques. The engineer, Mr

Charles Blaber, was also local. Most steep-grade railways adopted a gauge wider than standard but the Dyke line consisted of a three-foot-gauge double track, 840 feet long. To save engineering works, like the Sandgate line, the inclination varied, being 1 in 2.9 at the bottom, 1 in 1.5 in the middle, and 1 in 1.8 at the top.

The water balance method of operation was not used, partly owing to lack of water at the Dyke. As differing gradients with consequent variations in loading ruled out a self-working incline, the two cars were connected by two steel-wire cables passing round a drum driven by an engine. Again, lack of water placed a steam engine at a disadvantage and a Hornsby-Ackroyd oil engine of 25 brake horse-power was installed. This ran continuously, a clutch and reversing gear being provided. The gearing was such that the engine speed of 180 revolutions per minute rotated the drum at 17 revolutions per minute, and the cars moved at a little under three miles per hour. There was a brake on the drum and four brakes on each car which gripped the track. The brakes were applied automatically if, through the engine failing or the cable breaking, the tension on either or both of the wire ropes was withdrawn. The two cars, which were roofed but open-sided, were supplied by the Ashbury Railway Carriage Co., and seated 14 passengers. With regard to economics, the cost was £9,000, and at a single fare of 2d it was necessary to carry 275,000 passengers per annum to secure a satisfactory return on capital. The line was opened by Sir Henry Howorth, M.P., on Saturday 24 July, 1897, and, after three years of operation, it was clear that it was not an economic proposition. On 13 December, 1900 it was put up for sale, but there were no suitable offers, and so it was bought in for £390.

There is a paucity of information about the line, but it appears to have closed about 1908, and the tracks were removed by the end of the First World War. Although there were no heavy engineering works, despite the growth of vegetation, there are still indications of the position of the line and of its terminals for the determined railway archaeologist.

The first of the lines of the twentieth century was the East Cliff Lift constructed for Hastings Corporation by Easton, of Erith Ironworks, and opened in 1903. It joins the Old Town to the start of the Cliff Walk at the top of East Hill. This is a conventional line with two cars on parallel tracks 267 feet long, and inclined at 1 in 1.28, which makes it the steepest line in the south. The water tanks under the cars each hold 600 gallons which are discharged into a sump at the lower station. This does not drain away, as an electric pump is used to return the water to the top, so that in effect the line is worked by electricity with hydraulic transmission. The East Cliff Lift is still in use.[8]

In the following year a line was opened at Folkestone using the same principle of a water balance, with the water being pumped back to the top of the incline after use. It was situated about half-a-mile to the west of the original Leas Cliff line and was operated by the Metropole Lift Company, primarily to serve guests at the hotel wishing to reach the beach. During the invasion threat of 1940 it was disused, and after the war it was decided not to restore it. Demolition followed in 1951.

Two more short lines were opened before the First World War, one at Broadstairs and the other at Margate. The Broadstairs line was opened in 1910 and differs from the other lines which have been described in having only one car and one track of 5 ft 3 in. gauge. (The Sandgate line in effect consisted of two independent single lines.) It links the foot of the chalk cliffs at Viking Bay to Albion Street. The line is worked by an electric motor linked to the car by cable.

The installation opened at Margate in 1913 was rather similar, also consisting of a single car on a five-foot-gauge single track operated by electric motor and cable. The iron counter-balance goes up and down in a vertical shaft. Being only 69 feet long, this is probably the shortest of the inclined planes in the south of England.

If the four-track Folkestone line is counted as one, then a total of eight passenger-carrying inclines were opened in the south between 1885 and 1913. Of these, five remain in use during the summer season, although in some cases, traffic has declined. This is partly due to motor transport, although motorists and coach passengers tend to become pedestrians when they reach their destination. Also, there has been some decline in the number of long-stay holiday makers in the south-coast resorts. For these reasons, there seems little prospect of new cliff railways, and since the various degrees of restoration which accompanied re-opening after the Second World War, there have been no major changes. So the passenger-carrying inclines, whether one is waiting at a terminal or riding in one of the cars, still convey something of the atmosphere of the days before the First World War.

Pleasure Railways

All the lines described in this section are devoted to pleasure-riding, with most of the passengers leaving the train where they joined it. In a class on their own are lines provided mainly to allow preserved locomotives to be put in motion. For instance, the Hampshire narrow-gauge system consists of short lengths of track on private ground at Durley. The main interest lies in the locomotives which include examples from North Wales slate lines and 'Agwi Pet' which operated on the narrow-gauge system at Fawley Refinery. The premises are not open to the general public. The Wey Valley Light Railway, situated at Farnham, is different in character, having been constructed by Venture Scouts of the Moor Park Company. Three petrol locomotives and one diesel were obtained in order to use the line for pleasure-riding. On special occasions, additional locomotives are loaned from the Brockham Museum Association whose premises, near Dorking, are within easy reach by road transport. A third line combines locomotive preservation with the provision of a line for pleasure-riding at Hollycombe House near Liphook.

More common are lines provided in parks or pleasure grounds, where no policy of locomotive preservation is involved. These are usually commercial undertakings relying on pleasure-riders for their revenue. An interesting line operates in Hotham Park, Bognor, the track consisting of a plain circuit with no sidings. There are three platforms, one near the car park, one adjoining the coach park and a third near the zoo. Although booking offices are provided at both the coach park and the zoo, only that at the zoo is manned, the other platforms being used for setting down only. Most miniature railways have their engine and train sheds on spur lines, but at Bognor the shed consists of adapted steel air-raid shelters erected over the running line. During operation, the doors at either end are opened, and passengers may regard it as a tunnel. The track winds its way through the shrubs and trees in a very attractive manner.

The Littlehampton Miniature Railway, opened in 1948, differs in character, as it conveys passengers from a terminal near the beach to a lake in a park set back from the sea-front. Its track is fenced throughout. The main premises in Mewsbrook Park consist of a booking office, low platforms, and sheds for the locomotives, complete with turn-table. Whereas the Bognor line has only one petrol electric locomotive, the Littlehampton line added to its four steam locomotives a battery electric and a petrol engined locomotive from the Bognor Pier Railway.

The line opened in Brooklands Park, East Worthing in 1965, consists of a half-mile circuit of a lake with the shed for the petrol hydraulic locomotive and train on a short spur. There is one station, but rather unusually, the Brooklands line has substantial engineering work in a girder bridge crossing the stream which feeds the lake.

Drusilla's Tea Rooms at Berwick have an extensive pleasure ground attached, with a small zoo and other exhibits. The railway of 1947 consists of a simple circuit operated by one petrol engined locomotive and replaced a pre-war nine-inch-gauge line. The Kent Country Nurseries opened a system with petrol and battery electric locomotives near Ashford in 1970. This has ten-and-a-quarter-inch-gauge track. It is temporarily closed pending confirmation of planning permission.

The outstanding examples of 15-inch-gauge steam locomotives are to be found on the RHDR, but an interesting 4-4-2, built by A. Barnes & Co. of Rhyl runs on the Dreamland Miniature Railway in the pleasure grounds at Margate. This interesting line was designed as a circuit, with two overbridges, an underbridge and a viaduct just after the First World War. After the northern part of the circuit was removed to make way for new developments in 1924, the through station became a terminus, and linear operation was adopted. As a terminus, the station has two platform tracks and a centre engine release road, with a manually operated traverser at the buffer stops. While fantables were not uncommon, this must be one of the few surviving examples of a rail traverser outside a railway works. At present, however, its use is limited as the locomotive draws the train to the end of the line and propels it back, without use of the engine release road. In addition to the Barnes 4-4-2, another steam locomotive of the Bassett-Lowke 'Little Giant' class operated in Dreamland, but this was sold in 1968. The second locomotive is now driven by a petrol engine and was built in 1959.

A number of lines, instead of relying on parks to provide their passengers, were constructed near sea-fronts. The Southsea Miniature Railway, adjoining Southsea Castle, is a typical example. This relies on two petrol engined locomotives, but the comparable line on the beach at Hastings has three excellent steam locomotives. Their design is based on main line classes – an LMSR 'Royal Scot' of 1938, a GWR 'Saint' of 1938, and an 0-6-0 built in 1934. The normal traffic however, is now diesel-operated. The Hastings line has a terminal station with wooden buildings, and a separate running shed with workshop attached.

A short line at Hove, operated by a battery electric locomotive, appears to have an uncertain future.[9] The possibility of third rail electric traction was considered for the Sheppey Light Railway opened at Leysdown-on-Sea in 1973, but in the event, a diesel engine was obtained. The ten-and-a-quarter-inch-gauge track on the jetty at Margate should not be confused with the earlier manually operated line used for conveying luggage and stores in the days of the paddle steamers. The present line is passenger-carrying, and has a diesel locomotive.[10]

Pleasure railways clearly require far less capital than those which form part of the transport system, and therefore are far more ephemeral. They rarely include substantial earthworks and their removal leaves few traces. However, as sources of pleasure to generations of visitors to parks and seaside resorts, they should not be forgotten.

Fj 08325

Brighton Corp. Transp
VOLKS RAILWA
AQUARIUM to
BLACK ROCK
Fare 10d RETURN
Available on day of
issue only
Williamson, Printer, Ashton

Brighton Corp. Transport
VOLKS RAILWAY
BLACK ROCK to
AQUARIUM
Fare 10d RETURN
Available on day of
issue only
Williamson, Printer, Ashton
1851

Fj 08325

6

Private Railways

Whereas most of the public railways in the South of England have at least been mentioned, it is not intended to list all those carrying private traffic for a particular undertaking – the railway equivalent of a C licence lorry. Most of them fall into one of three categories: lines connected with public services, such as those serving hospitals or the gas and electricity industries; those operated by commercial undertakings, including the cement and paper industries; and lines serving defence establishments. While most of them carried freight only, a number did carry an appreciable passenger traffic. Length varied from the few yards of a small private siding to the appreciable mileage of, for instance, the Chatham Dockyard system. Where the length of private line was significant, the undertaking usually provided its own locomotives, but short sidings were operated by the main line company. One feature which often identified a private line was the provision of a gate across the track, marking the division between public and private railway.

Lines Constructed for the Public Services and Utilities

Around the turn of the century a number of large hospitals were constructed, usually by County Councils, and often in somewhat inaccessable places. One such was the Hellingly Asylum, where work commenced in 1899, on a site two miles north of the market town of Hailsham in Sussex. It was decided to link it to the LBSCR line at Hellingly by a single line branch about one mile in length. In November 1899, the Asylum Committee completed a formal agreement with the LBSCR by which the railway company was to build and maintain the track. It was specified that traffic would consist mainly of coal and other materials, such as food and clothing, all of which would be conveyed in truck-loads each of not less than one ton. The railway was used to convey building materials to the hospital during the construction period, and the traffic was worked by the contractor's steam locomotive. In 1903 the line was electrified and taken over by the East Sussex County Council.

The Hospital Committee had made a supplemental agreement with the railway which included some interesting details. As the asylum had its own power station, it had been decided to operate the line by electricity supplied from an overhead wire at 500 volts D.C. At the time, numerous electric street tramways were under construction and whereas the track was railway-type, the electrical equipment would have looked more at home in an Edwardian street. The wire was suspended from brackets supported by metal poles spaced out alongside the track. Passenger traffic was expected to consist of patients, visitors, attendants and asylum officials, and for their conveyance a four-wheeled tram-car with seating for 12 was purchased from the Brush Engineering Co. At Hellingly a wooden platform was constructed between the main line and the Asylum railway. This was on LBSCR property, and could be used between the hours of 8 a.m. and 6 p.m. on notice being given to the railway company.

A number of street tramways, including the Bolton Corporation undertaking, possessed electric locomotives for hauling freight wagons, and a similar machine went to Hellingly. It was rated at 14 horse-power, and could haul two loaded wagons. The performance of the locomotive would have been limited by the ruling gradient of 1 in 50. There were virtually no engineering works on the line but two roads were crossed on the level. The 'trains' doubtlessly surprised any motorist not familiar with the district.

Passenger traffic ended in 1931, and the platform at Hellingly was removed in 1932. By 1954, traffic was down to about one train per day, and arrangements were made with British Railways to rescind the previous agreements and to abandon the line. In fact, it lingered in intermittent use for some years. Final closure was in March 1959. Even then, on 4 April, 1959, a special 'train' consisting of the electric locomotive and a brake van borrowed from British Railways was run for a group of enthusiasts. The branch line which it joined did not last much longer, Hellingly station being closed in the June of 1965. Signs of this remain, but it requires a railway archaeologist to detect what is left of the hospital railway. The most impressive relic is the body of the tram-car, now in use as a pavilion on the sports ground.

The line to Park Prewett Hospital near Basingstoke was about one and one-third miles long, and apart from being slightly longer, differed from the Hellingly railway in a number of ways. It included quite considerable earthworks, and did not possess any rolling stock. Being worked by the main line company, motive power always consisted of a steam locomotive, but the tortuous curves and steep gradients made the use of standard passenger coaches virtually impossible.

The demand for accommodation for mental patients in Hampshire exceeded the capacity of the first hospital at Knowle near Fareham, and as early as 1891 there were proposals for a second establishment to serve the north of the county. Park Prewett Farm near Basingstoke was purchased in 1900, and plans for the buildings and the connecting railway were approved by the County Council in 1912. Joining the main line was not so straightforward as at Hellingly, and the LSWR agreed to construct a single line from the point where the hospital branch reached railway property parallel to their existing tracks for half-a-mile. This ended with a crossover on to the up goods line opposite the premises of Lilly & Co., and within the station limits of Basingstoke. One of the clauses of the agreement with the railway company, completed in October 1912, required the hospital to pay the LSWR for the construction of this siding and also rent for the land it occupied. It was completed by March 1913 before the rest of the hospital branch, in order to convey building materials during the construction period. However, work on the branch proper was in progress, and in a report made at the end of 1913, it is described as nearly completed.

An excellent description of the line with an account of its history by John Fairman appeared in the *Railway Observer* for March 1970. Mr Fairman states that the single-track connection ran parallel with the main line, rising at 1 in 289, as far as the gate at Winklebury which divided railway and hospital property. Beyond the gate a curve of seven-chains radius led on to a length of straight track climbing at 1 in 53 on a chalk embankment. The original plans had shown a level-crossing over the Basingstoke to Kingsclere road, but a bridge was substituted, and, in order to avoid approach ramps on the road, the railway ran under it with cuttings on either side. These provided the chalk for the embankment and also produced a dip at 1 in 55 in what was otherwise a steady climb up to the hospital. Having passed under the road, the railway swung west before completing a half-circle to bring it into the terminal at the back of the hospital. Adverse gradients of 1 in 70 and 1 in 53 were followed by a fall of 1 in 62 over the last few hundred yards into the terminus. There was a run-round loop with a weighbridge, the neck of the loop extending into the hospital's coal store.

The First World War had begun by the time the hospital was ready for opening, and, from 1916 until 1921, it was used by the Canadian Army. The construction of a passenger platform 40 feet long with a brick face indicates the intention of conveying passenger traffic, while a second platform of 120 feet with a concrete face, was, in effect, an extension to it. Mr Fairman thinks that the second platform might have been added about 1918 during the Canadian 'occupation'. Although both the agreement and the provision of platforms allowed for passenger traffic, he was unable to find any positive proof that it existed. On the other hand, he did find proof that after 1924 there was none.

A trial run in 1939 with eight coaches of passenger stock powered by a locomotive at each end satisfied the authorities that the curves and gradients made the line unsuitable for through passenger trains. Freight had, however, been operated continuously, and for most of the inter-war period there were two trains a week, running on Tuesdays and Fridays. To avoid the danger of wagons breaking away on the steep gradients, the locomotive always remained at the Basingstoke end of the train, propelling the loaded wagons to the hospital and drawing the empties back.

The hospital authorities were required to maintain the track to the satisfaction of the railway company's engineer, and, by 1950, he was unsatisfied. At this time, the railway authority was the Railway Executive who gave notice that it was no longer prepared to work the line, but would send coal and stores from Basingstoke by road. A period of doubt as to whether or not the track would be repaired lasted until 1954, when the hospital board decided to abandon it. The track was lifted by George Cohens in 1956.

In 1957, I was able to photograph the terminal station, the earthworks and the road bridge, but on a recent visit the bridge had gone, and the adjacent cuttings had been filled in. On the other hand, the embankment, the platforms, the weighbridge and the coal store all survive. The embankment can be seen from the main line and although the gate in the railway fence has been removed, a break in its alignment indicates the exact position at which the branch curved away. The tall chimney of the hospital remains as a reminder that for 37 years, the coal for the hospital boilers was delivered by rail.

The line to Netley Hospital was built rather later than the hospital itself, which was a product of the immediate post-Crimean-War period.

Florence Nightingale's work during that war had drawn attention to the shortcomings of the Army medical services, and in the years following 1856 a number of military hospitals were built. By far the largest of these was the Royal Victoria Hospital at Netley, on the shores of Southampton Water. It was provided with a pier so that soldiers returning from abroad could be landed directly from the troop-ships. In 1866 the Southampton & Netley Railway was opened, but it was 1900 before the siding from Netley station yard, down a steep gradient for about half-a-mile, to the hospital was completed.

The line was used for special trains and supplies. In 1943, as part of the preparations for the invasion of Europe, the track was relaid by American troops. The summer and autumn months of 1944 were probably the busiest in the history of the line, with ambulance trains often hauled by 4-6-0 locomotives of the former Great Eastern Railway, chosen for this work because they could run almost anywhere on the British railway system. Coaches were stored at the terminal in a single road carriage shed.

After 1945, use of the line declined. Four hospital coaches of LSWR origin were removed in March 1954, leaving three former LMSR coaches and a special brake van. These were finally removed in August 1955, and the carriage shed was dismantled. Under the circumstances it was rather a surprise to find, on a visit to the line in March 1959, that although the track was very overgrown and obviously disused, the station buildings had been recently repainted. Although by May 1966 the connection to Netley station yard had been removed, in the hospital grounds the station and adjoining track was still *in situ*. By this time most of the enormous hospital building, over a quarter-of-a-mile in length, was disused, and, in view of the colossal cost of maintenance, there was no reasonable alternative to demolition. Work began in September 1966, and the station was knocked down with the hospital it had served.[1]

Netley, Park Prewett and Hellingly were the only establishments with specially built sidings long enough to be regarded as private branch lines. Knowle, the Hampshire mental hospital near Fareham, had a short private siding, used mainly for coal traffic. At present, it is intact, but disused. Treloars Hospital for Cripples is situated west of Alton, adjoining the former Basingstoke & Alton line. As mentioned above, when through traffic ceased, the section between Butts Junction and Treloars Hospital continued to carry traffic, but, after some years of disuse, it was officially closed on 31 July, 1967.

Of a slightly different character was the Brookwood Necropolis

Railway. In 1852 when, with the passing of the Burials Act, the 'sanitary' movement was strong, a company was incorporated to open a cemetery beyond Woking on a large tract of Surrey heathland. This developed into the present Brookwood Cemetery which had a branch line railway opened in 1854 and two suitably designed stations. Special trains conveyed the mourners and the deceased from the private Necropolis station at Waterloo down to Brookwood. The railway company not only gained revenue from the initial journey, but in a period when death attracted more interest than at present, benefited from the subsequent pilgrimages of relatives.[2] (Incidently, on the traditional basis of charging what the traffic will bear, the rate levied for the conveyance of corpses was a high one.) The special trains consisted of hearse vans for the coffins and normal coaches for the mourners. The *Appendix* to the *Working Time-table* for 1934 stated: 'The Necropolis train on arrival at Brookwood is run into the siding which lies parallel with the down local line, and from the siding the train is propelled to the cemetery under the supervision of the guard. The section goes on to prescribe the manner of operating 'upon the completion of the work in the cemetery'. This consisted of setting down the coffins and the accompanying passengers at the two stations, North station for Nonconformists and Roman Catholics and South station for Anglicans. North station was about quarter-of-a-mile from the main line and South station half-a-mile further on.

A commercial postcard published before the First World War shows a train on the return journey, approaching North station on a single track bordered by a path which seems to have been used as a carriage drive. The brick-faced platform is lowered half-way along its length, perhaps to facilitate the unloading of coffins which would have been carried to the appropriate chapel, one on one side of the track for Nonconformists and one on the opposite side for Roman Catholics. The station had a special character which doubtlessly was a consequence of being constructed by a cemetery company. During the Second World War the Necropolis station at Waterloo was damaged by bombing, and when in 1941 this rather special traffic passed to the roads, the track in the cemetery was removed. The line of the railway may still be followed but the two stations have gone.[3]

In addition to hospital lines, local authorities maintained private sidings for the receipt of general stores, and also for more special reasons. For instance, the Metropolitan Borough of Southwark had a large, rail-served rubbish heap between Longfield and Meopham. (This was an exceptional arrangement; most of London's rubbish went down the Thames by lighters.) Brighton Corporation had a private siding for loading sand at Henfield between Shoreham and Horsham. But most of the sidings, such as those maintained by Brighton, Eastbourne, Folkestone, Tunbridge Wells, Hastings and Maidstone Corporations, were for general traffic, and none of them survive.

Water supply and sewage disposal usually involve pumping, and in the past this was carried out by coal-burning steam engines. However, the location of sewage works depended mainly on facilities for disposal, and water pumps were placed at sources of water, so not many of them were built near railways. At Southampton the sewage works did adjoin the railway, but coal appears to have been conveyed from the railway yard to the boiler house by road. Southampton, like many works, has relied on electric and diesel pumps for some years. While few sewage works were rail-connected, narrow-gauge internal systems for the conveyance of sludge were formerly common. Manual traction was the norm, but locomotives were not unknown. For instance the Apuldram Lane Works near Chichester still operate locomotive hauled 'trains' to carry sludge.

Water works, have also tended to transfer to diesel or electric power, but the Otterbourne Pumping Station of Southampton Corporation Water Undertaking, received coal by a private siding until 1968. It was moved from the siding to the boiler house in narrow-gauge hand-propelled trucks. Until steam pumping ended in this works in 1971, coal was delivered by road.

An unusually remote pumping station, with a private siding was still operating in the 1930s at Littlestone between Lydd and Dungeness. Other examples were to be found at Bedhampton and Falmer, but it would seem that since the closure of the Otterbourne siding, no water or sewage undertaking in the south has had a direct rail link.

The electricity and gas industries in the South have shown a comparable reduction in their railway linkage. The early electricity generating stations were usually town-based, and those at Eastbourne, Folkestone, Reigate, Southampton and Bognor were all rail-served. Now in some cases the works are closed, and in every case the private sidings have gone. Paradoxically, while a boundary fence sometimes gives the only faint clue to the position of a private siding, quite frequently short lengths of track survive in the electricity works themselves: Reigate and Southampton are both examples. Most of the works had their own electric locomotives, but no examples of the overhead wiring survive.[4]

Nearly all the new power stations in the south use oil or nuclear fuel, and are served mainly by water transport, unlike Richborough, which received coal by rail from the nearby Betteshanger Colliery.[5] In addition to supplying fuel, railways may also be concerned with the conveyance of heavy electrical gear and the disposal of waste products. For instance, a section of the former Dungeness branch railway is retained to serve Dungeness Nuclear Power Station in this way. Before the war, transformer stations were frequently provided with private sidings. But the traditional small electric locomotive serving the conventional coal-fired town power station has gone from the south.

Since the Second World War, the gas supply industry has changed as fundamentally as electricity generating, and there are very few gas-works left in southern England. In 1934 at least 15 of the gas-works in the area being studied had rail connections. They varied in extent from such modest undertakings as the Cranleigh Gas-Works, to the large plants at Eastbourne, Southampton and at Hilsea near Portsmouth. Even after 1945, most of the works had a sufficient length of rail track to justify ownership of their own locomotives, including Eastbourne, Dover, Glyne Gap near Hastings, Broadstairs, Hilsea and Southampton.

The massive rationalization of the gas industry which began in the 1950s, resulted in numerous closures, the construction of a pipeline network, and an increasing use of oil fuel. In the 1960s natural gas grew in importance. The sites of most gas-works can still be recognized by gas-holders, which may be storing gas produced miles away, and sometimes by the remains of the old retort houses in which coal gas was once made. Hilsea Works, at present, not only retains some of its retort houses, but also the overhead monorail which fed them with coal. Much of Hilsea's standard-gauge rail system survives at ground level, together with a diesel locomotive, and, usually carefully protected in its shed, a steam locomotive.

In their traditional form, gas-works and electricity plants not only received coal by rail or water, but also sent away coke and ash respectively. But unlike manufacturing industry, their main products were distributed by pipe or by wire. Their traditional links with the railways belong to the past, as do their traditional appearance and character.

Lines Constructed for the Government

The railway installations of the defence services had more in common with those of the public services than with commercial undertakings, in that they carried supplies inwards but there was little outward traffic. However, the principal munitions store for H.M. ships based on Chatham and Sheerness Dockyards had both inward and outward traffic. It was sited at Lodge Hill, a suitably secluded area about two-and-a-half miles north of Strood. The Chattenden Naval Tramways Order of 1901 authorized the construction of a standard-gauge railway from Lodge Hill down to Kingsnorth Pier on the River Medway.

In fact, only part of the line was built at this time; from the munitions depot to exchange sidings at Sharnal Street on the SECR Port Victoria branch. Since the union of the SE & LCD, the Port Victoria branch had lost its function of providing SER competition for Sheerness traffic, and the SECR offered to sell the line from Sharnal Street to Port Victoria Pier on the Medway to the Admiralty. This offer might well have been taken up. (Elsewhere, during the First World War, the Admiralty acquired the Stokes Bay branch and pier from the LSWR for their own use.)

However, in the event, Lodge Hill was connected to the river by another line, built to the unusual gauge of 2 ft 6 in. Initially, this was constructed as an exercise by the Eighth Railway Company, Royal Engineers. They arrived at Chattenden Barracks from Egypt in 1886, and built the line, which ran from their barracks down to Upnor Hard, before they left for South Africa in July 1899. It is possible that work was started immediately on their arrival, as the makers' dates for the first four locomotives to operate on the line were 1885, 1891, 1897 and 1897 respectively. This may well have been the first railway in Britain built by the Royal Engineers, who later pursued their railway activities on a far grander scale on the Longmoor Military Railway near Liss in Hampshire. Writing in the *Railway Magazine* in May 1941, Mr J.R. Hayton suggests that the 2 ft 6 in. gauge was chosen to match up with a number of lines under construction in the British Empire at the time, but especially to give experience that might prove useful in the North-West Frontier area of India. However, the Chattenden & Upnor, which in a sense was the forerunner of the Longmoor Military Railway, became a part of the naval defence system.

As explained above, the Chattenden Tramway consisted of a single-track standard-gauge line linking the magazine at Lodge Hill to the SECR at Sharnal Street, and providing the main route into the magazine for munitions from Woolwich and other centres. The rest of the tramway to Kingsnorth Pier was not constructed, and the offer to purchase the SECR line to Port Victoria Pier was not taken up, transport to the Medway being provided by the Chattenden & Upnor line.

The official date of the transfer of the Chattenden & Upnor from the War Department to the Admiralty was 2 April, 1906, although it is possible that the Admiralty had been working the line from 1904. The break of gauge in the naval magazine was immaterial, as there was no 'through' traffic. On grounds of security, the Chattenden & Upnor was never on show to the public, but it could be seen, both where it crossed the main road from Strood to Grain, near Chattenden Barracks and also on the minor road leading down to Upnor Hard. The main road was crossed by a substantial girder bridge supported by four metal columns. Before the Upnor road was reached, the single line forked, the eastern arm crossing the road on its way to Upnor Hard, and a western arm crossing the same road about 100 yards to the west to serve Islingham Barracks near Frindsbury. This western arm was disused before the Second World War.[6] Both level-crossings were gated, and a signal-box controlled the working of the junction. Adjoining the signal-box, steel plates, laid on the ground and backed by a handrail, provided a simple station. Passenger trains ran from here to Lodge Hill Munitions Depot.

The Chattenden and Upnor was replaced by a military road in 1961, some of its stock being sold to another 2 ft 6 in.-gauge-line, the Welshpool & Llanfair, which at the time was about to be re-opened by a group of railway enthusiasts.[7]

The standard-gauge link between the magazine and Sharnal Street station was also closed in 1961. As mentioned above, the original plan included an extension of this line beyond the Sharnal Street exchange sidings to a pier on the Medway at Kingsnorth. In 1915 a munitions factory and some airship hangers were opened on the edge of the saltings about one mile from Sharnal Street, and the line was extended to serve them. Rather surprisingly, both major and minor roads near Beluncle were carried over the line on bridges instead of level-crossings. Shortly afterwards, the line was extended to the river, with bridges carrying it over some minor stretches of water. This provided a convenient alternative to Upnor for the supply vessels delivering munitions to warships at Sheerness.

After the First World War, the munitions factory was taken over by Holm & Co., and became a chemical works. The firm took over the railway from Sharnal Street to the pier. This was one of the few occasions when a defence line was resold to a commercial undertaking. In November 1925, Holm & Co. regularized the position by applying for a Light Railway Order to bring the line up to standard for carrying public passenger traffic. (They also sought powers to convey public goods

33   A special passenger train on the Hellingly Mental Hospital Railway consisting of a
BR brake van hauled by the hospital's electric locomotive. This ran on 4 April, 1959
although official closure of the line took place in the previous month.

34   North station on the Brookwood Cemetery line. The daily train was returning
from South station.

35   The platform of North station, Brookwood Cemetery still in existence on 23 November, 1974.

36   The train ferry, 'TF4', at her berth in Southampton in 1918. With her adjustable deck, no link span was required, but the span visible to the left was necessary for the fixed-deck vessel, 'TF2'.

37 A special train in the private station at Bisley on 23 November, 1952, after official closure. It consisted of an ex-LSWR two-coach motor set, with LSWR M7 class No. 30027, built at Nine Elms in 1904, and scrapped in 1959.

38 The private station at Bisley on 16 May, 1964. At this date the platform survived, and the wooden buildings were in use.

39 Riflemen joining their 'train' at Bisley for the journey out to the ranges, about 1913. The tram-type locomotive and the toast-rack car were owned by the National Rifle Association.

40 The War Department station at Deepcut Camp on the extension to Blackdown was opened in 1917, and this photograph was taken at about that time. The train, with a W.D. locomotive is entering the station from the Bisley direction. A Canadian army construction team are said to have been responsible for the log walls and north American style.

41   The booking hall at Deepcut Camp station complete with W. H. Smith and Son's bookstall and a stove in the waiting-room. The table and benches were presumably provided for the necessary filling in of forms.

42   A special train organized by the Railway Correspondence & Travel Society on the Longmoor Military Railway on 4 October, 1958. The four-coach train consisted of two Maunsell coaches normally used on boat trains and marked for continental second class, and two Bulleid open coaches. It was hauled over the LMR from Liss to Bordon by 2-8-0 No. 400, 'Sir Guy Williams', built by the North British Locomotive Co. in 1943, and withdrawn in 1965. This view, taken as the train approached Longmoor, also shows the 75-cm-gauge line of 1948.

43 The motive power depot at Longmoor on 4 October, 1958. The locomotives are all War Department standard austerity saddle tanks, from l. to r. as follows: 186 ·Manipur Road', built Vulcan Foundry 1945, sold to National Coal Board, Maerdy Colliery, 1961; 118 'Brussels', built Hudswell Clarke 1945, adapted to W.D. Standard 1958; running on Keighley & Worth Valley Railway since 1971; 181 'Insein' built Vulcan Foundry 1945, sold to National Coal Board, Cambrian Colliery, 1961; 152 'Rennes', built Robert Stephenson & Hawthorn, 1945, sold to National Coal Board, Mountain Ash Colliery, 1962.

44 Aveling & Porter of Rochester produced a version of their road steam vehicles to run on rails, and these were not uncommon on Kentish industrial premises. A geared well tank of 1926 at the Holborough Works of A.P.C.M. Ltd on 26 June, 1946. It is now preserved on the Bluebell Railway.

45　A R.C.T.S. special train on the Sittingbourne & Kemsley Railway on 30 March, 1974. The locomotive was 0-4-2 saddle tank 'Premier', built by Kerr Stuart in 1905. The photograph at Burley crossing shows, beyond the steam pipe at the side of the track, the Kentish marsh scenery traversed by the line.

46 LSWR B4 class 'Corrall Queen' on 16 December, 1972, her last day at Dible's Wharf, Southampton, before transfer to the Bluebell Railway. She bore the BR No. 30096, was built at Nine Elms in 1893, and until her journey to Sussex, had spent all her working life in South Hampshire.

traffic but this clause was successfully opposed by the Southern Railway.) Order No. 476 was granted in November 1926, and a second Order, No. 490 of July 1929, transferred the powers to a subsidiary, the Kingsnorth Light Railway Company. In fact, public passenger traffic was never carried, but private freight traffic was increased by the opening of the works of Berry Wiggins, who produced oil and bituminous substances. Unfortunately, a dispute occurred between Berry Wiggins and the Kingsnorth company as a result of which the former constructed their own private siding about half-a-mile in length direct to the Port Victoria branch. While the Berry Wiggins siding is still in use, the Kingsnorth Light Railway was closed in 1940. Its most striking relic is an overbridge, which despite the road being diverted away from it, survives at Beluncle.

The Hundred of Hoo provides this interesting example of a line built for defence purposes but later transferred to commercial use. A comparable situation existed in the Dover area. The Naval Works Act of 1897 authorized the construction of a harbour of refuge of 600 acres. This involved the building of massive breakwaters with concrete or granite blocks. Most of the gravel for making the concrete was taken from a large pit at Stonar near Sandwich. Some of it was mixed with cement to make concrete blocks on this site, the remainder being conveyed to one of two block-making plants at Dover. Transport by sailing barge was used, but in view of the urgency of the work, a rail route was also provided.

At the Stonar end this consisted of just over half-a-mile of standard-gauge track, crossing the river Stour to exchange sidings with the SECR at Richborough. From this point, the main line was used as far as Martin Mill. A new line, nearly four miles long, branched off just south of the station and ran parallel with the main line for a mile, the difference in level increasing steadily as the latter cut down to the northern end of Guston Tunnel. A sharp curve changed the direction to south-east and the line crossed two roads, one by a bridge and one by a level-crossing, to reach the top of the cliffs. Below, another alignment descended to the harbour by means of an oblique platform hewn out of the face of the cliff. The scale of the engineering works, including both embankments and cuttings is surprising for a temporary line but in this case 'temporary' covered about ten years of intensive use.

Moreover, at an early stage the possibility of converting part of the line to a 3 ft 6 in.-gauge passenger line with electric traction was considered. In 1909 a Light Railway Order authorizing the conversion was obtained.

Traffic would have been provided by new housing estates built along the line, but quite apart from this, the spectacular run along the cliffs would probably have commended the trams to pleasure-riders. However the scheme failed to materialize and most of the pleasant country which might have been plastered with houses remains inviolate. The original flat-bottom standard-gauge track was removed by 1937.

Having failed to become an electric tramway, over one-and-a-half miles of the line was restored during the Second World War, and this was extended by about one mile of new line running parallel with the coast. The new route resembled a letter U, inclined at about 45 degrees to north with the top of one arm at Martin Mill station and the other ending at St. Margaret's. The purpose was to provide a lengthy firing range for rail-mounted guns which could be kept in Guston Tunnel on the nearby main line during the day and brought out on to the former contractor's line at night for the bombardment of the French coast.[8]

A visit in May 1956 revealed that much of the track laid in the Second World War was still down, the chairs being mostly marked SECR with dates between 1899 and 1919. At Martin Mill the remains of an engine shed survived. With the exception of one overgrown cutting, the line could be followed fairly easily as far as the bridge under the main Dover to Deal road. In the cutting beyond were still to be seen the brick-built entrances to the underground magazines, and the loading platforms from which the artillery train was provided with its supply of ammunition for the night's bombardment. As the new section of line was just a mile long, and every salvo was fired from a different point, the German forces would have had difficulty in getting a fix on the guns. The firing line was fairly straight and level, running between the 300- and 350-foot contours with few earthworks, and in the 1950s it was not too difficult to trace.

On a recent visit, however, considerable difficulty was experienced in establishing the exact position of this unique line. In contrast, the route down the face of the cliff following the harbour construction line is still easy to find. Indeed, it is so prominent, that unless it is deliberately removed, it will remain a clear-out feature for many years to come.

One of the more extensive railway systems of the First World War was that serving the Port of Richborough. This branched off from the SECR Deal branch three-quarters-of-a-mile south of Minster, and, like the contractor's line to Dover Harbour, displayed remarkable longevity. Extensive marshalling yards were constructed near the junction with a motive power depot near by. The lines served the train ferry dock and the new wharf, which were specially constructed, and a number of industrial plants including a munitions works. After the war, just as the Kingsnorth line was let to Holm & Co., the Richborough Port lines went to Pearson & Dorman Long. The company's plans for the development of a Kentish iron and steel industry were frustrated by successive trade depressions, but the tracks stayed down. Their retention during the 'phoney' war period of 1939 is easily explicable, and some use was made of Richborough in 1944 and 1945.

By 1953, improvements to the Sandwich to Ramsgate road had removed some of the level-crossings, but the most impressive of them, three tracks wide, still remained. Not only were the tracks still down, but rolling stock in varying stages of dereliction was to be seen, including the 0-6-0T locomotive 'St Anselm', which Pearson & Dorman Long had purchased from the Inland Waterways and Docks Executive after the First World War. This was finally removed in 1954. Even in 1956, rails were down in the marshalling yard and although the buildings of the motive power depot had gone, the coaling ramp and the water crane still stood out on the riverside marshes. At the water's edge the link span of the First World War train ferry survived, and some attempt was being made to revive the use of the wharf. Now the site of the yard and the motive power depot has been completely obliterated by the new power station and the rail link which serves it. But surprisingly, the remains of the train ferry dock still remain.

Their historical value is very considerable as the war-time ferries at Richborough and at Southampton were the first cross-channel train ferries. These developed from barges which were towed over from Richborough, and later from Poole and Southampton, to continental destinations. A suggestion that a train ferry would facilitate shipments to inland destinations by rail was made by the chairman of a South American railway, and taken up by Sir Guy Granet and Sir Sam Fay of the Railway Executive.[9] Three oil-fired train ferry steamers were ordered in January 1917, and services from Richborough and Southampton began in February 1918. The continental terminals for the Richborough services were at Calais, with a 44-mile crossing, and at Dunkirk 69 miles away. The corresponding port for Southampton was Dieppe with a 127-mile crossing. One advantage of the train ferries was the time saved at the terminals, but on the Southampton–Dieppe route a greater proportion of time was spent at sea.

The carrying capacity of the Southampton route was increased, not by ordering a fourth new steamer, but by retrieving one which had been built in 1914 for service in crossing the St Lawrence River in Canada. She differed from the other three vessels in not being constructed to operate from a link span. Instead, variations in water level and of the ship as she was loaded, were compensated for by raising or lowering the train-carrying deck with hydraulic jacks. Berths were constructed for her at Cherbourg and adjoining the link span at Southampton. She returned from Canada, her name was changed from 'Leonard' to 'TF4' and on 6 November, 1918 she made the first of a total of 12 round trips from Southampton to Cherbourg. After the war, her train ferry tracks were removed, and she survived until 1932 as the tanker 'Limax'.

The junction for the train ferry terminal adjoined the down bay platform at the old Southampton West station, and ran into a marshalling yard with seven tracks, located roughly on the site of the present down side car park. From here the track passed at the back of the Corporation Power Station, at the back of Pirelli's Cable Works and on to the Army's marshalling yard, which had 12 tracks. In order that the vessels could load at low tide, the link span was located at the end of a causeway and probably would have projected a little beyond the water-side edge of the present Mayflower Park. (The Park is on reclaimed land and formed part of a great dock reclamation scheme, most of which was carried out between 1929 and 1934.) Apart from the marshalling yards at the station end, the line was essentially military, and the siding into Pirelli's Cable Works was operated by the Army. However it does seem odd that after the war powers were not obtained to retain the siding to Pirelli's. (The power station had a direct connection with the main line.)

Despite their heavy consumption of supplies, aerodromes have usually relied on road connections, but during the First World War some of them in the south had rail links. From Eastchurch Aerodrome on the Isle of Sheppey, a private siding led on to the Sheppey Light Railway. This was no more than a siding, but on the Isle of Thanet a branch just over three miles long ran from the Kent coast line, half-a-mile west of Birchington, to Manston Aerodrome. There were no significant engineering works, and the roads were crossed by four level-crossings. About one mile of line at the Manston end ran on the west side of the road, past Cheeseman's Farm. It had disappeared, almost without a trace, by the early 1930s.

Another line associated with air transport was the branch, just over one mile in length, which ran from the goods yard of Farnborough Station on the LSWR main line to the Royal Aircraft Establishment at Farnborough. This not only included two level-crossings but also ran down

the middle of a road in Cove. Although used for carrying general supplies, the main function of the railway was to carry coal for the R.A.E.
generating station, and when this went over to oil fuel in 1968, the line
was closed. A steam locomotive was used, and especially after the
electrification of the main line, its intermittent sorties out of what is
locally known as 'The Factory', across the main road, and down the
middle of an Edwardian street, never failed to arouse interest. Its final
run was faithfully recorded on film by the R.A.E. Photographic Unit.
The last steam locomotive to operate on the line was named 'Invincible',
and built by Hawthorn Leslie in 1915. She is now stored near
Southampton.[10]

The railway installations of the War Department varied in extent
from a private siding at Dover Priory to the extensive system of the
Longmoor Military Railway. The siding at Fort Brockhurst on the
Gosport branch was out of use before the line was closed, but the long
siding at Aldershot, about one mile on the London side of the station is
still served.

The branch line from Brookwood on the LSWR main line, to Bisley,
involved the War Department, the LSWR and the National Rifle Association. When the N.R.A. range was moved out from Wimbledon to
Bisley, a railway was built to a station opened in July 1890 which
adjoined the rifle ranges. Special passenger trains were operated by the
LSWR with a locomotive at each end, but the branch was never owned by
the main line company. The station was not included in Bradshaw or in
the Railway Clearing House Handbook of Stations, and the passenger service was usually confined to the annual shooting season. The branch
left from a bay platform on the up side of Brookwood station and ran
obliquely down the embankment, parallel with the main line for about
half-a-mile towards Farnborough, and then left railway property, crossing over a road and the Basingstoke Canal, to run through heath and
woodland for another half-a-mile to its terminus.[11] Apart from the
bridges over the road and canal there were no engineering works of
note; the Cowshott Road was crossed by a level-crossing.

At the station, before the First World War, riflemen transferred to
another 'train' which operated on a narrow-gauge tramway leaving
the station at the Brookwood end and skirting the ranges which extended
for about one mile to the north-east. Contemporary photographs show
the motive power, provided by a steam tram locomotive with 'Wharn-
cliffe N.R.A.' painted on the bodywork. The 'train' consisted of vehicles
resembling open, toast-rack tram-cars, with a low footboard and

wooden seats crossing the full width, similar to those still operating in Douglas, Isle of Man. At the present time, part of this line is still sometimes used for carrying ammunition, motive power being provided by a small diesel locomotive.

During the First World War, the line from Bisley Camp was extended for about three miles to serve camps at Pirbright, Deepcut and Blackdown. Construction was undertaken by the War Department which authorized freight traffic as far as Deepcut from 25 July, 1917 and passengers from 1 August, 1917. The extension to the three camps was taken up in the 1920s, but passenger trains were run during the shooting season as far as Bisley Camp station, until 1952. During the Second World War, track was relaid between Bisley and Pirbright, but removed shortly after the end of the war.

When it had been announced that there would be no service in 1953, the Railway Correspondence Travel Society organized a special train which traversed the Bisley branch on 23 November, 1952. On this occasion instead of a train with locomotives at each end, a LSWR push-pull set of two coaches, previously used on the Plymouth to Turnchapel service, was used. (At the time its normal duty was on the Clapham Junction to Kensington service.) The locomotive was No. 30027 of the LSWR M 7 class. It was a rather cold dry day, typical of late autumn and entirely appropriate for visiting a line that had already been abandoned. The platform, backed with rhododendron bushes, was grass-grown from lack of use.

Nearly 12 years later in May 1964, I revisited the line with members of the Southern Counties Railway Society. The track had been removed from beyond the point at which it left railway property, but the girder bridge over the canal was still in position. The walk along the line to Bisley was difficult, but possible for the dedicated. The station platform had survived, and also the two wooden station buildings, which not being constructed by a railway company, always looked decidedly unrailway-like. Various additional buildings, including a private garage almost on the line of the railway, obscured but did not conceal evidence of a former station.

From Bisley to Pirbright, the course of the line proved easy to follow, but the only relic was a loading dock on the outskirts of Pirbright Camp, possibly associated with the temporary extension of the Second World War. However, at Pirbright two relics, one definite and the other speculative, were discovered. First, we found the concrete-faced platform of Pirbright Station; and second, what was very probably an engine shed. During the First World War the Army worked the traffic between Brookwood and Blackdown, and a photograph showing a passenger train entering Deepcut Camp station indicated that they used at least one powerful tank locomotive which could certainly have been kept at Pirbright.

The whole of the extension line ran on War Department property, and although at present no special steps are taken to exclude the public, use of cameras may precipitate a challenge from the Brigade of Guards, who now occupy Pirbright Camp. With this in mind, on our 1964 visit we used the normal roadway to get from Pirbright Camp station to Deepcut.

At Deepcut Station not only the concrete-faced platform, but also the large wooden building survived, in use as a regimental museum for the Royal Army Ordnance Corps. It was built of timber by Canadian troops, the walls being made not from planks, but with logs. A number of picture postcards showing views of the station were issued. Presumably these were intended for purchase by the troops stationed there during the First World War.

I have seen only two of these views, one of which, as mentioned above, shows a down passenger train running into the station. The other shows the view inside the booking-hall, most of one side of which is occupied by a bookstall operated by W.H. Smith & Son. There is a bare wooden floor and a home-made table, with benches. An open door reveals a free-standing stove, which is either in a waiting-room or in the booking-office. The booking-office window has a barrier in front of it with 'In' and 'Out' painted on the wall to ensure that intending passengers circulate behind the barrier in due order. Electric lighting is provided. Apart from the bookstall manager, there are three soldiers in the picture who were probably on the station staff.

I have not been able to ascertain whether or not through tickets to main line destinations were issued, but as military personnel probably travelled free on the Blackdown branch, this may well have been the purpose of the booking-office. Blackdown appeared to have had little more than a platform, similar to that at Pirbright, but if it was still there, I failed to find it.

The Blackdown extension was very characteristic of its period, when steam railways were at their zenith, and nothing approaching it was attempted in the Second World War. It was however, strictly for transport purposes, whereas the Longmoor Military Railway, like its predecessor, the Chattenden and Upnor, had an important training function.

The camps at Tidworth, Bulford, Blackdown, Bordon and Long-moor were all constructed for troops returning from the Boer War. All were associated with railway construction, but only Blackdown, Bordon and Longmoor come within the present area of study. Of the three, the lines based on Longmoor have a far longer and more compli-cated history.

The first line to be constructed had something in common with the Brighton & Rottingdean Seashore Electric Railway as it consisted of about four-and-a-half miles of two 18-inch-gauge tracks with their centre lines 20 ft 6 in. apart, linking Longmoor and Bordon. Its first traffic consisted of 68 huts, placed on trolleys running on the parallel tracks and hauled by steam winch, steam ploughing engine or horses, depending on the degree of difficulty of traction. Troops were being moved from Longmoor to Bordon, and it was decided that this was the best way of moving their huts with them. Agreement was reached between the LSWR and the War Department to build a branch line from Bentley, between Farnham and Alton, to a terminal at Bordon, and this standard-gauge line was opened in 1905.[12] The Royal Engineers started work on a corresponding standard-gauge line from Bordon to Longmoor and this was complete by 1907, although the approach cuttings and overbridge at Whitehill were not finished until 1910. After the end of the First World War when military railways were prone to extinction, the Longmoor line was extended for about three miles from Longmoor to Liss, on the direct Portsmouth line. The work was carried out between 1924 and 1933. Since 1908 the line had been called the Woolmer Instructional Military Railway, but in 1935 its name was changed to the Longmoor Military Railway.

During the Second World War, the LMR provided instruction for as many as 27,000 trainees per annum. Extra mileage was necessary for practice in constructional and repair techniques, and also in operating. A loop line for continuous running was required, and so an alignment which had been used between the wars was brought back into use in 1943. This was the Hollywater loop, which consisted of about four-and-a-quarter miles of new line, the circuit being completed by about two miles of the existing line between Longmoor and Whitehill, which was provided with double track.

After the war, the emergency training railways at Melbourne in Derbyshire and the Shropshire & Montgomeryshire Railway between Shrewsbury and Llanymynech were closed down, and Longmoor became the main railway centre for the British Army. It was self-contained, apart from the transfer of freight wagons.

Its passenger service, although not public, was probably the nearest approach to main line practice on any private railway, and interesting examples of second-hand coaches were used. In this collection, the LNWR, LSWR, SECR and BR were all represented.

Most of the locomotives were built for the War Department, although there were some interesting exceptions. For instance, No. 2531 an ex-GWR 0-6-0 of the Dean Goods class was used for practice in derailment by explosives, and therefore always appeared in a rather battered condition. 'Gazelle', a minute 0-4-2 well tank, acquired with the Shropshire & Montgomeryshire Railway had been built by Dodmans of Kings Lynn for a showman in 1893. She is now preserved with 'Woolmer' an 0-6-0 saddle tank of 1910 on the parade ground at Longmoor.[13]

The stations were provided with conventional platforms, and in most cases were fully signalled. There was a great variety of signalling arrangements as soldiers had to be trained to operate any type of equipment they were likely to encounter.

Although locomotives were sent away for major overhauls, the workshops at Longmoor were equipped to deal with all running repairs. Exceptionally, main line passenger stock was transferred to the LMR at Liss or at Bordon. For instance, in the summer of 1953, ten coach trains from Waterloo conveyed Army Reservists through to the LMR station at Weaver's Down, between Longmoor and Liss. Motive power from Bordon was provided by the LMR and it seems unlikely that main line stock ever ran on the LMR behind a main line locomotive. For instance a railway enthusiasts' special run in October 1958 was hauled from Liss to Bordon by W.D. No. 400, a 2-8-0 built in 1943. On this occasion, the main line locomotive, No. 30120, a 4-4-0 of the LSWR T 9 class ran light over the LMR and this would seem to be one of the few occasions when BR motive power appeared at Longmoor.

In 1965, the Railway Squadrons of the Royal Engineers became part of the newly formed Royal Corps of Transport. Public interest in the LMR was increasing, and in the late 1960s a highly successful series of open days were held, when the general public had the opportunity to ride on LMR trains. By this time the only railway access was via Liss, as BR had withdrawn its passenger service to Bordon in 1957. In 1966 its freight service was abaondoned, and the track was removed during the following year. The LMR closed its station at Bordon, and removed about half-a-mile of track. The new terminal then consisted of the wooden platform at Oakhanger.

Perhaps inevitably, the Ministry of Defence decided that training in railway work could be undertaken without the expense of maintaining its own private railway, and the decision was taken to close the LMR. The closure was marked by an appropriate ceremony on 31 October, 1969. Train A consisting of the three saloons (LNWR of 1910, LSWR of 1920 and LSWR of 1909) ran to Oakhanger and back, hauled by 2-10-0 No. 600, 'Gordon'. Train B was hauled by 0-6-0 saddle tank No. 196, 'Errol Lonsdale' to Liss and back. At the time of writing the disused railway is still intact and it is hoped that preserved steam locomotives will run over about a mile between Liss LMR station and Liss Forest. Seven of these are stored in the running sheds at Longmoor, including two ex-Southern Pacifics – No. 34023, 'Blackmore Vale' and No. 35028, 'Clan Line'.[14]

The Longmoor Military Railway was unique among private railways in that, although it carried considerable traffic, its operation was an end in itself. It showed its effectiveness in the part played by the Royal Engineers in repairing and running railways all over the world during the Second World War.

The principal Admiralty dockyards of the south, at Sheerness, Chatham and Portsmouth were all established before the coming of the railways, and in the two latter cases, rail communications did raise problems. However both Chatham and Portsmouth became rail-connected and acquired extensive internal railway systems.[15] Sheerness was easier of access. A long siding left the main line short of the original terminal station, crossed the road by an ungated crossing and entered the dockyard through a massive wooden gate. The dockyard has now been sold to a commercial undertaking, and although the track is still down, it is disused.

Clarence Yard at Gosport has also lost its railway system, but Priddys Hard, to the north of Gosport, retains its railway.[16] In fact its traffic justifies the retention of a stump of the main line from Fareham to Gosport.

An unusual system was based on the landing stage on Haslar Creek, Gosport. A standard-gauge single track led directly into the Haslar Hospital and was used for the conveyance of men on stretchers. The rolling stock comprised one four-wheeled carriage, and the motive power consisted of six to eight sailors. Alongside was a narrow-gauge line which diverged in front of the hospital and ran down to the sea wall.

Here it forked, one arm following the road at the back of the sea wall to Fort Blockhouse (now H.M.S. *Dolphin*) and the other following the sea wall in the opposite direction to the Zymotic Hospital.[17] Passenger traffic on the narrow-gauge was also catered for by a single carriage likened to an 'upright piano'.[18] However, in addition, the narrow-gauge was used for carrying materials for the repairs of the sea wall. A similar track connected the Monkton Hutments with Fort Gilkicker, and the two lines were apparently connected.

Further west, narrow-gauge tracks served the rifle ranges near Browndown. At Lydd in Kent a narrow-gauge system continues to serve the rifle ranges. The standard-gauge tracks which connected the ranges with the main line at Lydd were lifted in the mid-1920s.

Most of the supply depots constructed or developed during the Second World War, had rail connections. Examples of those still provided with their own locomotives, are to be found at Ashford, Hilsea near Portsmouth, Liphook and Botley. While there has been some decline in the mileage of private railways owned by the Government, it remains the largest single operator in the south of England.

Lines Constructed for Industry and Commerce

Industrial activities may increase the utilization of existing tracks or may lead to the construction of new lines. At present, the tendency is to use road transport to and from a convenient railhead, but where bulk consignments were being delivered by rail, as at Richborough Power Station or the new cement works at Northfleet, new railways were built. Not only lines of standard gauge giving connection to main lines are of significance but also the narrow-gauge tracks of internal systems some of which lead to road or to water transport.

Chalk, Cement, Lime and Whiting

It is probable that the first railway to be constructed in the south connected a chalk quarry and lime-works at Offham, about one mile north of Lewes, to the Ouse Navigation. This is the object of research by Mr K. Leslie and members of the Sussex Industrial Archaeology Group, but superficial inspection indicates the general character of the line. It consisted of a double-track inclined plane, which was probably self-acting, i.e. descending wagons loaded with chalk or lime would pull up wagons either empty or loaded with coal for the lime kilns. Detailed survey may reveal such details as the gauge of the line and whether, apart from the necessary passing place, it had three or four rails. It was constructed about 1809, and reputedly designed by Mr Rand, a local schoolmaster. (He could either have seen similar inclined planes working in other parts of the country, especially in the north east, or have read accounts of them.) The incline and the works at Offham seem to have gone out of use in the 1890s.

Many lime-works were old establishments with local markets and had no direct connections with the railway. However, some used the railway for coal inwards and lime outwards traffic. The Associated Portland Cement Company owned lime-works at Buriton about two-and-a-half miles south of Petersfield on the Portsmouth Direct line. On one of the three sidings, instead of the usual catch point to derail any runaway wagon, a catch hook was provided. This was lowered when the siding shunt signal was off, but normally it was in a raised position. The *Western Appendix* to the *Southern Railway Working Time Table* states:

'A length of chain is attached to the hook, and in the event of a wagon running away from the private siding towards the railway company's property, the axle of the wagon engages with the hook which is then released from a socket and the gradual running out of the chain attached retards the wagon until it is eventually brought to a stand.'

Now this ingenious piece of apparatus, and the sidings that went with it, have all been removed.

Peppers at Amberley not only possessed a private siding, but also an unusual locomotive to work it. This was similar in design to a road traction engine with the cylinder on top of the boiler, and was constructed by Aveling & Porter of Rochester. A number of these road-type locomotives with gears, were in use, especially in the brick and cement industries.

Cement-works are in a sense, descended from lime-works, although the scale of operations is far greater. There are three working in Sussex, but none in Hampshire. Of the Sussex works one is situated on the River Adur and two on the Ouse. The former is located at Upper Beeding between Shoreham and Bramber, and was of sufficient importance to cause the retention of the railway from Shoreham as far as the works when the rest of the Shoreham to Horsham line was closed in 1966. Both the works on the Ouse used water transport. (In fact, vessels going to Southerham Works were the usual reason for operating the drawbridge on the East Sussex main line.) The Rodwell Works, situated further downstream and served by the Newhaven branch line was linked to its jetty by a cableway, as well as retaining a siding for rail traffic. However the greatest concentration of cement-works is found in Kent on the lower Thames and on the Medway. The railway between Dartford and Gravesend is more involved with cement than any other line in the country, but this falls outside the range of the present study.

On the Thames below Gravesend, there have been two works at Cliffe. The first consisted of a chalk quarry, a cement-works, a whiting-works and two wharves, which, from about 1870, were connected by a narrow-gauge steam railway. This was, of course, before the construction of the Hundred of Hoo branch, and being isolated, Francis & Co. like many of the manufacturers, selected their own gauge – in this case 3 ft 8½ in. The works closed about 1920, but subsequently the railway was used informally. While the last of the steam locomotives lingered in its shed until 1943, in the 1930s a lightkeeper used to sail down the line each day. Writing in the *Railway Magazine* for June 1937, Mr J.R. Hayton stated that Mr J.W. Slater had

'equipped the chassis of a truck, originally belonging to the cement company that owned the quarry, with two masts carrying lug sails and a jib, and this makes full use of the stiff sea breezes that blow across the exposed lonely lower reaches of the Thames'.

When the wind failed to serve, the alternative motive power was Mr Slater's donkey.[19] The Alpha Cement Company's works adjoined. This was a modern works, with a narrow-gauge line linking wharf, works and quarry, which was closed in 1969. A standard-gauge siding was opened in 1961 to the Hundred of Hoo branch, and this continues in use for gravel traffic.

About 20 cement-works have operated on the Lower Medway, of which seven are listed as having had railways of particular interest.[20] Of the four that are closed, the Burham Works had a standard-gauge system, although on the east bank and therefore unconnected to the main line. It extended from the river wharves via the works to the quarries for about two miles, including a tunnel about one-third-of-a-mile long. It was closed about 1938.

Peters's Wouldham Hall Works was also on the east bank, but with a route mileage of half-a-mile, and a gauge of 4 ft 3½ in. Lee's Works at

Halling used a 4 ft 3 in.-gauge for internal traffic, but had a standard-gauge siding to the main line. Like Peters's Works, it closed shortly before the Second World War. Batchelor's Clinkham Works was located north of Halling station and like a number of works, had track of more than one gauge. The siding to the main line was of standard gauge, but there were internal lines of two-feet-gauge and 3 ft 9 in.-gauge. The present Halling Works of the Rugby Portland Cement Company was built since the war on an adjoining site. Its internal two-feet-gauge system went out of use in 1973, but it retains a standard-gauge siding. The other operational works are both owned by A.P.C.M., situated at Wickham and Holborough, near Snodland, and have ceased to use railways apart from their connections to the main line. Movement from quarry to works is now undertaken by road transport or pipeline.

In some cases, evidence of railways remain. For instance, the Crown and Quarry Works at Frindsbury, near Strood, was closed in 1963, but the course of the line from Strood dock may be easily followed. A 4 ft 3 in.-gauge system continues to operate at the Smeed Dean Works near Sittingbourne but the 3 ft 7½ in.-gauge line to East Hall claypits has been closed. Chalk is conveyed by pipeline from the Highsted Chalk Pit whose internal system is operated, somewhat surprisingly, by electric locomotives. Particularly in north Kent, the cement-works railways were a very distinctive part of the railway scene.[21] With their multiplicity of gauges and their characteristic well tank geared locomotives by Aveling & Porter of Rochester, they possessed a unique character which persisted at least into the 1950s.

Gypsum, Clay, Bricks, Pottery, Glass, Sand and Gravel
One of the essential ingredients of cement is gypsum, and most of this comes from the mines at Mountfield in Sussex. In an indirect way this is associated with Kentish coal, as it was borings for coal in the early 1870s that led to the discovery of gypsum. To convey the product to the SER Hastings line, a siding over one mile in length was partly opened in 1876, and completed in 1877. It has usually been worked with the gypsum company's own locomotives, although they have occasionally been hired from the main line company. Traffic is exchanged at a siding about half-a-mile on the London side of Mountfield Halt. In addition to the cement works, British Plaster Board and Gyproc of Rochester receive large quantities of gypsum by rail.

Of the clay-based industries, brick production has been important throughout the railway era, but there has been little production of pottery in the south. Before the advent of the railways, although it meant dispensing with the advantages of specially constructed kilns, bricks were often made in clamps at the building site on which they were required. (In fact, temporary brick-works sometimes served major tunnels and viaducts on the railways during the construction period – those at Penge used clay taken from the tunnel working.) Rail transport reduced the cost of coal for small local works, but at the same time exposed them to competition from large-scale plants. There was a concentration of brickmaking for the London market between Sittingbourne and Faversham. Transport of bricks to London, with a return cargo of coal, was usually by sailing barges, and if works did not adjoin a creek, they frequently had a narrow-gauge railway leading to a convenient wharf. In some cases, Sittingbourne being an example, the scale of operations was such that internal railways were used to convey the clay from the pits to the brick-works. A typical example may be seen at Conyer, near Teynham. One works, recently closed, adjoined the creek, and for many years relied mainly on sailing barge transport. Another two were located about three-quarters-of-a-mile inland, near Teynham and each had its own railway leading down to a wharf. Despite some years of disuse, careful observation will still reveal the two routes, one from Barrow Green and one from Frognal.

Like coal-merchants, builders' merchants frequently based themselves on railway goods yards, but the development of road transport and large-scale building operations has encouraged the dispatch of bricks from the major works direct to sites. There were a number of smaller brickyards using Wealden clay, most of which were provided with private sidings. Pluckley on the SER and Keymer on the LBSCR were typical. The greatest concentration of brick-works in Hampshire was in the Fareham area, famed for its 'Fareham reds'. All the Fareham works have now closed down, partly owing to competition from the Bedfordshire and Peterborough works, assisted in their invasion of Hampshire by road transport.

As mentioned in the description of the railway to Fareham and Gosport, although production has ceased, the disused siding to Funtley Works survives.[22] The opposite situation exists at Bursledon Works on the Netley line, where the works is still active but the private siding has been removed. The only clues to its existence are a short length of track near the main entrance, and the railway-style concrete gate-post which once supported the gate at the railway company's boundary.

Terracotta was produced on a large scale by Blanchards at Bishops

Waltham, but both the works and the branch line which served it have been closed for some years. Whereas in north Kent the narrow-gauge systems were of some length, linking clay pits, works and water transport, shorter internal systems connected pit and works. Good examples also survive at Midhurst in Sussex and Selborne in Hampshire.

Some of these tracks are of a temporary nature, and this is also true of the lines which at one time were in general use in sand or gravel pits. However, a few pits had more permanent lines, leading to water, road or rail transport. A surviving example is to be found at Oare near Faversham. The pottery at Queenborough on the Isle of Sheppey is served mainly by water and road transport. Also at Queenborough, Pilkingtons have a glass-works which uses sand brought by rail from Buckland, near Reigate. Like the pottery, the works is situated on a siding, about one mile in length, which runs from the Sherness branch at Queenborough to a wharf on the Swale, and is operated by Settle, Speakman & Co. Coal comes in by water, but some of the glass and pottery products are moved away by rail.

Coal and Oil

Coal is the only product of southern England which has been responsible for the formation of a public railway company, and the story of the Kent coal-field is mentioned in Chapter 4. All four colleries had sidings which they operated themselves. Only Betteshanger had a line of significant length measuring about two miles from the pit to the junction with the main line. As a fuel, coal has been subjected to increasing competition from mineral oil, and one major refinery has been constructed in the south (Fawley, on the west side of Southampton Water comes just outside the area of this study). A small refinery was established on the Isle of Grain before the Second World War, and this has now developed into the extensive Grain Refinery.[23]

Petroleum products are conveyed to storage depots at various points on the railway system. Traffic from Grain to the large storage depot at Hamble on Southampton Water goes by sea, but from this point considerable quantities are dispatched by rail. A siding just over one-and-a-half miles long runs from exchange sidings adjoining Hamble Halt to the depot, with its pier and water frontage. A feature of unusual interest is that the single line runs across an aerodrome, used principally by the College of Air Training. Needless to say, stringent safety precautions are enforced to prevent trains crossing when planes are using the runways. Locomotive power on the siding now consists of diesel locomotives owned by Shell-Mex & B.P. For oil products, there are also a number of minor distribution centres with rail connections, such as that at Wye in Kent. Coal distribution centres with their own locomotives exist at several points such as Cory's Rochester wharf. At present, Corralls maintain one of the last working steam locomotives in Hampshire at Dible's Wharf in Southampton.[24]

Other Industries

Before the railway era, breweries were to be found in almost every kind of settlement, varying from the large establishments in London to small village breweries. The railways of the south were involved with brewing, although there was nothing equivalent to the amount of malt brought up from East Anglia by the Great Eastern Railway, or the barrels of beer conveyed by the Midland from Burton-on-Trent to the vaults under St Pancras Station. The London breweries drew most of their barley and malt from East Anglia, but relied on Kent and, to a much lesser extent, on Surrey and Hampshire for hops. But whereas maltings were frequently located in East Anglian railway yards, both to receive their coal and barley, and to send away their malt, oast houses for roasting hops were usually found on the farms. Although really large-scale concentration of brewing awaited mechanical road transport, some concentration took place in the railway age, with horse and cart operating from the railheads.

Thus in Kent, Shepherd Neame at Faversham, and Style & Winch, and Fremlins of Maidstone all expanded greatly. But the most interesting brewery railway was at Alton in Hampshire, where the siding extended for about 300 yards from a junction with the Mid-Hants Railway. This was situated at the point of transition from embankment to cutting, just over a quarter-of-a-mile on the Winchester side of Alton station. The siding is now disused, but in times past it was employed to bring in coal and barley, and to dispatch beer; hops were delivered by road from local hop gardens in the Alton and Farnham districts.

Traditionally, flour-milling was carried out in watermills and windmills but the railways, by providing cheaper coal for the inland towns, favoured the development of steam power associated with metal rollers as opposed to grindstones. A number of mills, including those at Ashford, Crowborough and Robertsbridge were served by private sidings. Unfortunately, partly because of the development of the North American railways, mills, using imported grain and sited in the ports, competed strongly with the inland mills. However some of them still operate, that at Robertsbridge continuing to use its own private steam locomotive until very recently.

Gunpowder mills, with their principal raw materials of charcoal and saltpetre, using water power and steam power were well-established by the 1840s, especially in the Tonbridge, Dartford and Faversham districts of Kent. The physical relationship between the railways and the established gunpowder works was negative. In some cases, such as at Ramhurst, near Tonbridge, there was, first, a fear that the railway bridge over the Medway would throttle the water power, and, second, that there was a danger of explosion from sparks from the locomotives. The railway may have enabled some of the works to survive longer by providing cheaper coal, but already gunpowder was giving place to more powerful explosives. Partly because of the concentration of the defence services in the south, and the location of the principal arsenal at Woolwich, while the manufacture of gunpowder declined, that of other explosives continued, probably reaching a peak during the First World War. In the Second World War, the danger of aerial attack led to a far greater dispersal of munitions manufacture, most of it well away from the vulnerable south. But in the First World War what was probably the greatest concentration of plants in Britain was sited on the marshes to the north-west of Faversham. By 1916 there were four factories employing around 5,000 people, about half of whom were women.

Needless to say, these could not all live in Faversham, and each day large numbers arrived at Faversham station from as far west as the Medway Towns and as far east as the Isle of Thanet and Dover. They were then faced with a walk of nearly three miles down to the marshes at Uplees. Not surprisingly there were complaints, and it was mainly to increase the efficiency and the reliability of the labour force that a narrow-gauge line, a little over two miles long, was opened from Davington on the outskirts of Faversham, to a terminal at Uplees. It came as close as possible to Faversham, consistent with avoiding demolition of property. It was constructed and operated by the Admiralty and its opening in November 1916 was not advertised. However, in a recent paper on the Davington Light Railway, Mr M. Minter Taylor has brought together a great deal of information about this 'secret' railway.[26] The gauge was 3 ft 3 in., which was probably selected to conform with that used in the internal system in the factories. (This does not explain the somewhat unusual choice of gauge for the factory system.) Although the new line was primarily passenger-carrying, it was also used to convey mines, bombs, shells and the like to Davington where they were transferred to motor lorries. However, a high proportion of the output of the works continued to be sent away by sailing barge. An obvious step would have been a branch to the main line railway and this was planned from a point between Davington and Oare to the SECR about one mile west of Faversham, but it was never constructed. The only engineering works of note were the bridge over Oare Creek and the bridge under the road from Oare to Harty Ferry. In fact, as the railway passed under the road at a very oblique angle the underbridge was 80 ft 6 in. long and was usually described as a tunnel. It remains as an unmistakable railway relic. Signs of the stations at Uplees and Davington do exist, but are only perceptible to the fairly practised railway archaeologist. This is not surprising for such an ephemeral railway. By 1920 all four factories were closed down and the whole complex, including the railway was sold by auction.

The three locomotives which had operated the passenger and freight traffic on the Davington railway went back to their manufacturers, Manning Wardle, for repair and subsequent disposal. There were 12 passenger coaches, operated in three four-coach sets. They were of the toast-rack type, open-sided but provided with tarpaulins to keep out some of the wind and rain, to which the marshes were much exposed. The question of smoking compartments did not arise, but some entire trains were for 'Ladies Only'. These were the later trains in the morning, between 7.00 and 8.00 a.m. and the earlier ones at night between 5.00 and 6.00 p.m. A standard fare of 2d return was charged, although it is unlikely that anybody other than works employees was carried. The Davington line was on a small scale compared with the narrow-gauge system in Woolwich Arsenal, which also carried passengers, but this comes outside the present area of study.

While the munitions industry is unlikely to produce any more railways in the south, the paper-making industry has the distinction of having provided one of the few industrial railways which is being preserved. The industry is old-established, especially in Kent, in the Darent and Medway valleys. A number of the pre-railway sites are still in use, notably on the Darent at South Darenth, on the Dour at Dover, on the Stour at Chartham, and in the Maidstone district. These were selected mainly because of the availability of suitable water for processing, and for power, although most of them went over to steam many years ago. Even if railways passed near them, as at Turkey Mill on the River Len, just east of Maidstone, they did not always construct private sidings. In the case of Turkey Mill, the railway was on a viaduct, above the level of the works, but this would not have been an insoluble difficulty if direct rail connection had been desired. In fact, when the Maidstone and Ashford line was authorized in 1880, the paper company had a clause inserted requiring the railway to provide a roof over the viaduct for the protection of its paper. Although this roof has now been removed, the high side walls, from which it sprung, have survived. In contrast to Turkey Mill, Hayle Mill was served by a long siding from Tovil, near Maidstone.

The modern mills produce a greater variety of products for a wider market and are located on the Thames, Medway and Swale. The principal Thameside works are west of Gravesend, but the Reed Group has some mills at New Hythe on the Medway. Coal is brought by rail from the Kentish coal field, and a standard-gauge railway system is operated. Wood pulp and pulpwood are, however, unloaded into lighters at Rochester, and brought up the Medway. (In 1969, as an experiment, lighters were loaded overseas, carried on a specially designed ship, and off-loaded into the Medway, thus avoiding transhipment.) The problem of transhipment into barges was avoided by the proprietors of Edward Lloyd's mill (now Bowaters) at Sittingbourne in an interesting way. The mill was served by sailing barges coming up Milton Creek from the Swale to a wharf. The wharf and mill were connected by a railway just over a quarter-mile long. The barge link was eliminated by the construction of two docks which could be reached by steamers. Ridham Dock, on the Swale, accommodated the larger steamers bringing in wood pulp, pulpwood and china clay, while coal was brought nearer the works, to Grovenhurst Dock.

Constructional work began at Ridham in 1913, but there were delays during the First World War, when the Admiralty established a salvage depot on the site, with a standard-gauge connection to the Sheerness branch railway. In 1919, Ridham Dock was returned to its owners, who had built a new line to connect it to their Sittingbourne works. In one sense this was a branch of their original line, but as it was about three-and-a-half miles long, for operating purposes it became the main line. It was laid with single track of 2 ft 6 in. guage. Like the lines from the great London terminals, numerous streets had to be crossed at the Sittingbourne end and this was done by a viaduct of reinforced concrete, about half-a-mile long.

Before the First World War, it had been decided that as an alternative to attempting to expand on the restricted site at Sittingbourne a second works should be built roughly half-way along the railway at Kemsley. This was completed in 1924, the narrow-gauge line was doubled between Kemsley and Ridham Dock, and additional steam locomotives were purchased to handle the traffic for the two mills. The new Kemsley Mill being in an isolated position on the marshes, similar to the Uplees munition works, employees had difficulty in reaching it from the town so until 1968 a regular service of workmen's trains was provided. The coaches were wooden and box-like but, unlike the Davington coaches, they were equipped with sides as well as roofs. In addition to the narrow-gauge railway system the standard-gauge siding from the Sheerness branch was extended to serve both Ridham Dock and Kemsley Mill. Steam raising was carried out at Kemsley with steam pipelines to serve Sittingbourne. A conveyor carried the waterborne coal from Groven-hurst Dock, Kentish coal being brought in by the standard-gauge rail connection. An aerial ropeway for carrying pulpwood connected Ridham Dock and Kemsley.

In 1969, Bowaters were advised that the railway was not the most economic means of meeting the group's internal transport requirements. However, within the Bowater organization there was a feeling of attachment to the railway, and it was decided to investigate the possibility of a suitable society to take over the section from Sittingbourne to Kemsley which could be conveniently severed from the rest of the firm's transport system. In addition to the track, Bowaters offered five of the steam locomotives, one diesel, five of the passenger coaches, and a number of wagons. The choice fell on the Locomotive Club of Great Britain, and the line was formally handed over to them at a ceremony on 4 October, 1969. At the present time, regular services for passengers operate at weekends from March until October. It is fortunate that one of the most highly developed of the private railways of the south should have been enabled to survive in this way.

But the typical private railway is more likely to be of interest to the railway archaeologist than the enthusiast for railway operating. Many abandoned lines have left signs of their existence. One example, about three-quarters-of-a-mile in length, ran from the LCDR Kent coast line, a mile west of Herne Bay, down to a jetty at Hampton. This was authorized by the Herne Bay Fishery Act of 1864, and enabled sea food, including fish and oysters, to be speedily dispatched for the London market. Oysters declined and so did the Herne Bay Fishery. But the line which probably consisted of a standard-gauge single track is still represented by a low curving embankment crossing a field near the former junction. Motive power consisted of a horse, or, under appropriate weather conditions, a sail. At Hampton most of the jetty has gone, but enough remains to indicate beyond doubt the site of the landing place. In terms of the total economic activity of southern England such a feature is not very significant. But in its time, it was highly significant for those whose money had built it, for those who worked on it, and, indirectly, such people as the oyster-eaters of London.

Privately owned railways show so many variations that few generalizations are of value. However, most of them were owned by their own principal users. One exception, already mentioned is Settle, Speakman's line at Queenborough, which serves a number of industrial establishments. Another interesting exception was the Chapel Tramway Company which owned land, track, and, for most of its existence, one locomotive to serve wharves and other establishments in Southampton. It escaped nationalization, and, as late as 1960, acquired a new locomotive.[27] However, it has now succumbed to road competition. Perhaps the extremes are represented by short lengths of narrow-gauge track in a sand pit on the one hand, and the Longmoor Military Railway, virtually indistinguishable from a main line, on the other.

Appendix 1
The Colonel Stephens Railways

If any one person could be described as the 'Stephenson' of the light railways, it would be Colonel Stephens. He was born in 1866, and his period of greatest activity coincided with the peak of the light railway movement from about 1896 until 1914. His military title was acquired by serving with the Royal Engineers, and during the First World War he commanded the Kent (Fortress) Battalion. Although he was an engineer, because he frequently accepted payment from light railway companies in shares instead of cash, he became much involved in their management. In fact, my interest in light railways was sparked off by the appearance in 1936 of one of the first publications of the Oakwood Press, with the title *The Colonel Stephens Railways*.[1] This booklet gave descriptions of five lines – the East Kent, the Kent & East Sussex, the West Sussex, the Weston, Clevedon & Portishead, and the Shropshire & Montgomeryshire – and having read it, I was at once fired with the strongest desire to see them all. I managed four of them, but was too late for the West Sussex.

Without question, the Colonel Stephens railways formed a coherent group. The Colonel, who was general manager, engineer, and loco-motive superintendent of each of the lines, operated what was unkindly called his 'old iron empire' from an office at 23 Salford Terrace, Ton-bridge, Kent – a building lacking the plaque which it surely merits. By the time of his death, most of the companies were bankrupt and his title had changed to general manager and receiver. His successor was Mr W.H. Austen.

Colonel Stephens's work as an engineer was not confined to the companies he managed. For instance, in the south he was responsible for the engineering of the Rye & Camber, and the Sheppey. There was a limited exchange of locomotives between the companies of his group, not encouraged by the apparent lack of enthusiasm of the main line companies for having Colonel Stephens's rolling stock on their tracks. One common service however was the printing press maintained at Rolvenden. But the strongest link between the companies was their general atmosphere, emanating from their simple iron or wooden stations, their second-hand and sometimes hybrid rolling stock, and their pleasantly informal operating practice.

Somewhat surprisingly when Colonel Stephens died in October 1931, he was not awarded an obituary notice in *The Times*. However a note was published on his will, which included the valuation of his gross estate at £30,197 without indicating how much of this was attributable to his light railway interests. His pictures and drawings, then on loan to the Tate Gallery, were left to the nation, but his light railways were not mentioned.

Appendix 2
Opening and Closure of Light or Independent Railways

TABLE 1

This list includes all the railways built under Light Railway Orders and some not owned by main line companies which carried passenger traffic. It excludes lines not open to the general public such as the Longmoor Military Railway and the Hellingly Hospital Railway. It also omits cliff lifts and pleasure railways.

Against each line is written the year of opening or closure, the operating company at the time, the number of the chapter in which it is described and the route mileage opened or closed. Four of the lines did not carry freight apart from baggage – the Herne Bay Pier (HBP), Volk's (VER), Brighton & Rottingdean Seashore Electric (BRSER) and the Ramsgate Tunnel (TA). For the remainder, the dates given apply to both passenger and freight traffic, except in cases of appreciable time gaps where the particular service being provided or withdrawn is identified.

		Operating Company	Chapter No.	Route Miles Open	Route Miles Closed
1832	Pier Entrance to Pier Head, Herne Bay	HBP	5	$\frac{3}{4}$	—
1864	Pier Entrance to Pier Head, Herne Bay	HBP	5	—	$\frac{3}{4}$
1883	Aquarium[1] to Chain Pier, Brighton	VER	5	$\frac{1}{4}$	—
1884	Chain Pier to Children's Playground (Paston Place)	VER	5	$\frac{1}{2}$	—

		Operating Company	Chapter No.	Route Miles Open	Route Miles Closed
1894	Fort Brockhurst to Lee-on-the-Solent	LSR	2	3	—
1895	Rye to Golf Links (Rye Harbour)	RCT	5	$1\frac{1}{2}$	—
1896	Paston Place, Brighton to Rottingdean	BRSER	5	$2\frac{3}{4}$	—
1897	Chichester to Selsey Town	WSR	3	$7\frac{1}{2}$	—
1898	Selsey Town to Selsey Beach	WSR	3	$\frac{1}{2}$	—
1899	Pier Entrance to Pier Head, Herne Bay	HBP	5	$\frac{3}{4}$	—
1900	Robertsbridge to Rolvenden	KESR	3	12	—
1901	Basingstoke to Butts Junction, Alton	LSWR	2	$12\frac{1}{2}$	—
	Queenborough to Leysdown	SECR	3	$8\frac{3}{4}$	—
	Childrens Playground (Paston Place) to Black Rock	VER	5	$\frac{1}{2}$	—
	Paston Place, Brighton to Rottingdean	BRSER	5	—	$2\frac{3}{4}$
1903	Rolvenden to Tenterden Town	KESR	3	$1\frac{1}{2}$	—
1904	Selsey Town to Selsey Beach	WSR	3	—	$\frac{1}{2}$
1905	Bentley to Bordon	LSWR	2	$4\frac{1}{2}$	—
	Tenterden to Headcorn	KESR	3	8	—
1908	Golden Links (Rye Harbour) to Camber Sands	RCT	5	$\frac{1}{2}$	—
1912	Shepherd's Well to Wingham Colliery (to freight)	EKLR	4	$10\frac{1}{4}$	—
1914	Pier Entrance to Pier Head, Herne Bay	HBP	5	—	$\frac{3}{4}$
1916	Shepherd's Well to Wingham Colliery (to passengers)	EKLR	4	—	—
1917	Basingstoke to Butts Junction, Alton	LSWR	2	—	$12\frac{1}{2}$
1924	Basingstoke to Butts Junction, Alton	SR	2	$12\frac{1}{2}$	—
1925	Wingham Colliery to Wingham, Canterbury Road	EKLR	4	1	—

		Operating Company	Chapter No.	Route Miles Open	Route Miles Closed
	Eastry to Richborough Port (passenger to Sandwich Road only)	EKLR	4	$4\frac{1}{2}$	—
	Pier Head to Pier Entrance, Herne Bay	HBP	5	$\frac{3}{4}$	—
1927	Hythe to New Romney	RHDR	3	$8\frac{1}{4}$	—
1928	New Romney to Pilot Halt	RHDR	3	$4\frac{1}{4}$	—
	Eastry to Sandwich Road (closed to passengers)	EKLR	4	—	—
1929	Pilot Halt to Dungeness	RHDR	5	$1\frac{1}{4}$	—
1930	Fort Brockhurst to Lee-on-the-Solent (closed to passengers)	SR	2	—	—
1932	Basingstoke – Butts Junction, Alton (closed to passengers)	SR	2	—	—
	Bentworth and Lasham to Treloars Siding	SR	2	—	$3\frac{1}{2}$
1933	Aquarium[1] to Aquarium[2]	VER	5	—	$\frac{1}{4}$
1935	Fort Brockhurst to Lee-on-the-Solent	SR	2	—	3
	Chichester to Selsey Town	WSR	3	—	$7\frac{1}{2}$
1936	Thorneycroft's Siding to Bentworth and Lasham	SR	2	—	$8\frac{1}{4}$
	Ramsgate Harbour to Ramsgate, Hereson Road	TA	5	$\frac{3}{4}$	—
1939	Ramsgate Harbour to Ramsgate, Hereson Road	TA	5	—	$\frac{3}{4}$
	Rye to Camber Sands	RCT	5	—	2
	Pier Entrance to Pier Head, Herne Bay	HBP	5	—	$\frac{3}{4}$
1940	Hythe to Dungeness (closed to public)	RHDR	3	—	—
	Aquarium to Black Rock	VER	5	—	$1\frac{1}{4}$
1946	Hythe to Maddiesons Camp (re-opened to public: passengers only)	RHDR	3	—	—

		Operating Company	Chapter No.	Route Miles Open	Route Miles Closed
	Ramsgate Harbour to Ramsgate, Hereson Road	TA	5	$\frac{3}{4}$	—
1947	Maddiesons Camp to Dungeness (re-opened to public: passengers only)	RHDR	3	—	—
1948	Aquarium to Black Rock	VER	5	$1\frac{1}{4}$	—
	Shepherd's Well to Wingham, Canterbury Road (closed to passengers)	BR	4	—	—
1950	Queenborough to Leysdown	BR	3	—	$8\frac{3}{4}$
	Eastry to Richborough Port	BR	4	—	$4\frac{1}{4}$
1951	Eythorne to Wingham, Canterbury Road	BR	4	—	$9\frac{1}{2}$
1954	Robertsbridge to Headcorn (closed to passengers)	BR	3	—	—
	Tenterden to Headcorn	BR	3	—	8
1957	Bentley to Bordon (closed to passengers)	BR	2	—	—
1961	Robertsbridge to Tenterden	BR	3	—	$13\frac{1}{2}$
1965	Ramsgate Harbour to Ramsgate, Hereson Road	TA	5	—	$\frac{3}{4}$
1966	Bentley to Bordon	BR	2	—	$4\frac{1}{2}$
1967	Treloars Siding to Butts Junction, Alton	BR	2	—	$\frac{1}{4}$
	Thorneycroft's Siding to Basingstoke	BR	2	—	$\frac{1}{2}$

TABLE 2

This shows the greatest mileage open to traffic during 1832, 1864 and for each year from 1883 to 1967 inclusive. There were no changes between 1832 and 1864, 1864 and 1883, or since 1967. The 'high summer' of the minor railways lasted from 1929 to 1931 with 91 route miles available. The present $16\frac{1}{2}$ miles is made up of 15 miles carrying passengers (VER and RHDR) plus part of the East Kent Light Railway carrying coal traffic.

1832	$\frac{3}{4}$	1910	$61\frac{3}{4}$	1939	$65\frac{3}{4}$
1864	0	1911	$61\frac{3}{4}$	1940	$64\frac{1}{2}$
1883	$\frac{1}{4}$	1912	72	1941	$64\frac{1}{2}$
1884	$\frac{3}{4}$	1913	72	1942	$64\frac{1}{2}$
1885	$\frac{3}{4}$	1914	72	1943	$64\frac{1}{2}$
1886	$\frac{3}{4}$	1915	$71\frac{1}{4}$	1944	$64\frac{1}{2}$
1887	$\frac{3}{4}$	1916	$71\frac{1}{4}$	1945	$64\frac{1}{2}$
1888	$\frac{3}{4}$	1917	$58\frac{3}{4}$	1946	$65\frac{1}{4}$
1889	$\frac{3}{4}$	1918	$58\frac{3}{4}$	1947	$65\frac{1}{4}$
1890	$\frac{3}{4}$	1919	$58\frac{3}{4}$	1948	$66\frac{1}{2}$
1891	$\frac{3}{4}$	1920	$58\frac{3}{4}$	1949	$66\frac{1}{2}$
1892	$\frac{3}{4}$	1921	$58\frac{3}{4}$	1950	$53\frac{1}{2}$
1893	$\frac{3}{4}$	1922	$58\frac{3}{4}$	1951	44
1894	$3\frac{3}{4}$	1923	$58\frac{3}{4}$	1952	44
1895	$5\frac{1}{4}$	1924	$71\frac{1}{4}$	1953	44
1896	8	1925	$77\frac{1}{4}$	1954	36
1897	$15\frac{1}{2}$	1926	$77\frac{1}{4}$	1955	36
1898	16	1927	$85\frac{1}{2}$	1956	36
1899	$16\frac{3}{4}$	1928	$89\frac{3}{4}$	1957	36
1900	$28\frac{3}{4}$	1929	91	1958	36
1901	$47\frac{3}{4}$	1930	91	1959	36
1902	$47\frac{3}{4}$	1931	91	1960	36
1903	$49\frac{1}{4}$	1932	$87\frac{1}{2}$	1961	$22\frac{1}{2}$
1904	$48\frac{3}{4}$	1933	$87\frac{1}{4}$	1962	$22\frac{1}{2}$
1905	$61\frac{1}{4}$	1934	$87\frac{1}{4}$	1963	$22\frac{1}{2}$
1906	$61\frac{1}{4}$	1935	$76\frac{3}{4}$	1964	$22\frac{1}{2}$
1907	$61\frac{1}{4}$	1936	$69\frac{1}{4}$	1965	$21\frac{3}{4}$
1908	$61\frac{3}{4}$	1937	$69\frac{1}{4}$	1966	$17\frac{1}{4}$
1909	$61\frac{3}{4}$	1938	$69\frac{1}{4}$	1967	$16\frac{1}{2}$

TABLE 3

This shows the net gain or loss of route mileage in each decade from 1890 to 1969. The maximum growth rates were achieved in the decades before and after the First World War. The slight decline during the war reflected war-time conditions rather than a long-term trend. This became apparent in the 1930s when, in the face of motor competition, mileage fell by $25\frac{1}{4}$. Inspection of Table 2 will show that the gain during the 1940s is misleading. Providing that Tilmanstone Colliery remains open, the 1970s may well be the first decade with no change in mileage.

1890–1899	$+15\frac{1}{2}$	1930–1939	$-25\frac{1}{4}$
1900–1909	$+33$	1940–1949	$+2$
1910–1919	-3	1950–1959	$-17\frac{1}{2}$
1920–1929	$+32\frac{1}{4}$	1960–1969	$-19\frac{1}{2}$

Appendix 3

Opening and Closure of Passenger Stations on Light or Independent Railways 1832-1965

This list defines the points at which passengers could join or leave lines described in this book. The more important establishments, such as Tenterden Town on the KESR, consisted of simple buildings with conventional platforms; at the other extreme, Prince of Wales halt provided no more than hard-standing at the side of the track and a name-board. They were all open to the general public, and private stations, such as Golden Sands on the RHDR or the well-built platforms in the grounds of Park Prewett Hospital, are omitted. Also excluded are the boarding points on cliff railways and short pleasure lines.

Each entry begins with a number which indicates the position of the station on the map and diagrams. Next comes the name and this is usually the present name, or that at the time of closure, as shown in time-tables and on station name-boards. Earlier names are shown in brackets and are also cross-referenced. The county in which the station is to be found is shown as follows: H – Hampshire, K – Kent, Su – Surrey and Sx – Sussex. This is followed by the number of the chapter in which the station appears. Next come the initials of the company which provided the service at the opening date.

The dates given are of the first and, where applicable, the last year in which a service was provided. There is, of course, no indication of the proportion of the year of opening or closure during which a station was served. Temporary closures of considerable duration, such as that of Black Rock, are shown. To assist in locating their sites, grid references are given for all closed stations. Finally, an indication is given of what was still to be seen in 1972. The code used is as follows:

  a Main buildings demolished
  b Main buildings in use for railway or for other purposes.

The following list, added to those provided in Volumes One and Two, covers all the 487 passenger stations in southern England.

408	Aquarium (1st Station)	Sx	5	VER	1883–1933 (TQ 314038)	a
409	Aquarium (2nd Station)	Sx	5	VER	1933–1940 1948	b
410	Ash Town	K	4	EKLR	1916–1948 (TR 286581)	a
411	Bentworth & Lasham	H	2	LSWR	1901–1917 1924–1932 (SU 669418)	b
412	Biddenden	K	3	KESR	1905–1954 (TQ 853393)	b
413	Black Rock	Sx	5	VER	1901–1940 1948	b
414	Bodiam	Sx	3	KESR	1900–1954 (TQ 782250)	b
415	Bordon	H	2	LSWR	1905–1957 (SU 773362)	a
416	Botolphs Bridge Halt	K	3	RHDR	1927–1939 (TR 124329)	a
417	Brambledown Halt	K	3	SECR	1905–1950 (TQ 964716)	a
418	Browndown Halt	H	2	LSR	1894–1930 (SZ 581993)	a
419	Burmarsh Road Halt	K	3	RHDR	1927–1940 1946–1948 (TR 107305)	a
420	Camber Sands	Sx	5	RCT	1908–1939 (TQ 952188)	a

Canterbury Road, Wingham (See Wingham, Canterbury Road)

421	Chain Pier, Brighton	Sx	5	VER	1883–1884 (TQ 316038)	a
422	Chalder	Sx	3	WSR	1897–1935 (SZ 860991)	a
423	Chichester	Sx	3	WSR	1897–1935 (SU 858042)	a
424	Children's Playground (Paston Place)	Sx	5	VER	1884–1940 1948	b

425	Cliddesden	H	2	LSWR	1901–1917	a
					1924–1932	
					(SU 638496)	
426	Dungeness	K	3	RHDR	1928–1940	b
					1947	
427	Dymchurch	K	3	RHDR	1927–1940	b
					1946	
428	Eastchurch	K	3	SECR	1901–1950	a
					(TQ 985704)	
429	East Minster-on-Sea	K	3	SECR	1902–1950	a
					(TQ 946728) ·	
430	Eastry	K	4	EKLR	1916–1948	a
					(TR 304552)	
431	Eastry South	K	4	EKLR	1925–1948	a
					(TR 302545)	
432	Elmore Halt	H	2	LSWR	1910–1930	a
					(SZ 568997)	
433	Elvington (Tilmanstone Colliery Halt)	K	4	EKLR	1916–1948	a
					(TR 283506)	
434	Eythorne	K	4	EKLR	1916–1948	a
					(TR 282495)	
435	Ferry	Sx	3	WSR	1898–1935	a
					(SZ 856960)	
436	Fort Gomer Halt (Privett)	H	2	LSR	1894–1930	a
					(SZ 590998)	
437	Frittenden Road	K	3	KESR	1905–1954	b
					(TQ 843408)	
438	Golf Links (Rye Harbour)	Sx	5	RCT	1895–1939	b
					(TQ 944192)	
439	Greatstone	K	3	RHDR	1928–1940	b
					1947	
440	Harty Road Halt	K	3	SECR	1905–1950	a
					(TR 008705)	
441	Headcorn	K	3	KESR	1905–1954	a
					(TQ 387439)	
442	Herriard	H	2	LSWR	1901–1917	a
					1924–1932	
					(SU 668451)	
443	High Halden Road	K	3	KESR	1905–1954	b
					(TQ 877368)	

Holiday Camp (See St Mary's Bay)

444	Hunston	Sx	3	WSR	1897–1935 (SU 859012)	a
445	Hythe	K	3	RHDR	1927–1940 1946	b

Jesson (See St Mary's Bay)

446	Junction Road Halt	Sx	3	KESR	1901–1954 (TQ 771243)	a
447	Kingsley Halt	H	2	LSWR	1906–1957 (SU 778391)	a
448	Knowlton Halt	K	4	EKLR	1916–1948 (TR 288522)	a
449	Lade Halt	K	3	RHDR	1928–1940 1947	b
450	Lee-on-the-Solent	H	2	LSR	1894–1930 (SU 562003)	b
451	Leysdown	K	3	SECR	1901–1950 (TR 033708)	a

Littlestone (See New Romney)
Littlestone Holiday Camp (See Maddieson's Camp)

452	Maddieson's Camp (Littlestone Holiday Camp)	K	3	RHDR	1928–1940 1947	b
453	Mill Pond Halt	Sx	3	WSR	1910–1911 1928–1935 (SZ 858978)	a
454	Minster-on-Sea	K	3	SECR	1901–1950 (TQ 954723)	a
455	New Romney (Littlestone)	K	3	RHDR	1927–1940 1946	b
456	Northiam	Sx	3	KESR	1900–1954 (TQ 834267)	b
457	Ovingdean	Sx	5	BRSER	1896–1901 (TQ 360024)	a

Paston Place (See Children's Playground)

458	Paston Place, Brighton	Sx	5	BRSER	1896–1901 (TQ 325034)	a
459	Pier Entrance	K	5	HBP	1832–1864 1899–1939 (TR 173683)	a

460	Pier Head	K	5	HBP	1832–1864 1899–1939 (TR 169693)	a
461	Pilot Halt	K	3	RHDR	1928–1940 1947	b
462	Poison Cross	K	4	EKLR	1925–1928 (TR 308557)	a
463	Prince of Wales Halt	K	3	RHDR	1927–1928 (TR 142339)	a
	Privett (See Fort Gomer Halt)					
464	Ramsgate Harbour	K	5	TA	1936–1939 1946–1965 (TR 386649)	a
465	Ramsgate, Hereson Road	K	5	TA	1936–1939 1946–1965 (TR 389662)	a
466	Rolvenden (Tenterden)	K	3	KESR	1900–1954 (TQ 864328)	a
467	Roman Road, Woodnesborough	K	4	EKLR	1925–1928 (TR 318573)	a
468	Rottingdean	Sx	5	BRSER	1896–1901 (TQ 369021)	a
469	Rye	Sx	5	RCT	1895–1939 (TQ 925206)	a
	Rye Harbour (See Golf Links)					
470	St Mary's Bay (Jesson; Holiday Camp)	K	3	RHDR	1927–1940 1946	b
471	Salehurst Halt	Sx	3	KESR	1929–1954 (TQ 749241)	a
472	Sandwich Road	K	4	EKLR	1925–1928 (TR 317585)	a
473	Selsey Beach	Sx	3	WSR	1898–1904 (SZ 864936)	a
474	Selsey Bridge	Sx	3	WSR	1897–1935 (SZ 856940)	a
475	Selsey Town	Sx	3	WSR	1897–1935 (SZ 859938)	a
476	Sheerness East	K	3	SECR	1901–1950 (TQ 932734)	a

477	Shepherd's Well	K	4	EKCR	1916–1948 (TR 258483)	a
478	Sidlesham	Sx	3	WSR	1897–1935 (SZ 860971)	a
479	Staple and Ash	K	3	EKLR	1916–1948 (TR 274576)	b
	Tenterden (See Rolvenden)					
480	Tenterden St Michael's	K	3	KESR	1912–1954 (TQ 883352)	a
481	Tenterden Town	K	3	KESR	1903–1954 (TQ 883335)	b
	Tilmanstone Colliery Halt (See Elvington)					
482	Warren Halt	K	3	RHDR	1927–1928 (TR 078260)	a
483	Wingham, Canterbury Road	K	4	EKCR	1925–1948 (TR 236573)	a
484	Wingham Colliery	K	4	EKLR	1916–1948 (TR 252571)	a
485	Wingham Town	K	4	EKLR	1925–1948 (TR 244571)	a
486	Wittersham Road	K	3	KESR	1900–1954 (TQ 867288)	a
487	Woodnesborough	K	4	EKLR	1925–1948 (TR 298564)	a

Appendix 4
Steep-Grade Railways and Pleasure Lines

This list includes lines which carry passengers but not freight, with track gauges varying from ten-and-a-quarter inches to six feet, described in Chapter 5. They are open to the public unless otherwise stated, but in many cases during the summer season only. Portable and private lines are excluded. The following information is given:

(a)   Reference number on Maps Nos 1 and 2
(b)   Name and situation of line
(c)   County
(d)   Grid reference of main station or other point of access
(e)   Track gauge or gauges
(f)   Motive power – steam (s), internal combustion (IC), battery electric (E), hydraulic (H)
(g)   Open or closed in 1972

(a)	(b)	(c)	(d)	(e)	(f)	(g)
P1	Hampshire Narrow-Gauge Light Rly., Durley	H	SU 522173	1' 11½" & 2' 0" & 3' 0"	S/IC	Open (1)
P2	Southsea Miniature Rly.	H	SZ 642981	10¼"	IC	Open
P3	Hollycombe House, Liphook	H	SU 852295	2' 0" & 4' 8½"	S/IC	Open
P4	Drusilla's Tea Rooms, Berwick	Sx	TQ 524048	2' 0"	IC	Open
P5	Hastings Miniature Rly.	Sx	TQ 825094	10¼"	S/IC	Open

(a)	(b)	(c)	(d)	(e)	(f)	(g)
P6	Hotham Park Miniature Rly., Bognor	Sx	sz 938995	$10\frac{1}{4}''$	IC	Open
P7	Brooklands Miniature Rly., East Worthing	Sx	TQ 178034	$9\frac{1}{2}''$	IC	Open
P8	King Alfred's Amusements, Hove	Sx	TQ 283044	$10\frac{1}{4}''$	E	Open (2)
P9	Littlehampton Miniature Rly.	Sx	TQ 036014	$12\frac{1}{4}''$	S/IC/E	Open
P10	Sheppey Light Rly., Leysdown	K	TR 033708	$2' 0''$	IC	Open
P11	Kent Country Nurseries Challock	K	TR 009508	$10\frac{1}{4}''$	IC/E	Open
P12	Margate Miniature Rly.	K	TR 353713	$10\frac{1}{4}''$	IC	Open
P13	Dreamland Miniature Rly., Margate	K	TR 349707	$15''$	S/IC	Open
P14	Wey Valley Light Rly., Farnham	Su	su 848472	$2' 0''$	IC	Open
P15	Leas Cliff, Folkestone	K	TR 227356	$5' 10''$	H	Open
P16	Leas Cliff, Folkestone	K	TR 227356	$4' 10''$	H	Open
P17	Leas Cliff, Folkestone	K	TR 317352	—	H	Closed 1940
P18	Sandgate	K	TR 208353	—	H	Closed 1918
P19	Broadstairs	K	TR 398677	$5' 3''$	E	Open
P20	Margate	K	TR 360714	$5' 0''$	E	Open
P21	West Hill, Hastings	Sx	TQ 824097	$6' 0''$	IC	Open
P22	East Cliff, Hastings	Sx	TQ 828096	$5' 0''$	H	Open
P23	Devil's Dyke, Poynings	Sx	TQ 258115	$3' 0''$	IC	Closed c. 1908

Appendix 5

Lines Constructed for Public Services, Utilities and the Government

This list includes lines built for their own traffic, passenger and/or freight, by the Government, other public authorities and public utilities described in Chapter 6. They vary from extensive systems such as the Richborough Port lines (65 track miles) to short sidings, such as Otterbourne Water Works. The following information is given:

(a) Reference number on Maps Nos 1 and 2
(b) Name and situation of line
(c) County
(d) Grid reference of point of access (not necessarily open to public)
(e) Track gauge or gauges
(f) Worked by main line locomotive (M), or own motive power (P)
(g) Connected to the main line for through running (C), or not connected (U)
(h) Open or closed in 1971.

Lines and Sidings Constructed for Public Services and Utilities

(a)	(b)	(c)	(d)	(e)	(f)	(g)	(h)
A1	Hellingly Hospital	Sx	TQ 595125	4' 8½"	P	C	Closed
A2	Park Prewett Hospital	H	SU 613540	4' 8½"	M	C	Closed
A3	Royal Victoria Hospital, Netley	H	SU 464077	4' 8½"	M	C	Closed
A4	Brookwood Necropolis	Su	SU 956567	4' 8½"	M	C	Closed
A5	Brighton Corporation	Sx	TQ 318059	4' 8½"	M	C	Closed
A6	Eastbourne Corporation	Sx	TV 614995	4' 8½"	M	C	Closed
A7	Maidstone Corporation	K	TQ 746557	4' 8½"	M	C	Closed
A8	Knowle Hospital	H	SU 557097	4' 8½"	M	C	Closed

(a)	(b)	(c)	(d)	(e)	(f)	(g)	(h)
A9	Treloars Hospital	H	SU 708384	4' 8½"	M	C	Closed
A10	Otterbourne Waterworks	H	SU 468234	4' 8½"	M	C	Closed
				& 2' 0"	P	U	Closed
A11	Littlestone Waterworks	K	TR 068202	4' 8½"	M	C	Closed
A12	Bedhampton Waterworks	H	SU 706064	4' 8½"	M	C	Closed
A13	Falmer Waterworks	Sx	TQ 346086	4' 8½"	M	C	Closed
A14	Motney Hill Sewage Works, Rainham	K	TQ 829683	2' 0"	P	U	Open
A15	Apuldram Lane Sewage Works, Chichester	Sx	SU 843038	2' 0"	P	U	Open
A16	Southampton Power Station	H	SU 415121	4' 8½"	P	C	Closed
				& 2' 0"	P	U	Closed
A17	Folkestone Power Station	K	TR 208366	4' 8½"	M	C	Closed
A18	Eastbourne Power Station	Sx	TQ 622011	4' 8½"	M	C	Closed
A19	Dover Gas Works	K	TR 307424	4' 8½"	P	C	Open
A20	Glyne Gap Gas Works	Sx	TQ 763079	4' 8½"	P	C	Closed
A21	Hilsea Gas Works	H	SU 663027	4' 8½"	P	C	Open
A22	Woolston Tip	H	SU 436115	4' 8½"	P	C	Open

Lines and Sidings Constructed for the Government

B1	Brookwood to Bisley	Su	SU 939577	4' 8½"	M	C	Closed (1)
B2	Bisley to Blackdown	Su	SU 913578	4' 8½"	P	C	Closed
B3	Lydd Ranges	K	TR 035200	4' 8½"	P	C	Closed
				& 2' 0"	P	U	Open
B4	Longmoor Military Railway	H	SU 794313	4' 8½"	P	C	Closed
				& 75 cm	P	U	Closed
B5	Chattenden & Upnor	K	TQ 757716	2' 6"	P	U	Closed
B6	Chattenden Naval Tramway	K	TQ 787744	4' 8½"	P	C	Closed
B7	Kingsnorth Railway	K	TQ 790742	4' 8½"	P	C	Closed (2)
B8	Chatham Dockyard	K	TQ 764703	4' 8½"	P	C	Open
				& 1' 6"	P	U	Closed
B9	Sheerness Dockyard	K	TQ 910750	4' 8½"	P	C	Closed
B10	Portsmouth Dockyard	H	SU 642012	4' 8½"	P	C	Open
B11	Bedenham to Priddys Hard R.N. Armament Depot	H	SU 591027	4' 8½"	P	C	Open
B12	Stonar to Richborough	K	TR 329602	4' 8½"	P	C	Closed (3)
B13	Dover to Martin Mill	K	TR 333437	4' 8½"	P	C	Closed (3)
B14	Richborough Port Lines	K	TR 336622	4' 8½"	P	C	Closed

(a)	(b)	(c)	(d)	(e)	(f)	(g)	(h)
B15	Southampton West to						
	Train Ferry Dock	H	SU 417111	4′ 8½″	P	C	Closed
B16	Hoo Ness Island	K	TQ 783703	2′ 6″	P	U	Open
B17	Manston Aerodrome	K	TR 324669	4′ 8½″	P	C	Closed
B18	Royal Aircraft						
	Establishment,						
	Farnborough	H	SU 867557	4′ 8½″	P	C	Closed
B19	Aldershot, M.o.D.	H	SU 875513	4′ 8½″	M	C	Open
B20	Ashford, M.o.D.	K	TQ 998434	4′ 8½″	P	C	Open
B21	Hilsea, M.o.D.	H	SU 664039	4′ 8½″	P	C	Open
B22	Liphook, M.o.D.	H	SU 843313	4′ 8½″	P	C	Open
B23	Botley, R.N.						
	Victualling Depot	H	SU 483165	4′ 8½″	P	C	Open
B24	Haslar Hospital, Gosport	H	SZ 619988	4′ 8½″	P	U	Closed
				& n.g.	P	U	Closed (4)
B25	Clarence Yard, Gosport	H	SU 617004	4′ 8½″	P	U	Closed
B26	Eastchurch Aerodrome	K	TQ 985706	4′ 8½″	M	C	Closed
B27	Rustington Aerodrome	Sx	TQ 058025	4′ 8½″	M	C	Closed (5)
B28	Bisley Rifle Ranges	Su	SU 941585	2′ 0″	P	U	Open (6)

Appendix 6
Lines Constructed for Industry and Commerce

This list consists of a selection of lines built for their own traffic by industrial and commercial undertakings, and described in Chapter 6. It includes examples of internal systems, such as that operating in the Highsted Chalk Pits, and connections to the main line, such as that serving the oil product storage depot at Hamble. Most of the lines carried freight only, but a few, such as the Davington Light Railway, conveyed the labour force. Lower reference numbers are given to the longer systems and higher numbers to the shorter. The following information is given:

- (a) Reference number on Maps Nos 1 and 2
- (b) Name and situation of line
- (c) County
- (d) Grid reference of point of access (not necessarily open to public)
- (e) Track gauge or gauges
- (f) Worked by main line locomotive (M), or own motive power (P)
- (g) Connected to the main line for through running (C), or not connected (U).
- (h) Open or closed in 1971.

Chalk, Lime, Cement and Whiting

(a)	(b)	(c)	(d)	(e)	(f)	(g)	(h)
C1	A.P.C.M. (formerly Alpha)[1] Thames Works, Cliffe	K	TQ 721756	4' 8½"	M	C	Open (2)
				2' 0"	P	U	Closed

(a)	(b)	(c)	(d)	(e)	(f)	(g)	(h)
C2	A.P.C.M. (formerly Francis) Cliffe	K	TQ 724763	3' 8½"	P	U	Closed
C3	A.P.C.M. (formerly Burham Brick, Lime & Cement) Burham	K	TQ 717608	4' 8½"	P	U	Closed
C4	A.P.C.M. Crown and Quarry Works, Frindsbury	K	TQ 749691	4' 8½"	P	C	Closed
C16	Lime Works, Offham	Sx	TQ 402115	(3)	P	U	Closed
C17	Lime Works, Buriton	H	SU 737198	2' 0"	P	U	Closed
				& 4' 8½"	M	C	Closed
C18	Amberley Lime Works (Pepper & Son)	Sx	TQ 028119	4' 8½"	P	C	Closed
C19	A.P.C.M. Rodmell Works	Sx	TQ 436065	2' 0"	P	U	Open
				& 4' 8½"	M	C	Open
C20	A.P.C.M. Upper Beeding Works	Sx	TQ 197086	4' 8½"	P	C	Open
C21	Rugby P.C.M., Southerham Works	Sx	TQ 426094	4' 8½"	P	C	Open
C22	A.P.C.M. Holborough	K	TQ 706624	2' 0"	P	U	Closed
			& TQ 691619	3' 0"	P	U	Closed
			& TQ 706624	4' 8½"	M	C	Open
C23	A.P.C.M. (Smeed, Dean) Sittingbourne Works	K	TQ 919646	2' 0"	P	U	Closed
				& 3' 7½"	P	U	Closed
				& 4' 3"	P	U	Open
C24	A.P.C.M. Highsted Chalk Pits	K	TQ 908620	4' 8½"	P	U	Open
C25	A.P.C.M. (Martin Earle) Wickham Works (4)	K	TQ 728678	2' 0"	P	U	Closed
				& 4' 8½"	M	C	Open
C26	Rugby P.C.M. Halling Works (5)	K	TQ 704650	2' 0"	P	U	Closed
				& 4' 8½"	P	C	Open
C27	British P.C.M. (Lees) Halling	K	TQ 708633	4' 3"	P	U	Closed
				& 4' 8½"	P	C	Closed
C28	Batchelors, Clinkham Works	K	TQ 703650	2' 0"	P	U	Closed
				& 3' 9"	P	U	Closed
				& 4' 8½"	P	C	Closed
C29	Peters, Wouldham Hall Works	K	TQ 712631	4' 3½"	P	U	Closed

APPENDIX 6

Sand, Gravel, Gypsum, Clay, Bricks and Pottery

(a)	(b)	(c)	(d)	(e)	(f)	(g)	(h)
C5	British Gypsum, Mountfield	Sx	TQ 730199	$4'\,8\frac{1}{2}''$	P	C	Open
C6	Barrow Green, Teynham to Conyer	K	TQ 962646	$2'\,0''$	P	U	Closed
C7	Frognal to Conyer	K	TQ 958646	$2'\,0''$	P	U	Closed
C30	Ace Sand and Gravel, Oare	K	TR 013625	$2'\,0''$	P	U	Open
C31	Midhurst Whites, Midhurst	Sx	SU 877212	$2'\,6''$	P	U	Open
C32	Bursledon Brick Co.	H	SU 500098	$4'\,8\frac{1}{2}''$	M	C	Closed
C33	Funtley Brick	H	SU 562083	$4'\,8\frac{1}{2}''$	M	C	Closed
C34	Keymer Brick	Sx	TQ 322192	$4'\,8\frac{1}{2}''$	M	C	Closed
C35	Pluckley Brick	K	TQ 920434	$4'\,8\frac{1}{2}''$	M	C	Closed
C36	Blanchards, Bishops Waltham	H	SU 552177	$4'\,8\frac{1}{2}''$	M	C	Closed
C37	Cremer, Whiting and Co., Oare	K	TQ 998613	$2'\,0''$	P	U	Open

Coal and Oil

(a)	(b)	(c)	(d)	(e)	(f)	(g)	(h)
C8	N.C.B., Betteshanger Colliery	K	TR 336528	$4'\,8\frac{1}{2}''$	P	C	Open
C9	Shell Mex & B.P., Hamble	H	SU 474075	$1'\,8''$	P	U	Open
				$\&\ 4'\,8\frac{1}{2}''$	P	C	Open
C10	Berry Wiggins, Kingsnorth	K	TQ 808730	$4'\,8\frac{1}{2}''$	P	C	Open
C38	N.C.B. Chislet Colliery	K	TR 213629	$4'\,8\frac{1}{2}''$	P	C	Closed
C39	N.C.B. Tilmanstone Colliery	K	TR 287503	$2'\,0''$	P	U	Closed
				$\&\ 4'\,8\frac{1}{2}''$	P	C	Open
C40	N.C.B. Snowdown Colliery	K	TR 246512	$4'\,8\frac{1}{2}''$	P	C	Open
C41	Corrals Ltd. Southampton (Bull's Run)	H	SU 432123	$4'\,8\frac{1}{2}''$	P	C	Open
C42	Storage Depot, Wye	K	TR 048472	$4'\,8\frac{1}{2}''$	M	C	Open
C43	Shell Mex & B.P. Grain Refinery	K	TQ 870752	$4'\,8\frac{1}{2}''$	P	C	Open

Other Industries

(a)	(b)	(c)	(d)	(e)	(f)	(g)	(h)
C11	Davington Light Railway	K	TR 009618	$3'\,3''$	P	U	Closed

(a)	(b)	(c)	(d)	(e)	(f)	(g)	(h)
C12	Bowater-Lloyd, Ridham Dock to Sittingbourne	K	TQ 916664	2' 6"	P	U	Closed (6)
			& TQ 918684	4' 8½"	P	C	Open
C13	Settle, Speakman & Co. Queenborough	K	TQ 912719	4' 8½"	P	C	Open
C14	Herne Bay Oyster Fishery	K	TR 158683	4' 8½"	(7)	C	Closed
C15	Pollock, Brown & Co. Southampton	H	SU 437127	1' 11½"	P	U	Open
			& 4' 8½"		P	C	Open
C44	Watneys, Alton Brewery	H	SU 719392	4' 8½"	M	C	Closed
C45	Pledges Mill, Ashford	K	TR 010422	4' 8½"	M	C	Closed
C46	Hodsons Mill, Robertsbridge	Sx	TQ 732241	4' 8½"	P	C	Open
C47	Express Dairy, Billingshurst	Sx	TQ 089252	4' 8½"	M	C	Closed
C48	Cellactite and British Uralite, Hoo Junction	K	TQ 703738	4' 8½"	M	C	Closed
C49	Reed Paper Group, New Hythe	K	TQ 716593	4' 8½"	P	C	Open
C50	Chapel Tramway, Southampton (8)	H	SU 428117	4' 8½"	P	C	Closed
C51	Dennis Motors, Guilford	Su	SU 975506	4' 8½"	P	C	Closed

NOTES

1 For the Leadhills Light Railway, constructed in Scotland, it was estimated that the adoption of narrow gauge would have saved 14 per cent of the cost of cross drains, 18 per cent in earthworks, 48 per cent on culverts, and 64 per cent on overbridges and viaducts.

2 All lines with Light Railway Orders under the 1896 Act are included. Two lines – Lee-on-the-Solent and the West Sussex – with certificates granted under the 1864 Act are also included, but the Allhallows extension of the Hundred of Hoo branch, authorized under section 2 of the Railways Act of 1921 is excluded.

3 The Gosport system served Haslar Hospital and other establishments. Manual power was also much used in sewage works, and in pumping and generating stations.

Chapter 2

1 This was the well-recorded 2-4-0 tank locomotive, 'Scott', built by George England in 1861, and obtained from the LSWR. It was not of course, possible to operate indefinitely without a second locomotive, and this was an 0-6-0 saddle tank locomotive, 'Lady Portsmouth', built by Manning Wardle in 1879.

2 In particular, in the period between 1909 and the First World War, LSWR Nos 9 and 10 were in use on the line.

3 Because of the demands of mobilization, the Lee-on-the-Solent Railway was closed during the first month of the war, September 1914.

4 In addition to the devious route from Gosport involving a change at Fort Brockhurst, with an average speed of 12 miles per hour, the train was no faster than the buses.

5 Closure to traffic was on and from 30 September, 1935; No. 2239 was removing empty wagons.

6 E.C. Griffith: *The Basingstoke & Alton Light Railway 1901–1936*, 1st Edt., Farnham, 1947.

7 The 'A.M.B. Hospital Camp' was the Absent-Minded Beggar Hospital and Convalescent Camp, later Treloar's Hospital. It was founded under the auspices of the 'Absent Minded Fund' which was devoted to welfare work during the Boer War.

8 The Bordon Light Railway was one of the few lines subsidized by the War Office. An agreement of 1903 between the LSWR and War

Office provided for the latter to make good any deficiency between the amount of the net revenue and the interest at $3\frac{1}{2}$ per cent on the capital cost of construction. In 1926 the SR Traffic Committee recorded that there was no net revenue, and the War Office was paying the full amount of the interest. By 1935 the latter was stated to be ready for a fresh agreement to make good the losses on working the line up to a maximum of £500 per annum for a ten-year period.

9 In April 1915, special traffic at Bordon included 50 troop trains and 8,000 soldiers on leave (information from Alan A. Jackson).

Chapter 3

1 Colonel Stephens, the 'Sir Herbert Walker' of light railways (see Appendix 1).

2 E.C. Griffith: *The Hundred of Manhood & Selsey Tramway later known as the West Sussex Railway 1897–1935*, 1st Edt., Farnham, 1948.

3 This comment came at the end of a delightful description of a journey on the line which appeared in *Railway Magazine*, Vol. 2, (1898). On that occasion the 10.15 a.m. from Chichester left at 10.33, after one wagon was attached in front and one at the rear of the train. At Hunston, the water-supply system attracted attention:

'Imagine, O reader, an elevated platform supported by four rough timber piles, and a small cistern with a pump thereon, the latter being assiduously worked by a small boy in his shirt sleeves, whistling and happy. A pipe led down into a little stream trickling in a ditch by the side of the road from which the small boy pumped up the water with all his might'.

Shunting took place at further points, and, after Sidlesham, there were three trucks in front of the engine, and the passenger coach and two more trucks behind. Selsey Town was reached at 11.30, 40 minutes later, 15 after the train was due to return to Chichester. The return journey was accomplished in 35 minutes, despite an additional call, presumably at Hoe Farm Halt, where a farmer stopped the train by waving a red flag.

4 By 1915, traffic was sufficient to encourage the drafting of a Light Railway Order for a branch to Wittering, and retrospective legal status for the existing 'main' line. This came to nothing, but the legal position of the 'main' line was regularized in 1924 by the

issue of a Certificate under the Railway Construction Facilities Act of 1864. (The Lee-on-the-Solent Railway's legal status was similarly based.) At the same time the name was changed to the West Sussex Railway although locally, the line continued to be called 'the tramway'.

5   M. Lawson Finch: *The Rother Valley later the Kent & East Sussex Railway*. 1st Edt., Sevenoaks, 1949.

6   M. Lawson Finch: *op. cit.*

7   The first two sets were provided with Ford engines at both ends, one or the other being used according to the direction of travel. One set was disposed of in the mid-1930s; the other, together with the Shefflex, went for scrap in 1941.

8   Since this was written in 1972, the hopes of the society now transformed into the Tenterden Railway Company have been partly realized. The section between Bodiam and Robertsbridge, with its level crossings over the busy A21 and A229 roads, has been abandoned and the necessary Light Railway Transfer Order for operating between Tenterden and Bodiam was obtained in November 1973. Passenger traffic began in the spring of 1974 between Tenterden and Rolvenden, and an official re-opening ceremony was performed by the Rt Hon. William Deedes, M.P., on 1 June, 1974.

9   *Railway Magazine*, Vol. 19, p. 330.

10 *Railway Magazine*, Vol. 9, p. 288.

11 *The Romney, Hythe and Dymchurch Railway*, London, 1926.

12 In 1972 ownership passed to a consortium, headed by Messrs McAlpine and Hollingsworth.

Chapter 4

1   *Railway Magazine*, Vol. 29, p. 470.

2   A.E. Ritchie: *The Kent Coal-field*, London, 1920.

3   This would have connected with the Channel Tunnel.

4   In addition, the Tilmanstone Colliery branch appears to have had a workmen's service at this time. Miners were conveyed from Shepherd's Well about 6 a.m., and returned about 2 p.m.

5   *Railway Magazine*, Vol. 80, p. 179.

6   R.W. Kidner: *The Colonel Stephens Railways*, 1st Edt., Sidcup, 1936.

Chapter 5

1 The ten-and-a-quarter-inch gauge of pleasure lines such as the Hastings Miniature Railway, and the 18 feet of the Brighton & Rottingdean Seashore Electric Railway.
2 Alan A. Jackson: *Volk's Railway, Brighton, 1883–1964*, 3rd Edt., London, 1973. This describes the history of both Volk's, and the Brighton & Rottingdean Seashore Electric Railway.
3 K. Turner: *Pier Railways*, Lingfield, 1972, and A. Winstan Bond: *Modern Tramway*, April 1968, p. 127.
4 Machines for both vending and such amusements as the revelation of 'What the Butler Saw'. There was also a restaurant and a marquee for an orchestra or band.
5 E. Course, *Railways of Southern England: The Main Lines*, London, 1973.
6 This was probably of three-foot gauge and survived until the jetty suffered extensive damage in the storms and floods of the winter of 1952/1953. After repairs, the jetty was re-opened but closed again in October 1974, when the ten-and-a-quarter-inch-gauge railway was sold to Mr Pay of Margate. Information from Thanet Central Library and Mr Pay.
7 The rope-worked inclines on the Canterbury & Whitstable are described in Volume Two, Chapter 1, and the industrial line at Offham in Volume Three, the present volume, Chapter 6.
8 By the end of 1973, there were plans to substitute electric for hydraulic operation.
9 It had certainly disappeared by 1974.
10 It was closed in 1974; see section on Other Railways on Piers and Jetties, above.

Chapter 6

1 See E. Course: *The Southampton & Netley Railway*, Southampton, 1974, for more details of this line.
2 Brookwood Station, which served the cemetery, was opened in 1864 when the junction for the branch was moved to the west. Details of the main line station are given in Volume One.
3 South station was demolished after ignition by vandals in 1972; buildings of North station have gone but the platform survives.
4 At the time of its closure in 1972, some of the poles for supporting the live wire survived at Southampton Generating Station.
5 This arrangement had ceased by 1970.

6   It was abaondoned by 1941.

7   See A. Gray: *Isle of Grain Railways*, Lingfield, 1974.

8   Mr G. Balfour has located 30 railway gun positions in Kent alone. These were not confined to disused lines, but were also kept at such places as Shepherd's Well, Eythorne and Staple on the EKLR.

9   See E.A. Pratt: *Railways and the Great War*, London, 1921, also *Proceedings of the Institution of Civil Engineers*, Vol. 110, and *The Engineer*, 10 January, 1919.

10 'Invincible' subsequently went to the Wight Locomotive Society headquarters at Haven Street.

11 LSWR ownership ended on the far side of the bridge over the canal.

12 See Chapter 2.

13 Subsequently the two locomotives have been stored under cover.

14 Opposition from local inhabitants brought about the abandonment of this project.

15 The connection from the main line to Chatham Dockyard is described in Volume One, Chapter 2, and that to Portsmouth Dockyard in Volume One, Chapter 7.

16 See Volume Two, Chapter 7.

17 The Zymotic Hospital dealt with infectious cases, and it has been suggested that the availability of two gauges ensured that cases went to the appropriate hospital.

18 Information from Mr E.J. Holmes, who recalled the line in use about 1910.

19 See A. Gray: *op. cit.*

20 Listed in Appendix 6.

21 See B.D. Stoyel and R.W. Kidner: *Cement Railways of Kent*, Lingfield, 1973.

22 See Volume Two, Chapter 7.

23 See Volume Two, Chapter 5.

24 Formerly BR No. 30096 of the LSWR B4 class, constructed in 1893. This locomotive was handed over to the Bulleid Locomotive Society on 16 December, 1972, and transferred to the Bluebell Line. Subsequently, the only working steam locomotive to be found in Hampshire was at the Marchwood Military Port.

25 Both the breweries served, Watney's and Courage's, have ceased brewing, and the siding was lifted in 1972.

26 M. Minter Taylor, *The Davington Light Railway*, Lingfield, 1970.

27 'Lord Fisher', an 0-4-0 saddle tank, built by Andrew Barclay in 1915, at present on temporary loan to the Somerset & Dorset

Railway Circle at Radstock. The owners of the Chapel Tramway were the companies who used it.

Appendix 1
1 R.W. Kidner: *The Colonel Stephens Railway*, 1st Edt., Sidcup, 1936.

Appendix 2
1 Aquarium (1st Station).
2 Aquarium (2nd Station).

Appendix 4
1 By special arrangement only.
2 Closed by 1974.

Appendix 5
1 Opened under a joint arrangement between the War Office, the National Rifle Association and the LSWR.
2 This was an unusual case of a line built for the Government, in this case an extension of the Chattenden Naval Tramway, being sold to a private company.
3 Built by contractors for the Admiralty's Dover Harbour contract.
4 Width of narrow-gauge (n.g.) tracks not ascertained.
5 No record of private locomotive at Rustington so presumably siding worked by main line locomotive.
6 National Rifle Association and War Office.

Appendix 6
1 A.P.C.M. – Associated Portland Cement Manufacturers Ltd.
2 Cement-works closed 1969 but siding in use for gravel traffic.
3 Gauge of this early incline not known.
4 A.P.C.M. Wickham Works virtually on site of Martin Earles, but a new works.
5 Rugby Portland Cement Manufacturers Ltd, Halling Works, adjoins site of Batchelor's Works.
6 Sittingbourne to Kemsley re-opened for passengers only – see Chapter 6.
7 Not known if Herne Bay Oyster Company provided its own motive power.
8 Chapel Tramway Company was owned jointly by the firms that used it.

Index

Adams, William 96, 97
Adisham 81, 86
Admiralty dockyard railways 144–5
Admiralty Pier Railway 115–16
Adur R. 146
'Agwi Pet' (locomotive) 122
Amberley Siding 146
Albert, Prince 119
Aldershot 139
Alton, see also Basingstoke and Alton line 11, 20ff., 42, 129, 142, 151
Appledore 39, 43, 46
Ash 42, 83, 91, 101
   Town Station 101, 102
Ashford 39, 40, 47, 48, 97, 103, 123, 145
   line 43
   Works 29, 50, 97, 98
Ashford Chronicle 46
Austen, W. H. 157
Axminster 97

Banjo Groyne 108, 110
Barnstaple 96
Basingstoke 20ff., 42, 127, 128
Basingstoke and Alton line 11, 20–30, 42, 129
Battle 77
Beattie, W.G. 96, 97
Beckley 44
Belunde Bridge 135
Bentley 31, 142
Bentley and Bordon line 16
Bentworth 22
   and Lasham 23, 26, 27, 29, 30
Berwick 10, 123
   Drusilla's Tea Rooms 1, 13, 123
Betteshanger Colliery 79, 86, 93, 132, 150
Biddenden 46, 47, 48
   Road Station 47, 51
Birchington 81
Birdham 32
Birling Gap 10
Bisley Camp 139, 140
Blaber, Charles (engineer) 120
Blackdown Camp Station 140, 141, 142
Bluebell Railway 97
Bodiam 49
'Bodiam' (locomotive) 42
Bodiam Castle 11, 39, 44
   Station 41
Bognor Regis 35
   Hotham Park railway 122
   Pier Railway 123
Bordon 31, 142, 143
   branch line 7, 11, 31
   Light Railway 31
Botley 145
Botolph's Bridge 68
Bournemouth 11, 15
Bowaters Railway 13
BR 43, 143
   Southern Region 49, 50, 94, 98, 105, 126, 143
Bradshaw (railway guides) 3, 35, 139
Bramber 146
Brambledown 58ff.
Branch Line Society, the 52
Breweries' railways 151
Brick works' railways 148–9
Brighton 48, 97, 107ff., 114
   and Rottingdean Seashore Electric Railway 13, 107, 109–11, 118, 142
   Aquarium 75
   Chain Pier 110
   Paston Place 75
   Works 52
Brighton main line
   lines and stations east of 8
   lines and stations west of 9

Bristol 42
Britannia Inn Halt 70
British Association, the 77
British Rail *see* BR
Broadstairs Lift 121
Brockham Museum Association 122
Brookwood 139
   Station 139, 141
Brookwood Necropolis Railway 129–30
Browndown 17, 18, 19, 20, 145
Bulford Camp Station 142
Burmarsh Road 68
   Halt 68
Burr, Arthur 78, 86, 87
Burr, Dr Malcolm 79, 84, 85, 87
Bury Road 17
Butt's Junction 30, 129

Camber 111ff.
Camber Sands 54, 111ff.
Canterbury 50, 73, 81ff., 118
   West Station 81
Castle, Mrs Barbara 53
Cement works' railways 14, 146–8
Chalder 36
   Station 35, 37
Channel Tunnel Co. 77–8
Chapel Tramway Co. 156
Chatham Dockyard 13, 125, 144
Chatterden and Upnor Tramway 7, 133, 141
Chatterden Naval Tramway 11
'Cheltenham' (locomotive) 52
Chichester 12, 32ff., 129
   Canal 32, 34, 37
   Station 34
Chichester Observer 34, 35
Chislet Colliery 74, 79
Cliddesden 21ff.
Cliffe 13, 147
Coal export 104
Colne Valley and Halstead Railway 57
Colonel Stephens Railways, The 100, 157
Cranbrook 10, 40
Cuckmere Valley Railway 10

'Daddy Long Legs' 110
Daily Express, The 37
Davington Light Railway 152–3
   Station 153
Deal 73, 81, 86ff.
   branch 87, 89ff., 136
Deepcut Camp Station 140, 141
Defence, Ministry of 144
Devil's Dyke steep-grade railway 118, 119–20
Dolphin, HMS 145
Dorking 122
Douglas, Isle of Man 140
Dover 42, 78, 81ff., 115, 116, 135, 136
   Colliery 78
   Harbour 8off., 93, 136
   Marine Station 116
   Priory Siding 139
Dover Express, The 85
Drellingore 73, 74, 86
Drusilla's Tea Rooms *see* Berwick
Dungeness 11, 54
Durley narrow-gauge railway 122
Dymchurch 62ff.

Ealing Studios 43
   The Loves of Joanna Godden (film) 43
Eastchurch 56ff.
   Borstal 59, 61
   RAF airfield 59
East Guldeford 112, 114
East Kent coalfield 76ff.
East Kent Light Railway *see* EKLR

186

Eastleigh
Shed 43
Works 29, 50, 60, 96, 97
Eastry 72ff.
South Station 87, 105
Eaton Hall Railway 63, 67
EKLR 11, 12, 42, 49, 72–106, 157
after 1945, 99–106
later developments 92–5
rolling stock 95–9
Elmore Farm Halt 18, 19
Elvington 74
Eyethorne 73, 82, 83, 88, 89, 102, 105

Fairbourne Railway 63
Fairman, John 127–8
Fareham 17, 20, 28, 127, 129, 149
Farleigh 25
Farnborough Royal Aircraft Establishment line 138–9
Farnham 122, 142
Faversham 10, 81, 150, 151
Fawley Refinery narrow-gauge railway 122
Finch, Lawson, *The Rother Valley Railway*, 42ff.
Firbank, J.T. 21
Flyington Halt 105
Folkestone 65, 118
Lift 121
Fordwich 83
Fort Blockhouse 145
Fort Brockenhurst 16ff., 139
and Lee-on-Solent line 16–20
Fort Gilkicker 145
Fort Gomer 17, 19
Fredville boring 82
Frittenden 46, 48
Road Station 47

Gainsborough Pictures 42
'Gazelle' (locomotive) 143
General Strike, the 88, 91
GER 49, 129, 151
GNR 65
Godwin-Austen 77
Golf Club Halt 36
Golgotha Tunnel 83, 84, 106
Goodnestone 82
Gosport 13, 19, 37, 149
Clarence Yard 144
line 17, 139
trams 18
Government railways
list of 173–5
Grain Refinery 150
Great Eastern Railway *see* GER
Great Northern Railway *see* GNR
Greatstone 65, 66, 69
Great Western Railway *see* GWR
Greenly, Henry (locomotive designer) 64
Gresley, Sir Nigel 65
Griffiths, E.C. 20ff., 34, 35, 37
Grove 58
Guilford Colliery 73, 75, 79ff.
Guston Tunnel 135, 136
GWR 11, 20, 30, 42, 48, 49, 53, 95, 123, 143
Gypsum railways 148

Hailsham 125
Halling Station 148
Hamble Halt 150
Hampshire Herald and Alton Gazette 21
Harty Road Halt 58, 59, 61, 62
Haslar Hospital 144, 145
Hassocks Station 119
Hastings 38, 39, 41, 43, 46, 52, 97, 123, 124, 148
beach railway 123–4
East Cliff Lift 121
Hawkhurst 39, 41
branch 53
Hay, Will (actor) 42

Hayling Island branch 43
Headcorn 33, 39, 40, 42, 46ff., 97
Junction 50
'Hecate' (locomotive) 40, 48, 49, 98
Hellingley Mental Hospital line 7, 14, 125–6, 127, 129
Herne Bay 114, 115
Herne Bay Pier Railway 13, 58, 75, 114–5
Herriard 23ff., 42
'Hesperus' *see also* 'Ringing Rock' 48, 49
High Halden 46, 47, 48
Road 47, 51, 52
Hilsea 145
Hoe Farm Halt 35
Holborough Works 148
Holford 58
Hollingbourne 10
Hollycombe House railway 122
Hornby 'O' Gauge 12
Hornsby-Ackroyd (locomotive) 120
Horsham 146
Horsmonden 32
Horsted Keynes 97
Hove electric railway 124
Howey, Captain J.E.P. 63, 64, 67, 70
Hubbard, J.H. 119, 120
Hundred of Hoo line 135, 147
Hundred of Manhood and Selsey Tramway *see also*
West Sussex Railway 11, 21, 32–8
Light Railway 11, 55
Hunston 32ff.
Hythe 11, 54, 62ff.
Station 67
Hythe (Hampshire) pier railway 115

Ilfracombe 96
'Ilfracombe Goods' class 48, 49, 96
Independent railways 107–24
opening and closure of lines 159–64
Industrial and commercial railways, list of 176–9
Ivatts, E.B. 32

Jackson, Alan 109, 110, 113
Job, R. 94
Journal of the Society of Arts 77
Junction Road for Hawkhurst Station 41, 48
'Juno' 49

Kent 32ff.
Kent and East Sussex Railway *see* KESR
Kent Coal Concessions 78, 80
Kent coalfield 11
Kent Country Nurseries Railway 123
Kent Examiner and Ashford Chronicle 43–5
Kentish Gazette 85
KESR *see also* Rother Valley line 11, 29, 38–53, 85, 97, 157
Kingsley 31
Kingsnorth Light Railway 134–5, 137
Kipson Bank 34
Knowle 31
Mental Hospital 129
Knowlton 12, 105

Lade Halt 64, 70
Lambourne Valley Railway 57
Lamsham Station *see* Bentworth and Lamsham
LBSCR 10, 11, 19, 32, 36, 43, 48, 49, 50, 51, 125, 126, 149
LCDR 10, 53, 57, 59, 63, 116
Leas Cliff steep-grade railway (Folkestone) 118–9
Lee Britten 15
Lee-on-the-Solent 11, 15ff.
Station 20
Railway 7, 15–20, 32, 36, 37, 38, 55
Leysdown 11, 53ff., 124

Light Railways
  in east Kent 72–106
  in Hampshire 15–31
  in Kent and Sussex 32–71
  opening and closure of lines 159–64
  opening and closure of passenger stations 165–70
  in Southern England 7–14
Light Railways Act 10, 11, 15, 20, 39, 63
Light Railways Commissioners 10, 80, 81
Light Railway Orders 10, 31, 53, 57, 63, 64, 65, 72, 77, 80, 82–3, 84, 85, 87, 88, 89, 92
Lime works railways 145–6
Liphook 122, 145
Liss 31, 142, 144
Littlehampton Miniature Railway 122–3
Littlestone-on-Sea 63
  Road 68, 69
Little Stour R. 101
LMR 14, 31, 49, 133, 139, 141–2
LMSR 59, 123, 129
LNER 65
LNWR 143
Locomotive Club of Great Britain 52, 53, 105
London and South Western Railway see LSWR
London to Southampton main line 1
London Transport 1, 69
Longmoor Military Railway see LMR
LSWR 11, 17, 18, 19, 20, 21, 26, 29, 30, 31, 36, 48, 49, 50, 52, 94, 95, 96, 97, 129, 138, 139, 140, 143
Lydd-on-Sea 66, 145
Lyme Regis 97
Lympe 67
Lynton and Barnstaple Railway 64

Maddieson's Holiday Camp 66, 70
Maidstone 40, 46
Manston 14
  Aerodrome line 138
Margate
  cliff railway 13, 14, 121
  Dreamland Miniature Railway 123
  jetty railway 116, 124
  pier railway 116
Martin Mill 135, 136
Mate's Illustrated Guide 15
Maydensole 73, 84
Meon Valley line 19, 28
Mid-Hants Railway 151
Mill Pond Halt 35, 36
Minster 56ff., 87, 103
  East Station 58, 61, 62
  -on-Sea Station 57
Moat Farm Siding 101
Mongeham 73, 84
Monkton Hutments 145
Munitions on the rail 152–3

National Coal Board 94
Netley (Royal Victoria) Hospital line 13, 14, 128–9, 149
Newenden 44
Newmill Channel 41
New Romney 11, 63ff.
  line 43
  Station 63
Nine Elms 27, 29
NLR 49, 94
Northbourne 86
  branch line 74
North Downs 50
Northfleet cement works 145
'Northiam' (locomotive) 43, 97
Northiam 38, 40, 44
  Station 41
North London Railway see NLR

Oakhanger 31, 144
Oare 150, 153
Offham inclined plane 118, 145–6
Oil carriage by rail 150–1

Ottley, George, Bibliography of British Railway History 3, 4
Ouse R. 146
Ovingdean 110

Padgham Harbour 34, 36
Palmarsh 67
Paper-making 153–5
Park Prewett Hospital line 14, 127–8, 129
Pauling and Elliott 17
Pearsons and Dorman Long 81, 86, 88, 90, 92, 137
Pilot 70
'Pioneer' (car) 109–11
Pirbright Camp Station 140, 141
Pleasure railways 122–4
  list of 171–2
Pluck's Gutter 91
Poison Cross Station 85, 103
Portsmouth 20, 28, 31
  and Horndean Light Railway 107
  Dockyard 144
Port Victoria 56
Poulton Farm Siding 101
Poynings 119
Priddys Hard 144
'Pride of Sussex' (locomotive) 53
Prince of Wales Pier Railway 115–6
Private railways 125–56
  government 132–45, 173–5
  industrial and commercial 145–56, 175–9
  public services and utilities 125–32, 173–5
Privett 17, 18, 20
  Station 17, 19
Public service railways
  list of 173–5
Public utilities railways
  list of 173–5

Queenborough 53ff., 81, 150

Railway Clearing House Handbook of Stations 100, 101, 139
Railway Construction Facilities Act 7, 15
Railway Correspondence Travel Society 140
Railway Magazine 4, 53, 55, 59, 72, 94, 133, 147
Railway Observer 127
Ramblers' Association 53
Ramsgate 50, 81, 103
  Harbour 54, 116
  Hereson Road Station 54, 116, 117
  Tunnel Railway 13, 67, 116–8
Ravenglass and Eskdale Railway 63
Reading 42
Reculver 81
Redhill 42
Regulation of Railways Act 7, 39
Relph, Harry 59
RHDR 1, 11, 12, 13, 14, 62–71, 111, 118, 123
Richborough 72, 145
  Castle 73, 82
  Old Wharf 74
  Port 75ff., 136, 137
  Siding 74, 90, 91, 104, 132, 135
'Ringing Rock' (locomotive) see also 'Hesperus' 48
Ripple Colliery 73, 84, 85
Ritchie, Kent Coalfield 79
Robertsbridge 33, 38ff., 97
Robinson, Sir J. 15, 17
Rochester 151
Rodwell Works Siding 147
'Rolvenden' (locomotive) 48
Rolvenden 38, 40ff., 97, 158
Romney 62ff.
Romney, Hythe and Dymchurch Railway see RHDR
Romney Marsh 11, 12, 43, 63ff.
Rother (locomotive) 48
Rother Valley line see also KESR 21, 38–53, 58
Rottingdean 75, 107ff.
Royal Military Canal (Deal) 63, 67

Ryde pier railway 115
Rye 40, 68, 97, 111ff.
  and Camber Tramway 111–14, 157
  Golf Links Station 112, 113
  Harbour 111ff.

'St Lawrence' (locomotive) 50
St Leonards 39, 52
St Mary's Bay (Jesson) 64, 68–9
St Michael's Halt 46, 48, 51
Salehurst 41, 48
Sandgate 65
  Hill steep-gauge railway 119, 120, 121
Sand Hutton Railway 63
Sandling Junction 65
Sandwich 74, 81, 84, 90, 91, 92, 99, 104, 135
  Road Station 87, 99, 103
Scarborough steep-grade railway 118
Scott (engineer) 24
Scotter, Sir C.L. 20
SECDR 51, 116, 133
SECR 11, 50, 51, 52, 53, 58, 59, 60, 74, 79, 80, 81, 87,
  88, 89, 94, 99, 133, 135, 136, 143
Selsey 12, 32ff.
  Beach 32ff.
  Bridge Station 35
  Ferry 36, 37
  Station 36
  Tramway see Hundred of Manhood and Selsey
    Tramway
SER 39ff., 56, 63, 77, 91, 112, 116, 148, 149
Sevenoaks 50
Sheerness 53, 56, 60, 99, 150
  Dockyard 57, 144
  East Station 57, 60, 62
  electric trains 60
Sheffield Park 97
Shepherd's Well 72ff.
Sheppey, Isle of 53ff., 81
Sheppey Light Railway 1, 11, 53ff., 82, 83, 124, 157
Shoreham 146
Shropshire and Montgomery Railway 95, 157
Sidlesham 34, 36, 37
  Station 35
Sittingbourne 99, 154, 155
Snowdown 73, 85, 86
  Colliery 79, 82, 93
Southampton 137–8
  and Netley Railway 129
  West Station 138
South Eastern Railway see SER
Southend 114
  Pier 114
  Pier railway 106
Southern Counties Railways Society 140
Southern Railway see SR
Southern Railway Working Timetable 146
Southsea 17
  Castle 123
  Clarence Pier 17
  Miniature Railway 123–4
SR 19, 28, 37, 42, 43, 48, 59, 60, 63, 66, 69, 87, 90, 92ff.,
  116
Staple 101, 102
Steep-grade railways 118–22
  list of 171–2
Stephens, Lt-Col. Holman Fred (engineer) 32, 39, 41,
  42, 43, 44, 49, 51, 52, 55, 57, 58, 67, 82, 83, 84, 86,
  92, 95, 97, 101, 102, 106, 111, 157–8
Stirling, James (designer) 29, 97
Stodmarsh 84
Stonar 91, 104, 135
Stonehall 73, 74, 84, 85, 89
  Colliery 86
Sturry 91
Sussex 32ff.
Swindon 42, 95

Tankerton 58
Tay Bridge 41
'Tenterden' (locomotive) 43
Tenterden 10, 38ff.
  Railway 39ff.
  Station 40
  Town Station 45, 49
'Terrier' class (locomotives) 19, 48, 50, 52, 53, 59, 64, 65
Thanet Amusements Ltd 116
Thorneycroft's Works 24, 30
Tilden-Smith, R. 93
Tilmanstone Colliery 72ff.
Times, The 158
Tonbridge 42, 46, 47, 50, 52
Trade, Board of 7, 10, 17, 18, 20, 57, 77, 82, 102
Transport, Institute of 62
Transport, Ministry of 10, 36
Treloars Hospital 30, 129
Tunbridge Wells 38, 39

Uplees Station 153
Upnor see Chattenden and Upnor line
Upper Beeding 146

Venus 17
Victoria, Queen 49
Volk's Electric Railway 13, 107–9, 112

'Waddon' (locomotive) 59
Waldershare boring 82
Walker, Sir Herbert 48, 63, 87, 92
'Walton Park' (locomotive) 95, 98
War Department 134ff.
  lines 139ff.
Warren Halt 68
Watkin, Sir Edward 77
Weald, The 47
Weavers' Down Station 143
Weddington 91
Wells, H.G., Kipps 63
Welshpool and Llanfair line 134
Westcliff-on-Sea 55
West Hill steep-grade railway (Hastings) 119
Weston, Cleveland and Portishead Railway 42, 95, 157
West Sussex Railway see also Hundred of Manhood and
  Selsey Tramway 7, 14, 32ff., 157
Wey Valley Light Railway 122
Whitaker 77, 78
Whitehill 142
Whitland and Cardigan Railway 95
Whitstable 81, 118
Wickhambreux 84ff.
  Colliery 73, 74
Wickham Works 148
Winchester 27
  and Guildford line 26
Wingham 7, 72ff., 82ff.
  Canterbury Road Station 75, 88, 99, 101, 102, 106
  Colliery 74, 81, 85ff.
  Town Station 100
Wise, Prof. M.J. 3, 4
Wittersham Road Station 41, 44, 52, 53
Woking 42
Woodnesborough 83, 84, 86, 101, 102, 103
  branch line 73
  Colliery 73, 81, 85, 89, 102
'Woolmer' (locomotive) 143
Woolmer Instructional Military Railway 142
Worthing 123
  Brooklands Park Railway 123
Wye 151

Zborowski, Count 63
Zymotic Hospital 145